LICKING

THE

KNIFE

a memoir

SABRINA CAPPER

Publishing Services provided by Paper Raven Books LLC

Printed in the United States of America

First Printing, 2024

ISBN: 979-8-9916435-0-4

Dedicated to all the little girls in the dark

TABLE OF CONTENTS

AUTHOR'S NOTE

This book is challenging to read. It is challenging to live. It is a true story, it is my story, and I know it will not be easy for anyone to hear. I am including this note to my dear readers—please be careful. I love that you are interested in hearing my story. I am so tickled that you are here, reading my words, hearing my perspective of things never before told to the world. I cannot express what it means to be heard after a lifetime lived in silence. Even if you never go further than this, you are here, and that matters.

Beware: this book contains detailed accounts of child abuse, rape, torture and murder.

All of these events are told through a child's perspective, which is unique and unsettling. It is hard to absorb, to imagine any child living through such horrors. In using my inner child voice to narrate, I hope to give readers a softer, more honest approach to difficult events. As a child narrator, I am not recounting gory or gratuitous details, rather giving an honest account about what I saw and experienced. This includes using words and descriptions of unsettling scenes with childlike language and knowledge. If you are able to follow along, I hope to share a story of how one little girl grew on a different path and used it to shine. How my mind navigated through trauma and how I use it to grow.

I love that you are here to witness and educate yourself, but please be gentle. It's OK if you need to skip a few lines, or pages or chapters. It's OK if you need to put the book down and walk away for a while. It's OK if you feel uncomfortable or cry. It's OK to never make it past this page

because you know it's too much for you. It's safe to take care of yourself first.

If you do stay to listen, remember I am OK. I live a beautiful life. This struggle did not stop me from being the person I want to be, I am alive and well in my sweet home with my precious family. The family I made for myself, with love and kindness. I survived. I am healing. I hope sharing this story will help others see that that stuff like this happens, but it doesn't have to be in isolation. We can talk about it. We can help each other.

For those brave souls who continue to read this story, talk about it. Talk about how it affects you, how you relate, how it makes you feel. Write it down, make a video, sing a song… help me continue to break the silence.

THERAPIST NOTE

Dear readers,

I have had the honor of working with Sabrina through the unfolding of this story. If you are a survivor of abuse, please try to resist comparisons. Every journey is unique. *Licking the Knife* is a powerful story that may spark intense feelings inside you. Your mind might react in unexpected ways, or your body might have responses that surprise you. This is OK. Treat yourself with kindness and care.

It's important to remind you that most people spend their whole lives trying to heal from trauma. Some people bury memories, some turn to substance addiction, and some stay trapped in a cycle of abuse. Most of us find ourselves somewhere in between, hoping it gets better and pretending it didn't happen. Wherever you find yourself, there is help and hope available. Sharing your stories is the first step, saying it out loud—to a therapist, to a friend, or to the mirror. Talking about it is the first and hardest step you will take towards healing, and there are resources available to help (gethelp.com).

If you find this story hard to believe, I will tell you as a professional with decades of experience in this field, I have never had one second of doubt about the truth of these stories. Abuse is much more common than we want to admit, and much worse. Families and religious organizations perpetuate abuse by demanding secrecy and covering for abusers. If you have a child in your life that tells you something strange about an adult, like this brave girl did, believe them. Do not question their motives.

Children are not in the business of ruining adults' lives to have fun making accusations like this. Children cry out for help. It is our duty and responsibility to listen when they do.

For me, this experience has been astounding. Discovering new ways the body manifests what the mind will not acknowledge. We still don't fully understand why she was able to navigate survival and healing with such unique success at such a young age, but it's been fascinating to explore. Especially how her fractured young psyche did not severe completely into full Dissociative Identity Disorder. She has parts that carry memories completely separate from a conscious central core personality that has remained fully intact. Her process of allowing memories to reintegrate into consciousness is particularly difficult (and ongoing), necessitating the support of a team of professionals in addition to committed friends and family. Her healing is a testament to her willingness to accept help and do the work.

I hope you are inspired to use this story to start a conversation in your own circles. The more we are willing to bring into the light, the more we prevent the horrors of what can happen in the dark.

~RC, LPC, Jungian Analyst IAAP

"When you are not fed love on a silver spoon, you learn to lick it off of knives."

- LAUREN EDEN

PROLOGUE

AGE 46 LUCKY GIRL

I am a lucky girl. Everyone has said so my whole life. I am lucky I have such a loving family who cares so intensely for me. I am lucky companies hire me, pay my salary, and give me benefits. I am lucky my husband puts up with me. I am lucky my life is so perfect.

I am a lady. I always mind my manners and never speak out of turn. Attentive and thoughtful to the needs of those around me, I respect my elders and do as I am told. I can be trusted with secrets.

I am tough. I can endure pain. I can keep going when others fall. I persevere because I never give up. Giving up is a luxury so many take for granted.

I am a liar. I lie to the most important people in my life. I use omission and manipulation of words to stay as close to the truth as possible. I am as honest as I am able to be, but safety comes first.

I am a whore. I've had with sex men who are not my husband. I lost my virginity long before I knew what it was.

I am a wife. Through marriage, eternal bonds, and ritual. Only one of me, but so many claim me as their property.

I have endured these labels throughout my life. I earned them all. But I never asked for them. They have that one thing in common: the implication of choice. No one ever asks what labels I would like for myself.

I did not choose so many events that shaped my life, yet I carry these labels like stones in my shoes. Every step is heavy as I climb the mountain of survival.

So many people start miles ahead, throwing down boulders and spears of shame and fear—easier to defeat those below than to work their way

up. Those unlucky people who are born into privilege and stability are smothered by love and ambition. It's hard for them to climb when they are so comfortable in the middle, but the middle is only secure if they ensure no one below makes it.

They fear the strength they will create in those they left behind, that those scraping to climb will build new paths, forcing growth and accountability from those born at the top. They fear the wild determination they could create with just one little girl slipping by. If just one little girl suffers and endures and makes it to the top, what kind of monster will they have created?

And what will she do when she grows up? What stories will she tell?

AGE 4 VILLAIN

I am a villain. I know this because The Mother reminds me all the time so I don't forget. I am a big girl now, almost five years old. I should remember.

I don't forget, but sometimes she thinks I do, so she has to remind me with hits and kicks. I haven't forgotten since last year when I was too excited about hearing in Sunday school that Jesus loved me. He loves me, and He is always right so I can love me. I was too little to know that The Mother's love hurts and is real, and Jesus is just make-believe.

It's NOT OK to love me. I am an awful bad girl, and I deserve what I get, but I am lucky so I am still in a good family with a nice home, and I am grateful for what I get.

It's like our movie, *Snow White*. The beautiful Evil Queen is just trying to make sure she is pretty and her husband, The King, is happy. Then her stupid daughter has to mess everything up with her beautiful face and songs. The Evil Queen was only trying to protect her beautiful life before that awful girl came along. We don't like the part where Snow White gets rescued by seven men who are kind to her. The Mother says that's a bunch of crap.

We listen to the songs and wait for the beautiful Queen to transform into the powerful Crone. She is scary and mean, but her magic is strong enough to put Snow White to sleep so the Evil Queen can finally get some peace until the stupid Prince comes and takes her away.

It's not a nice trick that grownups play on kids, pretending that little girls being Disney princesses is such a fun game. I know I am like Snow White, beautiful and kind and everyone hates me. I will be punished for it for the rest of my life. It's not such a fun game, being a princess.

But I am only four, so maybe I can make it better. I don't believe in fairy godmothers, won't make that mistake again—but I do like puzzles. I do lots of them at school. Maybe I can find another way to put me together, so people can love me. Maybe I can live like Mowgli with the animals in the woods so The Mother won't have to put up with me. I wonder if we live near a jungle.

AGE 45 NYC

CHAPTER ONE

Life is golden. My adoring husband, Dave, my beautiful son, Jack, and I step into the deep carpet in the high-rise suite in Times Square. Our spring break adventure is off to an excellent start. No flight delays, available upgrades with my airline status, and now a room that looks just as good as it did on the internet. I think I finally have this life thing figured out.

A current TikTok trend loops in my head:

I don't dress cool so boys will look at me. I dress cool so a 13-year-old girl will pass me on the street and think, Damn, that girl is so cool.

I think my 13-year-old self would be fucking floored if she saw me standing here today. Perfect on-trend jeans and sneakers, denim collared shirt casually rolled up at the sleeves, designer sunglasses, and a fresh salon blowout. Casual, cool NYC vibe on point. Waltzing into this amazing suite with casual grace because this level of luxury is now attainable. Mind gently running possible dinner plans and evening activity ideas as I collapse on the bed next to the floor-to-ceiling views of Broadway.

It's an odd thing, achieving your dreams. I never looked too far into the future—I was too preoccupied with managing the present. Now I live in a lovely two-story home with a three-car garage, a pool, and a 200-year-old tree in the front yard. It backs up to a golf course, the green providing a non-impeded view of the copse of trees across the course. It's almost like a park in the evenings, with fireflies blinking and the pool's small waterfall babbling. It's our favorite family spot, sitting around in metal rocking chairs that squeak and sing as we chat and discuss life's adventures.

I have a husband who adores me and a son who is an incredible human. Working at a cool new tech start-up, making more money than I ever dreamed I could make.

This is it. It is all I ever wanted.

I take a moment to pause and be grateful. Not to God or to my lucky stars, but to my own inner voice that whispers that this is what matters. Sitting in a new city, about to enjoy an epic adventure with my incredible family that I created. Whatever happens in our lives, this is what matters, and this moment can never be taken away.

Yes, the room is a bit dated and in the middle of the biggest tourist district. But it has a separate room for our tween boy and an excellent view of all the Times Square excitement. A stark contrast to the fifth floor walk-up B&B in Murray Hill we stayed in 20 years ago when Dave and I traveled here in our early 20s. It still feels so luxurious to not count every dollar or panic when I realize there is an extra $25 per day "resort" fee. It is a luxury, and I revel in it still. So many trips I schemed and researched to have the most experience I could afford (and usually couldn't afford). Yet of all the stupid spending I have done in my life, travel is one thing I have never regretted. Not a single exorbitant fee or scammed euro, I treasure them all. Experience is the only true wealth in life.

So bringing my son to New York for his eighth grade spring break trip is an important investment and a special moment. It's what I have dreamed of, sharing something that means so much to me with a human I created. Enjoying the thrill of watching his face come alive as he steps foot in a new city and watching his perspective change for life. Seeing how others eat, communicate, celebrate, and live is an amazing gift. It's

knowledge that will help him see a world beyond his own experience. Knowledge that will be with him, always.

We are all bobbing in the waves and navigating what ups and downs come our way. I have always known that money is lovely, and makes life exuberant, but money can be lost in a blink of the eye. I have a nice home, nice cars, and cute shoes, but it won't last. We all lose a job or get scammed or make a bad investment and fall on financial hardship at some point. Financial experts agree wealth is cyclical. Sometimes you have it; sometimes you don't. As a parent, I like to focus my greatest resources on providing Jack with as many experiences as I can afford: things he can take with him wherever he goes in life, whatever his resources.

So as my son says, "Yeah, it's a'ight," and plops down on the settee overlooking the most famous theater district in the world, I let a slow smile creep over my lips. He may not be on a road trip with PB&Js or enjoying amusement rides like my family did growing up, but I willingly pay the price of enduring his spoiled comments because he is getting the kind of experiences that his fiercest competitors in life will take for granted. I am giving him advantages I never had, and no one can take this moment away from him. He will be able to use this to relate and add a unique perspective to other's stories, which is quite alluring to the privileged, if crafted the right way.

And my boy is going to be a master craftsman. This past year, he finally found his tribe... the theater kids. After years of benches, bleachers, weather, and uniforms, it finally made sense why he never quite fit in. Jack is just who we raised him to be, so it should not have taken us this long to figure out that he isn't a jock—he is a creative.

At 13, Jack isn't four feet tall just yet, but he is growing fast. His shining sandy brown hair is too long, constantly falling into his baby-blue eyes. A casual toss of the hair is constant, practiced to charm more than a few girls, I expect. He is beautiful. Made more so by the fact that he is kind and sensitive, not traits treasured traditionally in the teenage world. He has always been small, with the tabs pulled tight on his jeans and the size being smaller than his age. Now it's a time of maximum liability for being a smaller kid in a land of testosterone.

Dave and I are intentional about giving Jack the space he needs to explore what he is interested in, gender norms be damned. Beyond the traditional combat sports, he also tried dance, gymnastics, music, and voice lessons. At the time, he lost interest in them just as he had the sports, so we wrote them off like the others. But I suspect that, as with many young middle school boys, there may have been a hormonal-driven decision to take a chance on the theater class instead of math, bolstered by the safety of knowing his parents would support that decision.

What a luxury, having a parent you feel so safe with that you can make bold decisions. I have fought so hard to ensure that will always be true for him.

What an odd thought.

* * *

Accustomed to traveling together frequently, Dave and I eventually begin bustling around the suite putting things away. Working in a silent ballet of intuition that I share with someone whom I have lived life with for more than 20 years. I know he likes to hang things in the closet first. He knows to do that so he is out of my way while I arrange my toiletries.

I set up my nightstand while he gets ice. We chat and buzz and eventually collapse on the bed to take a rest after a job well done. Workers, both of us, to the core. But thankfully, we are partners, so the work is always shared.

As we do most times when settling into the hotel, I immediately reach for the remote to flip through and see what trashy TV is on. Dave lies back on the bed to relax with his dachshund videos on IG reels on the latest iPhone. After spending more than 15 years with Apple, I have come to accept he will work there for life. He loves being a part of something bigger than himself, the Apple brand being better than most. They have good benefits, treat their employees pretty well, and offer good stock options with few historic layoffs. So we have all the things to digitize our lives, causing more frustration than convenience more often than I would like, but this is just one thing I accept is part of this life with this man. It's not tough to accept. There are much worse things others shoulder.

I reach out absently, and his hand finds mine. More than two decades together and we still hold hands constantly. He still opens my door, pulls out my chair. He still flirts with me, tells me I am beautiful. This is what love feels like. Not the wild hot lightning that fades with smoke and burns, but the soft warm glow that comes from not having to look to see if someone is going to take your hand. The blind trust that his hand will find mine without having to say a word.

He has always worried about his lack of refinement—formal education, money, family. It took him a long time to realize how much I don't give a shit about those things. Anyone can read or pay to attend school. Not everyone can achieve the life we have with the challenges we have faced.

Survivors recognize the survivor in others.

Dave isn't fazed by my typical gasps and cackles from the unfiltered media, choosing to start to browse options for dinner. He knows he needs options now before we (and by we, I mean I) get hangry.

The work of a successful trip was divided long ago, on a month-long European backpacking trip Dave and I took in our 20s. When you have no money, but you want to travel, you have to get creative and learn how to save money. Dave was not good at either, so I did the planning, and we did Europe on the cheap.

To his credit, he trusted me from the start. Not many men immediately see the aptitude I have for canny financial maneuvering and trust me to make the decisions. Since I did the heavy lifting of planning and budgeting the trip, he took on learning the transportation systems and local laws.

In these days before the internet (yes, there was internet in the early 2000s, but we couldn't afford an AOL plan), we were doing all of our research at Barnes and Noble, where for three dollars you could get a cup of coffee in Starbucks and read as many books as you wanted. (And yes, we could have gone to the library, but what early 20s just-out-of-college kid wants to spend more time there?) We mapped and planned with Rick Steves like the rest of the cool kids in the '90s. It was the trip of a lifetime that we still reflect on fondly.

Dave, it turns out, has an excellent sense of direction and a good mind for navigation—not my strengths. London was our first new city to explore together, and I didn't quite trust that he knew where we were. Once we were heading down to take the tube, and I rushed to jump on a train that was about to leave the station. Breathless, I turned around and

saw the doors close behind me while Dave was back at the stairs, helping an elderly woman down to the platform. He waved as he continued to help the lady. He just chuckled as he watched me speed away.

Of course I panicked, this being the early days before cell phones. I didn't even have a calling card (you used to have to have a prepaid credit card to call overseas from a pay phone) and not like I would remember the hotel number anyway. I decide the only thing to do was to just go to the stop we marked on the map still clutched in my hand. I found the right train and emerged up the stairs of the tube to Leicester Square… and him smiling at the top. He didn't even look stressed, just amused. He knew I would find my way back to him.

By the time we reached the end of our trip, we were navigating the train stations like pros. He led the way through the busy stations and streets, I bought tickets, he navigated to the hotel, I planned activities, he marked maps. A couple of decades later, our system is a well-oiled machine of easy collaboration. It is by far one of my favorite things about our relationship—our ability to travel and enjoy the world's experiences together.

Dave suggests a local Italian restaurant within walking distance of the hotel that includes a convenient stroll through Times Square. Sounds like the perfect NYC dinner.

"I want to see the red stairs. And buy a NYC hat. Can we go to Krispy Kreme?" Jack is firing off requests quicker than I can process. Comments I would never have had the courage to ask when I was young.

You get what you get, and you don't throw a fit.

Both Dave and I grew up that way. "Be grateful for what you have; it's a privilege to have the opportunity just to be here." We have sacrificed so

much to ensure Jack feels heard and valued for his input. Going through the first years of your life being able to have input on what you want to see and do is a gift that neither of us received and are happy to provide.

Although it does cause a bit of eye-rolling and constant reminders of gratitude.

"Oh all right," I concede with a knowing look at my husband, "but only one. We are going to dinner. Any other things you want to see on the way?"

We bundle up in our new coats like unprepared Texans in an NYC spring chill and continue to chatter as we bustle out the door to explore the Big Apple.

* * *

I know NYC is the pinnacle of urban living, complete with homelessness, crime, and greed, but it feels somehow safer than back home. Yeah, there are all kinds in the big melting pot of NYC's citizens, but there are also rainbows and five-pointed stars, black power t-shirts and hijabs all existing together. No one is yelling hate or threatening violence like our libraries back home. I don't see any Karens threatening a deli worker or witness any walk-by racial slurs. Times Square is busy and bright and totally unique, yet quietly friendly.

What I do see are a few mothers watching kids play on a playground surrounded by tall buildings and people sitting outdoors inches away from blaring traffic, relaxed and chatting like the folks do back home. I point this out, make sure Jack sees how living here is different but the same. More than anything, I crave for him to know that the world is so

big and diverse, happiness can live anywhere. No matter who he wants to be, there is a place for him to fit in.

Dinner is a fantastic Italian restaurant, a social media recommendation of the kind of pasta they prepare tableside in a wheel of cheese. It makes for an excellent video to share with friends and is quite impressive, tasting as good as it looks. We enjoy a glass of wine, some good food, and discuss the wonders of New York. Excitement of the first day on a new adventure bubbles over like a champagne toast.

I don't post my photos of Jack with his cheesy noodles or in awe of Times Square. Those special moments captured in time are just for me. Social media isn't a very safe place for me so I haven't posted anything in over a year. Not since our adopted daughter, Destiny, took a turn for the worst. Not since I cut off all communication with my family back home in Oklahoma. And something about not prioritizing time to craft a snarky caption or adjust the lighting or respond to a comment still feels a little rebellious, but in a good way.

So the conversation and sweet pictures will be wrapped in the fuzzy memory of love and softened at the edges, but we do make plans to visit the MoMA the next day, resting before our evening show of preview week of *Sweeney Todd*. The night finishes in a warm Uber ride around the corner and sleepy dreams of adventures to come.

CHAPTER TWO

New York bagels are absolutely a fucking thing. They are the best, cannot be beat, and I love them. Getting a delicious, authentic NYC bagel and heading to the MoMA before our Broadway debut show is about as good as it gets in this life. The superior deliciousness of the perfectly toasted bagel with cream cheese oozing through the center. The awe and inspiration of consuming one of the most amazing collections of innovative artists' work at the Museum of Modern Art. The glow in my chest watching my son be captivated by just a few things—more than I was ever allowed at that age.

The Mother hates art. She doesn't get it. She can't do it. She is more of a puff paint kind of crafter which is absolutely the lowest of the low when it comes to the prestigious art hierarchy, according to The Grandmother. The Mother despises any kind of museum and vocally demeans any admiration of the work within. Only stuck-up and pretentious people like that kind of stuff.

The Grandmother was a porcelain atelier when she was alive, delicately painting doll faces for dolls that couldn't be touched. They sit on small shelves all over her house, looking blankly from their glass eyes and perfectly painted freckles over all the activity of our family. She was very proud of her exquisite collection, proud of her perfectly ladylike talent.

The Mother's sisters, Aunt Ivy and Aunt Robin, have appropriate talents too. Aunt Robin is the oldest, a beautiful voice she showcases frequently for family functions and at church. The Grandfather will ask her to sing before prayers or during Family Home Evening, us all joining

in but her leading us always. She has a nice vibrato and leads the church choir so she always helps us stay on pace. Sometimes, she would let me sit on her lap when I was little and sing me lullabies. The Mother is tone-deaf so singing in our house was a big no-no. Most assuredly, my love of music comes from being wrapped up in Aunt Robin's arms, being soothed with her soft songs.

Aunt Ivy is the youngest sister, the golden girl. She has always been the beauty of the family, with sparkling eyes, a quiet voice, and a heart of gold. It is from her I learned it was OK to really enjoy the abundance of mastery and creativity in artwork. She is a skilled painter, when she works on it. She is the people pleaser and the expressionist, always adding her own flourish to any canvas.

She is also the only woman in my family to have had a corporate career. Aunt Ivy worked for American Airlines as an accountant for 20 years, then was unceremoniously dumped in a mass layoff. The women in my family always laughed and scoffed at my aunt's misfortunes in both business and love. Corporate America in the '80s and '90s was not great for females, and in Oklahoma it was little better than the first season of *Mad Men*. Not that anyone in our family cared since women are not supposed to be working at all.

Our family joined the Church of Jesus Christ of Latter-Day Saints (aka LDS Mormons) when The Mother was in high school. The Grandfather demands a strict adherence to Mormon doctrine, a tight vise I was eager to break free of as soon as I moved out on my own.

Mormon doctrine is very discouraging of women having any focus other than being a wife and mother, but since her husband cheated on her and left Aunt Ivy as a single mother, her career was tolerated. I can't

imagine what she endured those years, facing the horrors of the male workforce and being a single Mormon mom. It couldn't have been easy. I know it wasn't.

The Mother is the middle child, beauty and grace above and below... but The Mother is the ugly duckling. She struggled in school and had learning disabilities. She wasn't very good at sports or auditions, so she gravitated to clubs and her church group where inclusion was not exclusive. She rebelled a bit in her early years and worked at a bar for a time, wildly inappropriate for a young righteous girl. Alas, this is where she fell into bed with a charming boy visiting from Alabama. She immediately came up pregnant, and a shotgun wedding was hastily arranged. I entered the picture as the light of my father's life and the thorn in The Mother's side.

This is not a story I know from growing up. The Mother maintained that my father met her, fell in love, and swept her off her feet. Now I admit my dad is pretty damn amazing, but suave he is not. Regardless, The Mother lived in a narrative of her own making from the beginning. She could twist a story to be whatever benefitted her as long as she was able to claim ignorance about key accountability points.

I tried to pretend The Mother was kind. She really liked to gather the most broken and damaged people as friends, people who were so sick or disabled or mentally ill, friends who allowed her to be the dominant force in the friendship. It was her most prized possession, the perception that she was a good person.

So I stroll along the large, bright corridors of the MoMA and enjoy the luxury of excellent creative works. I don't have to explain why I like it. I don't have to justify stopping to study a brushstroke or ponder a weird

modern expressionist piece. I can just absorb the feelings and technique of each piece without worry. How wonderfully freeing.

* * *

As we exit the MoMA drunk on colors and creativity, we head out into the cold afternoon light of the NYC spring. It's a bright day with a chilly breeze that smells of warmer weather to come. The trees are just beginning to bud, and the sunshine is warm enough to be comfortable in a sweater. We wander around, taking in the sights and sounds, letting Jack explore the city.

I can't ever remember being allowed to lead where our family would go when I was young. What a novel and perfectly ordinary idea, but odd. Why was that never a thing? I guess because of that one time when I was five and got lost at the Oxley Nature Park. I had been strong-willed and insisted I take a side path that would lead me back around to the welcome center. I was lost for hours. I was lucky they found me crying on the side of the road outside the reserve. Since then, trust in my navigational skills hasn't been great by anyone, including myself. Worked out well that I met Dave.

Jack has Dave's instincts for direction so we don't get lost. I enjoy absorbing his excitement of having the freedom to explore what catches his interest or stop to discuss something that looks interesting. Dave and I are happy to follow. Parents don't always have to lead the way.

We eventually head back to the hotel, chattering about how much time we have and what pieces we enjoyed in the museum. I feel very superior for splurging for a suite with two bathrooms. Just one more

thing I don't have to stress about as we make our way back to dress for dinner.

That's what money does—it lowers my stress level. Taxi fare ticks up because you get caught in traffic—it's OK. Your tickets you booked three months in advance are on the wrong day—it's fine. You can just buy them again. Your kid forgets to pack a hat even after you told him three times it would be cold, and he said it's not that cold—it's fine. You can buy a $40 NYC poly-blend beanie that will shred as soon as you get home. You can afford it. Ahhh, the best four words in the world.

* * *

Prioritizing time to rest and prepare for an evening's activities when traveling is essential to a memorable experience. When Dave and I were first dating, we booked a trip to NYC to visit a dear friend from college. Dave had never been to Manhattan so I insisted we see the most spectacular new Broadway show that just premiered to rave reviews. I knew we could never afford the exorbitant prices for a hit show that was already sold out months in advance, but I had a plan.

Before each show, the Gershwin Theater ticket office released the few remaining unsold or unclaimed tickets. This could be single seats or a block that was canceled last minute. A line would form early in the morning to score one of these prize seats at face value, usually four to five hours before the show. You could not leave to go to the bathroom, and you could not sit down (line monitors are very strict). So I devised a plan for us to stand in the line and take turns getting snacks and breaks in hopes of getting into the show.

However, my darling boyfriend hopped in line and insisted that I go to dance class at the Broadway Dance Center—no reason both of us should stand there. He didn't mind the cold. Surely we would get tickets in an hour or so. I could squeeze in a class, meet him with the tickets, and then we could go back to the room to get dressed for the show.

We did get tickets to the show… four minutes before curtain. I was horrified, walking into *Wicked*'s opening run on Broadway in dance pants and sneakers. We were cold, grubby, and tired sitting in single seats in the center orchestra just a few rows apart watching Idina Menzel defy gravity and Kristin Chenoweth delight in her popularity. At intermission, we took a quick look and head nod to meet in the lobby where we clasped hands and bubbled over with excitement at the wondrous story unfolding on stage.

Though I remember that story fondly, and still brag about catching that iconic performance on the cheap, it is tainted by the shame I felt sitting in the presence of such talent in my shabby clothes. Not just because I enjoy respecting the performances of the live actors with my effort, but also because I have been raised to constantly be thoughtful of how my outward appearance affects others. I must always be careful that I do not step out into the world without the proper armor and thoughtful consideration. It is my responsibility to ensure I look pleasing, proper, and beautiful without being too enticing or revealing; a sweatshirt at the theater is simply shameful.

Lesson learned: always incorporate time to prepare for an event and carry a few extra necessities with me just in case.

Preparing for this show is a luxurious contrast to that spontaneous day, with plenty of time for 'fit checks and shoe debates. We eat street

food for dinner, providing flexibility to nibble and enjoy the nighttime bustle without a waiter to keep informed. We saunter along the avenue in our dapper duds, eating steaming, wax-paper-wrapped deliciousness and enjoy being together in this great city.

Going to New York to see a Broadway show was ignited by our son's new love of musical theater. He was a bit surprised how easily we agreed to the trip just a few weeks before spring break. Usually, trips require months of planning. But it was the first time it was only the three of us traveling in a long time. Last year's spring break was the last with Destiny, such a heavy affair, and Dave and I were eager to give a more lighthearted experience to our son. Lucking into cheap flights and preview week tickets for the opening of *Sweeney Todd* with Josh Grobin and Annaleigh Ashford was just gentle confirmation that this was the best choice to make.

So as we approach the theater for Jack's first Broadway night—marquee lights brilliant, blustery wind blowing, line snaking around the block with buzzing excitement about the new show—it is downright magical. Entering the historic building, you can feel the echoes of the glorious voices of the past. People who feel the same awe and thrill at seeing expressive art live on stage are smiling and chatting in line at the snack bar, not caring at all about the exorbitant prices of popcorn and cheap wine. It's a timeless thing, to see a story told live by master storytellers, and we are all here to witness together.

This is what it's all for, this moment of happiness and sharing.

"This is amazing, Mom!" my son whispers over the armrest after the first few songs. And then Dustin Henderson bursts on to the stage and Jack bounces in his seat. Neither of us knew he was in the show, but

the shock is a zing of delight. *Stranger Things* fans from the beginning, he now sees that an actor can do a cool TV show and be in a Broadway musical. For the first time he sees someone who represents someone like him…and it is awesome! It's acceptable to be a young man, a performer, a sensitive artist, in the theater. *Dustin, you are an icon. Thank you for being visible*, I think as I miss his performance to enjoy my son's delight.

The show exceeds expectations. Talent that is honest, no filters or holding back, is a sight to behold. The walk home is filled with impromptu humming sessions with bouts of singing the chorus line together loudly with abandon. It is a night where you don't really talk about anything because your heart is speaking to the world. And you drop into sleep with a fullness that runneth over into dreams filled with song.

CHAPTER THREE

Waking up in a new city, the sounds and smells assault you before the sun. I can hear the cars honking instead of lawn mowers. Dave is already making a cup of crappy hotel coffee instead of his usual local-roasted French press. We are like country mice on holiday in the big city.

Early in my life, when I began to travel on my own, I packed every day with as many activities as I could manage. I was up at seven and going hard every minute to see all that I could with my time and budget. I had train schedules, promo days tagged, spreadsheets of sites with distances and costs; I wasn't sure I would ever be able to afford to travel to these places again; it was critical to do as much as my creative budgeting allowed.

Now, I schedule one activity a day and leave the rest unplanned. The best travel experiences often are the paths you didn't know to follow until you see them. Now that I have adult money, I can take vacations that are not centered around trying to absorb a world outside in one big bite. My favorite part of travel is still getting to see how others live and enjoy life, but I now don't push as hard to gobble it all in one setting. I have put in the time and work to feel more confident about my career and ability to make future earnings, take more trips. It's a dream realized and worth every sacrifice.

So as I lie drifting up towards full consciousness, I hear Dave and Jack as they whisper about a donut heist. They quietly creep out the door. I lie in bed just a few minutes in muted silence, soaking up the peace of the moment.

Life is like a storm, Alexander Dumas once said, *basking in the sun one moment and crashed on the rocks the next.*

So I make a conscious effort to pause and enjoy every soft, happy moment I get. Knowing my boys are safe and happy. Knowing, for the moment, we are basking in the sun.

The boys return with steaming Starbucks for me and confectioners' sugar crusting the tips of their fingers and the corners of their mouths.

"The biggest Krispy Kreme in NYC cannot be missed," Jack says with a grin.

I smile in return as I snuggle under the covers, still in my PJs, and gesture him over to jump into bed for a hug, sticky fingers and all. He lies with his head resting in the crook of my arm licking his fingers as he recounts the sights enjoyed on their morning excursion. It's not every day he sees a man painted like a statue that scares tourists.

We sit sipping and munching as we discuss our "free time" of the vacation. No plans, no tickets, no reservations. I have a list of four places that require no preplanning and are open today. I present all options to Jack and ask for his recommendations. This is a family trip; we make the decisions together. He really gets into reviewing the options, discarding some ideas and sharing his thoughts on the best activities. He carefully weighs the options and finally settles that a trip to Central Park is his top pick.

* * *

We head to Central Park lazily, not in a rush today. It's been a challenging few months for our family. I am relieved to see us all recovering and

relaxing. For the past four years, we've had my niece Destiny living with us, adopted all but in paperwork.

Destiny is the daughter of my sister, Rebecca. Rebecca was a veteran drug addict by the time she had Destiny, being a user of pills and other substances since she was 13. She tried to care for Destiny, but she was removed from the home by DHS within the first year at The Mother's insistence. The Mother then navigated the foster system, becoming vetted and approved to adopt Destiny legally and raise her for the next decade. The turn to teen was a tough situation for The Mother, and Destiny became so violent that I was able to convince The Mother to let Destiny come live with us.

Destiny has always been like a sister to Jack, so moving her in was like getting a sister full-time. At the time, I thought I was doing the right thing. Getting her out of that house, out of that church, out of Oklahoma. I was already living in a Dallas suburb with an excellent job. I had a kind husband, a lovely home, was financially stable, and had the emotional stability to help her get on her feet.

But I didn't know how deep the damage was. We welcomed her with open arms. We all gave the love, kindness, and acceptance we could offer. I researched and invested in physical and mental health resources, connecting multiple providers with complementary expertise to create a team of support for her. We did the absolute best job we could, but it wasn't enough. She left our home four months ago and has not contacted us since.

It's been hard on us all, but I worry most about Jack. It is devastating to a child to know you didn't do anything wrong, but you are being

punished anyway. Yes, it's difficult for everyone, but a child really has no resources to reconcile it with the basic principles of human morality being taught in our institutions. Destiny leaving and not saying goodbye or reaching out to him at all (even blocking him on social media) was rough for him. He is strong, and he learned to manage the void, but my momma bear inside just wants to fix it. I wish I could make her see that she doesn't have to punish Jack because she disagrees with me.

So Dave and I sit in the sun and watch our remaining child run and play in one of the greatest cities in the world. He climbs on rocks and shouts me to watch. Outwardly teasingly annoyed but secretly delighted, I turn to see him stand 1,000 feet tall and breathe in the confidence I will give my life to defend. The confidence that he is loved, safe, and supported and will be as long as I draw breath.

* * *

My life is an odd one, in so many ways, yet I always seem to find my way to a path I didn't even know was an option. A Tulsa, OK and LDS native, I took a chance in 2013 and moved my family to Dallas, TX. At the time, I was married to Dave with a darling four-year-old little boy, I had a job making $27K a year with benefits, and I was coaching a local dance team that gave me joy and fulfillment. I had dinner with my family every week. Was guilted into going to church for holidays and special occasions. It was no picnic, but we were doing OK.

Then one day I got a phone call from a college friend asking if I would be interested in a job in Dallas. I cannot believe I got that job. I was underqualified and had no intention of moving. But it was double my current salary and a chance at a new life away from my family. Escape.

I committed to my career to justify the upheaval. When Instagrammers and business gurus say you have to hustle to make it, I had no idea they were talking about what I was doing. I was learning software and certifications on the fly. I showed up at every social networking event, every happy hour. I returned phone calls and followed up on every detail. I listened, I took feedback, I learned. I succeeded. But I was fucking exhausted.

Entering Corporate America—every Dilbert comic made sense. The stupid legacy processes. The dinosaurs that roar and eat the young but contribute nothing. The political wars shamelessly throwing people's lives around like a hot potato. The absolute abandonment of any sort of ethical or moral code when shareholder value is on the line. It's soul-crushing. Especially when my job is to get the rawest form of the most heinous output and make it palatable.

Executives are not promoted for their kindness or compassion for others. At least none I have met. It's always, always "It's not personal, it's business."

But business is personal. I spent more time at the office than with my family. I used that money to provide a home and food for them. I compromised my integrity, framed my entire life around the company's timelines and demands—being a model ambassador for an entity. Companies now demand appropriate behavior and aligned views with The Company on personal social media accounts, yet they want to say business is not personal. Business couldn't be more personal. Anyone who says otherwise is doing something they feel bad about but will make them more money.

As we head back to the hotel, drowsy from too much sun and fresh air, I am content with the moment, but dwell on pondering what the next phase of my life looks like:

How do I not become another asshole executive? How does our family heal without Destiny?

There is no urgency to figure these things out today, and for that I am grateful. I have a steady job, a peaceful home, and two beautiful boys. I have time to plan for our future without being driven by duress. This is what I have worked so hard to achieve, and I am going to enjoy it.

CHAPTER FOUR

Returning home from a week-long vacation when working in Corporate America is always a chore. Though the Boomer generation likes to remind us how pampered we are getting the luxury of "paid time off," us Gen Xers know that it's not really vacation anymore but more of a permission to delay the instant response expectation (unless of course there is an emergency, then you know where to reach me), so I have blocked out my calendar for the next couple of mornings to give myself time to catch up.

Working as a Public Relations and Communications executive in a tech start-up is a wild experience, especially in comparison to the tightly run ship of a traditional manufacturing company. The CEO hides in his office and talks to employees on the other side of his door through a video chat. The C-suite leaders don't have budgets, strategies, or goals. Everything is "react and move fast." It's a good experience for me, learning to navigate new leadership ecosystems, but it does feel a bit silly. They seem like frat boys who won the lottery and are playing dress-up.

They are not serious people, as Logan Roy says. I tend to agree.

But they keep paying me, and the people are mostly lovely so I am happy enough to enjoy my coffee and morning notes recaps as I sit to prepare for my biweekly meeting with my boss.

She is an interesting lady, not at all like previous Human Resources (HR) folks I have been terrorized by in the past. I tend to struggle with HR relationships because I have to work so closely with them in my role. They realize real quick that if I am uncomfortable with their practices,

I ask a lot of questions that don't feel good. They do not like thinking about the people their "policies" actually impact.

"Morning! Good to see you," I chirp cheerily as I settle in front of the computer camera, checking that my fresh red lipstick and fun, funky glasses are giving that professional yet cool vibe I am going for. It's a tech firm; these things matter.

"Hey, morning," she says slowly, a bit more occupied than normal with a low pitch of voice that means things are still not resolving like she wants. "You doing OK? Everything with your trip turn out OK?"

"Oh yeah, it was great. We all had a really nice trip," I say with a smile. "Been taking it slow, catching up on what I missed. Have an important meeting with…"

"Hold on, hold on, let me stop you right there. Before you go into anything…" She stares at me through the screen as my voice fades out and I blink blankly.

"OK…" I feel the warning current tightening my spine. "Is everything OK?"

"Look, I'm sorry, but I don't want you to go into anything because we are letting you go today. Today will be your last day at this company. Do not remove anything from your computer or attempt to take anything. Your computer will lock as soon as we are off this call."

She pauses to take a breath; I just stare.

"This isn't a performance issue. I think you know the company is losing money. A lot of money last quarter," she explains, "and we have to cut expenses. You know we can't afford you anymore. You weren't really happy here anyway since we couldn't let you do the things you wanted to do."

I sit and stare. Blank.

"I didn't know the company was doing badly. That's not what I have been writing in the company news," I stammer. It's the only thing I can think to say.

"Oh, it's not good. We are having to cut a lot of people. This is a budgeting decision. This is not a performance issue. You didn't do anything wrong."

I am numb. I don't cry; I know that won't help. I just don't know what to say.

"Is there anything I can do to change this decision? Another role available?" My voice is squeaky, but I am determined not to cry. It's not professional to cry.

"No, the decision is final," she says, looking away. Shuffling papers uncomfortably. It's done.

There are a few other things said about insurance coverage, last day, and severance. I take a few notes without really looking at the words. I don't cry or scream or say much of anything really. I can't. I don't have any feelings at all—except one.

Fear.

* * *

I close the call, and my computer immediately goes to the lock screen with admin as the only user listed. I am locked out. Sure doesn't feel like I didn't do anything wrong.

I shakily open my phone and tap Dave's name, rattling the desk a bit as I set it down on speaker.

"Hey, what's up?" he answers. I can hear his coworkers laughing at a joke and chatting in the background.

"Dave. I lost my job. They laid me off. Can you please come home?" My voice rises and breaks on the end, numb, finally cracking under the pressure of the fear racing through my veins. "I don't know what to do," I finish weakly.

What a weird thing to say, I lost my job. I didn't lose it—I fucking know where it is. I didn't lose it—they kicked me out. Then why am I so worried?

"Oh no. OK, honey, I am on my way," he says urgently as I hear him gather his things and mumble to his coworker that he has to go for an emergency.

"OK," I say in a small, sad voice and hit the end button, rising from the chair as the emotion erupts through my mouth in a wail and a stream of tears leaks down my face. I collapse on my bed and weep into my pillow.

I don't know what to do. I don't know what to do. I don't know what I did.

I didn't do anything wrong. What did I do?

What will I do?

I won't go back.

* * *

For days, I let the raw emotion take its due. Hours on the couch, frantically applying for jobs. All jobs, any jobs, all the jobs. Watching videos on résumé improvements, looking at industry reports for clues

to who may be the best targets for proactive outreach. Looking into consulting opportunities. Making connections on LinkedIn.

Anything I can do to ease the panic of knowing income is stopping. The hum of fear is constant and exhausting. It grips my spine, shakes my hands, lies across my shoulders like Sisyphus's boulder. How can I be punished when I didn't do anything wrong?

Logically, I know I didn't do anything wrong. The company is a shit show and laid off lots of people. I am good at what I do. I am gifted at building narratives and strategies for millionaire executives to stay out of trouble and not sound like the assholes they are. That's my job, and just looking at the insanity on social media tells me my skills are in high demand. I am already getting paid a nice salary. I know I can get at least that if not more. I can even do this on my own if I want, start my own company. I am smart and capable... so why do I have all this fear?

CHAPTER FIVE

It's Tuesday again. I have been without a work email or business meeting or media reports for a week. It feels like a year. It feels like I am being lazy and neglecting my executive's needs. It feels like anyone who will find out will be disgusted to know me anymore without my pretty life and important job. I am so afraid of what will happen if I don't get a job soon. I am NOT going back. I don't care what I do—I am not going back to Oklahoma.

I can hear Dave multitasking in the kitchen as I lie still and stiff on the couch. He is an excellent cook and a lovely human, so it's not a good sign when he is using his I'm-not-dealing-with-this-now voice as he mumbles on the phone.

"What is it?" I don't really want to know, but I know it's polite to ask.

"Uh… your mom may show up here in a bit," he cautiously says as he wipes his hands on the tea towel at his waist and abandons his cooking dish. "I am telling her not now, but she is not responding to my texts."

"What?" I ask as the panic rises. I understand, but I don't understand. Why would she be coming here?

BANG BANG BANG

I jump up and squeeze my arms tight around my knees, pulling them to my chest and shaking uncontrollably.

Dave swears and turns off the stove. "Don't worry," he cajoles. "We will ignore them until they are able to coordinate a time that works for me. I can meet them somewhere after dinner. You don't need to deal with this right now," he finishes as he peeks around the corner into the

entryway where the dogs are barking insanely at the door. Our big lab/ Shepherd mix, Teddy, only whines like that when Destiny is around, so she must be out there too.

BANG BANG BANG BANG

BANG BANG BANG BANG BANG BANG BANG

BANG BANG BANG BANG BANG BANG BANG

The banging moves from the door to the windows. It's two, then three people, banging on the windows of the front room. There is someone peeking in the windows above the door and shutters. Teddy's excited whine flips to a protective growl that raises the hair on the back of his neck and on the back of my arms.

There is someone else out there who we don't know. I have only heard him growl like that once. It was a scary situation too. I sit frozen on the couch with my knees squeezed to my chest.

My mind goes black, and I see myself standing in the living room of my childhood home. I am shaking as I am now. The Mother next to me shakes and cries too. My brother is wild, crazy like that greedy guy at the end of Roger Rabbit who wants more billboards. He is yelling and swinging fists at The Grandfather and The Mother.

My flowered living room comes back into focus, and I feel my muscles aching from sitting in a tight ball shaking and crying like a scared child. I tuck my head down and cry harder, wishing they would go away and stop banging.

Then my mind clears, and I sit up, put my feet on the floor. *This is my house*. I worked hard for this house and these windows, and I don't have to deal with this shit in MY home.

This is my own house. I choose who is welcome here.

I stand up and start walking to the door. "I'm going out there," I toss casually at Dave as I get my flip-flops quickly. "This is my house, and they have no right to terrorize me here."

Dave pleads and cajoles in fearful gasps as I march past him to the front door. I gently push the whining and barking dogs away from the opening as I squeeze through, letting Dave take control of the doorknob from the other side to ensure their safety as I continue to charge out to four black car doors closing in the driveway.

I see The Mother in the driver's seat, Destiny and her boyfriend in the back. The Grandfather in the passenger seat—all smiling. Like this is the best part of a prank where they get to laugh at me falling down the stairs.

Something inside me breaks open, and red floods my vision like a rising of smoke.

"You don't come to my house and treat me like this!" I scream, pointing my finger at the beautiful home I have worked so hard for. "You don't get to come to MY house and bang on MY doors!"

The driver's side window slowly hums down, revealing The Mother's smiling face in full view. I know that smile, the Cheshire Cat smile. She is proud she has made me angry and lose control. She has delivered a performance that only happens every 20 years or so.

"Oh, honey, don't you want to talk about why we are here? The things you have done?" she purrs, lying back in the seat, ready to enjoy the entertainment.

"Are you fucking kidding me?!" I scream, oblivious to the trap. I have not lost my temper like this in a long time. There is too much flowing for me to listen to the hum of fear that's been pulsing for weeks and now is on hyperdrive. "I don't give a fuck about what you have to say," I

continue but stop short when my eyes adjust and I see what's in Destiny's hand.

The Grandfather sits in the passenger seat, cool as a cucumber and delighted like I haven't seen him in years. "Now you watch your mouth with that language, young lady," he says like he's speaking to a child who is being naughty. His soft, raspy voice is like a bucket of ice water in my veins. At 99 years old, he is not nearly as frail as he should be. And this little scene is giving him life.

I ignore him and jerk my gaze away to focus on the two heads in the back seat, my heart dropping out of my chest. First, I see her dark, wispy hair. Then her gigantic big teeth and cruelly narrowed black-lined eyes crinkling with delight behind the iPhone she holds like a torch in front of her. She knew seeing The Mother and banging on the door would piss me off, but she knew this would break me. I see the pride sparkle in her eyes that she has delivered the impossible—I have lost my temper, and she has it on video. Forever.

"You are recording me?" I ask dumbly to her shining face. "Why? Why do you want to show the whole world one of my most awful moments?" Tears stream down my face, all the fight in me dimmed by the malice in her brown eyes. I always did have a soft spot for Destiny. I always did try to see all the way to the inside, past the lies and the blackness in her.

"You know why," she sneers.

I stare at her, swallowing hard. She maintains we kicked her out. That's the story she tells. But it's not being kicked out if I ask you if you want to be here and you say no, then leave. There was no throwing clothes into the street, no hard arm grabs or shoves out the door. She said she didn't

want to be here, and we told her we wouldn't stop her from leaving. So she did.

Our house comes with rules, for protection and safety. Being an underage drug dealer is not acceptable. I won't apologize for enforcing that line; I have another kid and my own safety to consider.

"OK." I take a deep breath. "Just tell me I mean nothing to you, and I will never bother you again. Just tell me when I sat on your bed and listened to you and believed every word you said that it meant nothing to you, and I will walk away and never bother you again. Just look me in the eyes and tell me we, our little family, means nothing."

Her smile widens, and she replies with her specially crafted dagger, "Ha! I'm not giving you that kind of closure."

It hurts. Even through the armor of anger, it pierces deep. I gasp and tears leak in a steady flow as I gasp from the blow. She knew she had the knife; she was ready for this moment of violence. I don't think she prepared for what it would be like to stare at my face when she shoved it in. She turns away and stares at the man I am just now noticing on her right. Guessing that's the boyfriend, but thankfully, he stays silent. I don't think he had any idea what he was getting into.

She keeps her head turned to her boyfriend. He holds her hand and mumbles support under his breath. Tears stream and drip down both of our cheeks, pain and fear and anger in running rivers on our faces. She won't look at me again.

"Why don't we talk about what you did here?" The Mother interrupts the stare-down before someone gives in, obviously disappointed that I am not performing to the family legacy standard. "You sold her car and spent all the money." It isn't a question. She already knows we sold the

car months ago and told us to keep the money to pay for Jack's therapy. Which we did.

"Yeah, and tell Dave I want my tools back, little girl," The Grandfather chides, like he is going to give me a well-deserved punishment when we get back home, something he obviously would like to do very much. "Those tools are expensive, and I don't want them with someone like you and Dave," he says with a smug grin and a dismissive flap of his ancient, wrinkled hand.

"Oh, you can go fuck your tools," I blurt, surprising myself but not mad about it. "You are 99 years old. What the fuck are you going to do with a goddamn router or jig?" I demand with a harsh laugh.

I think Dave is behind me and says something about returning them, but I'll be damned if we give this man a fucking nail. "NO. We are not giving back the tools. You gave them to Dave, he uses them, and they are mine now. Possession is nine-tenths and all." The numbness and anger burning off, the despair creeping up my spine threatening to crumple me on the spot.

"And you," I step back just a bit, to get her rotting teeth out of zoom, "I can't believe that you have the audacity to come to MY house and bang on MY door considering the last time I was shaking inside my house and someone was pounding on the door, you were INSIDE, and it was my brother on a rampage. Remember that? He hit The Grandfather in the face, and he pushed you on the floor. I can't believe you would put me through that again... and YOU are the one on the outside banging. I can't with you. I can't. Get the fuck out of here and never come back."

I walk straight-backed and controlled to the door, never looking back at their gaping faces as they threaten to come back. But I cannot slow

even a step as I stumble the last few meters into the bedroom and melt into a wailing puddle. The grief, fear, anger, and hurt all come roaring out in tears and madness. What is happening? Why is this happening to me? Why does my family hate me so much?

* * *

Having a meltdown as an adult is different than when you are a child. As a child, you cry and scream, not caring who sees or what you hurt. It is a reckless abandonment of emotions enabled by the security that someone will care, pick you up, calm you down, and tell you it's alright. As an adult, it's a very different situation.

I am aware of my husband wrapping himself around me, trying to protect me and absorb my pain at the same time. I can hear the panic in my dog's barking, sensing my distress but not knowing what to do. I know it's my house, and I can choose to refuse company if I want to, especially if they are uninvited… but it's my family. Shouldn't my mother care that she is hurting me? Why doesn't Destiny love me anymore when all I ever did was love her? Why do I have a jagged, ripped-out hole in my heart where my family should be?

My mind is a black pit of yawning vastness, all the troubles of my past lying in wait to drag me down to drown in their pent-up misery. I know they are there, these tiny creatures with big, round, scared eyes. I can feel them waking, feel their hunger for attention so long ignored. My mind desperately bounces to every corner I can think of, looking for escape from the precipice. I feel like the little boy in the *Sixth Sense*, scared of my own mind and the ghosts only I can see.

I lie on the bed and let myself cry it out. I don't think I could hold it in anymore even if I tried. I cry like I haven't in decades, wailing like a wounded animal. The pain sluggishly washing through my muscles and vision, rendering me helpless long after there is no more moisture left to leak.

I have lost my career and faced the final blow from my family. I have never felt so empty and ashamed. Hopelessness wraps up my insides in a grey misty shroud, allowing my wasted body to finally release consciousness.

CHAPTER SIX

Therapy isn't something I discovered until my mid-30s. Working in big business, health insurance is a beating. My role as a communicator was to sit in rooms with top executives and help them communicate more clearly (and kindly) their decisions. This afforded me front-row seats to some disturbing and uncomfortable conversations— artful dodging of liability and creative justification of ruining others' lives. My job demanded I take the unfiltered content and make it appropriate for official communication from the office of the leaders.

It was an eye-opening experience on many levels. Surprisingly, the cultural aspect was the worst. I had so many unanticipated problems with more-tenured women undermining my work. I needed a resource who was unattached to outcomes where I could discuss pathways for success and focus solely on myself.

As fate would have it, I met my therapist in a moment of desperation with an employee assistance program (EAP). A random appointment with the first available provider at the closest in-network facility landed me in a chair with RC, soon to be one of the most important people in my life.

I am unique in that the random therapist accepting the dregs of the EAP business that day just so happened to be incredible. Her odd journey through life enabled her to be in the exact place with the right knowledge to help me. Opportunity knocks, and I know to hang on tight no matter how bumpy the ride.

So she knows that it is an emergency when I text her on her personal cell phone:

Me → The Mother, Grandfather and Destiny just showed up at my house and it's bad. Can you squeeze me in?

RC → I can see you tomorrow at 9 a.m. I hope you are OK?

Me → That works. Thanks for the quick reply.

She is someone who cares, and I fucking adore her for it. I medicate my mind enough to allow me some rest until the morning comes. Exhaustion and the gray frost of grief claim the hours in between. Who am I without my family?

* * *

I insist that Dave drive me to my therapy appointment the next day. I can't be trusted with driving. I feel like a mummy, an unraveling, dead-inside, walking corpse as I shamble from the car into RC's office. I didn't even bother with the mirror this morning, puffy eyes and messy bun—she doesn't mind, and I don't have the energy to care. But I see the lack of my usual luster on her concerned face as I step through the door.

"Hey," she coos as she gives me a hug, "come on in." She wraps me in a soft, warm arm as she ushers me into her little office. Her office is simple and cozy. An old-fashioned desk next to a worn floral-print couch, a few throw pillows. A little wicker basket sits at the far end of the couch with chenille blankets folded and ready for clutching. I slump into one of the two big chairs facing each other, a small coffee table between, and stare blankly at the floor-to-ceiling bookshelves behind the other chair. I hear the soft click of the lock and rustle of movement as RC closes the door, moving to sit in her chair quietly.

"Sorry I'm such a mess today. I appreciate you squeezing me in." Always polite, even when I am a zombie.

"Oh, it's not a problem. Tell me what happened," she says, sitting alert and ready. RC always reminds me of Marmee in *Little Women*. Soft clothes, soft cropped hair, soft kind eyes. Quick wit. Perfect partner for a trauma dump.

The words drop out like stones, hard and heavy. I can remember fear. That is the red that colors the clearest images—The Mother's smile, The Grandfather's burning eyes, Destiny's cheeks smiling. But as I struggle to tell the story, the details and perspective jumble together. I don't remember some things. Others, I see them happening in third person. I know I was there. I did it all; I just get stuck when I try and relive the details in order.

"I just don't understand," I finish, sniffing and wiping the damp tissue again across the rivers of salt running down my face. "Why does this stuff happen to me? First the job and now this. How much can a person take?"

I feel so depleted, empty, and blank. I can't feel any more, I have hit my max. My cup is empty, and there is none for anyone, including myself.

"OK, yeah, this is bad. But they are gone. They are not coming back." she says so confidently, I blink a few times to make sure I heard her right.

"Are you sure?" It's a tiny voice, scared and disbelieving. But I trust RC; she never wants to hurt me, and she always tries to say the right thing. If she believes they won't come back, I will believe her. I will make myself believe her. It's counterproductive to pay someone for their help and then not listen to them.

"Yes. And if they do, you call the cops," she says matter-of-factly, like it's a totally appropriate thing to do.

A tiny giggle escapes my lips, and I dip my head in embarrassment. "I can't do that." I can't even imagine how much trouble I would get in if I called the cops on The Mother and 100-year-old Grandfather.

"Yes you can! It's your house, and they are not welcome. It's called trespassing, and the police will escort them off your property." She says this through a laugh and a little extra bravado. It sounds like a perfectly reasonable idea, but my brain cannot compute the idea of calling the authorities on my family.

RC isn't surprised by my reaction; she doesn't let the jape go on. She is serious quite quickly when she sees that I am not able to comprehend. She knows I have an awful family. I have threatened legal action many times when helping Destiny, but the idea of using it to protect myself doesn't seem like a real thing. I mean, the police have never helped before.

The police don't care about little girls like me.

A few moments of silence pass while I try to put the words together to make sense. I can logically see that I am a law-abiding taxpayer with rights, but it feels completely foreign that I would be believed over a disputing mother and grandfather. Family squabbles are always "taken care of" by The Grandfather so the police don't have to be bothered.

"Let this go for a few days. You need to rest, and DO NOT look for work. Give yourself a little break and then we can touch base next week, OK?" she says as she picks up her appointment book and pencils in a note on the little Monday square.

"OK. I'll try to rest. If they come back, I'll call the cops," I say dutifully, making sure she sees that I have heard her and will do as she says. She wants me to get better so I need to do as she asks, even if it is hard.

She nods as she gives me another hug and walks me out the door. Dave is waiting in the car, sitting tensely, worry lines etched deep today. He gives a wave as she lets the door close behind me and I walk into the sunshine.

* * *

Depression is a thief, stealing moments and energy and leaving vast swaths of time unaccounted for. Sleep sometimes, sometimes lying just staring at the trees outside my window. Muscles aching with fire, but I haven't moved much in days. Movies and TV shows with filled little bars of progress that I don't remember seeing. It's like being a ghost inside a body wracked with aching.

Monday comes again. The sharp sting of the crisis has passed, settling into a heavy black river of sadness that puddles and drips inside me. I only feel safe on the couch or in bed. It's hard to eat or have a conversation. I am beyond panicked that I am not actively looking for a job, not that I want to but that I am putting my family at risk because I am not earning money. Ashamed and embarrassed of my family's behavior and my lack of employment, I revert to silence and isolation.

I sit quietly in RC's office, staring blankly at my hands.

"Your family is awful. You know this," she says kindly, encouraging me. "It's why you cut things off with them last year. They only care about themselves. Hurting you is just a means to an end," she finishes gently.

"I know," I sniff. "It just feels unbelievable. After all this time, all the work, all the logic in my brain… and I still can't believe that my own family doesn't love me."

The sadness ebbs just enough for a soft orange spark of anger to rise in my mind. "I mean, I am sure they do in their own way, but they do not want to see me happy or help me succeed. They only value blind obedience, loyalty, and silence." It hurts to say it out loud.

"That's right. That's not what love is. Or how you want to live your life. They are adults. They make their own choices." She pauses, searching my face to gauge where my sadness level sits in my eyes—currently not brimming over so better than when I came in. "I would never do something like that to my child, no matter how mad I was at them." She stops, seeing my face start to crumple again. "I would call and talk to them like a normal person!" she jokes just a little, to lighten the mood. "They are awful, and their behavior is unacceptable," she finishes honestly and clearly. These are words that are hard for me to hear, but I know they are true.

"I'm worried about our safety," I say as the fleeting smile fades. "Every time the dog barks or some random person knocks on the door, I break out in nervous shakes. I can't protect them." I hear the little girl's voice coming out of my mouth, and I feel even worse. I am a fucking adult; I hate that they make me feel like a scared little girl.

"So go buy a baseball bat or some mace," she suggests. "Have it ready if it helps you feel safer."

I stare at her with wide eyes. I can't even imagine committing violence. I have never thrown anything in anger. I can't even throw a pillow back

and forth yet, still working on that. I can't imagine being able to pick up a bat and hit a family member.

I lower my eyes and stare at my lap and mumble, "Maybe." I'm fading. It's exhausting working through this shit.

"So you're recovering a little, health-wise?" RC asks carefully, "No panic attacks or meltdowns?"

I look down at my lap, embarrassed. It's a valid question. "No, just took it easy this weekend. Trying to stay in touch with old friends. Doing yoga and meditation every day. Any healthy thing I can think to do." Always the optimist.

"Those are good. Be gentle with yourself. You need it," she says with a smile as we end our session. "We'll talk next week at our regular time."

"Sounds good," I say as I walk out the door, looking forward to climbing back to the safety of my pillows and blankets.

AGE 45 POKING THE OOZE

CHAPTER SEVEN

Two weeks pass. I slink into RC's office even messier than before (how is that even possible?!), and she chuckles like only your therapist can when they know you are down in the hole. RC squeezes my shoulder as I slip past her to the office and sink into the big easy chair.

"Uh, I am such a hot mess," I sigh mournfully. It's a familiar tune these days.

"Uh-huh, so, where do you want to start?" She settles herself, puts her hands in her lap, and gives me space to think of what to say.

"No bites in the job market. I can't understand why. PR is a mess right now. No contact from the family. It's been eerily quiet." It's good news, but it doesn't feel good. It feels ominous. I rush on, "So the same things keep happening to me. The definition of insanity is doing the same thing over and over and expecting different results," I say in a word salad, methodically laying out my conundrum, "but THE SAME stuff keeps happening to me over and over, and I can't seem to make different choices to keep them from happening." I pause to peek up at her from the focus of my nail picking. "What am I doing wrong?"

I am empty. It's like bobbing in the ocean on a raft, miles of ocean in every direction but not a drop to drink. I feel like taking action is the only way to solve the problem, but every action seems to toss me further into the waves. Setting me adrift even more in the empty sea of depression.

She gently chuckles. "You aren't doing anything wrong. Your company is run by idiots who are selfish. They would rather keep the money than invest in making a successful business. They couldn't afford you anymore.

You didn't do anything wrong." She says it gently, knowing I struggle with punishment for others' actions.

"Your family is crazy, so you cut them off. You did the right thing. They are not good people to have in your life. You are not doing anything wrong. You are just facing circumstances that most people never have to think about." She tilts her head to see if she can catch my eye, trying to give me some relief from the overwhelming guilt. I know she can't solve everything, but it does feel nice when she reminds me that I am not cursed or being cosmically punished for some transgression from my youth.

I feel horrible for letting my family down by losing my job—even if it's not my fault. I am the majority breadwinner for our family, and the loss hurts us all. I am hustling for hours every day, making contacts on LinkedIn, applying for jobs, and researching contract work. Anything to be productive again. To not think about what can happen if I fail.

I feel terrible for having such a heartless family, treating me and my family like we are the villains. Cutting off communication with The Mother last year was difficult, but necessary. It was just too hard seeing The Mother treat Destiny like she treated me. Seeing a child, a child you claim as your own, being degraded and hit is an eye-opening experience.

Foggy memories of punishments I remember receiving are shockingly awful when viewed through the lens of my own motherhood.

I know, but then one of my dear friends just scolded me to "stop being a victim" when I tried to talk to her about what was happening. And man, I am trying! I don't want to be a victim—I'm trying to fix it!" Tears run down my cheeks. It happens all the time now. "Another friend, someone I really respect and know is nice, told me I have to 'buck up

and deal with it.' Like I am being a baby about all of this." I'm frustrated and angry and embarrassed and totally empty. I know these people are my friends and care about me, but they are so callused and cold in this moment when I need them so fiercely.

"I can't get out from under this," I continue weakly, the angry fire gone as fast as it came. "It feels like every time I come up for air, another bomb goes off, and I get a lungful of toxic fumes before I sink beneath the surface again. I just need some buoyancy and clean air, just a little bit," I finish softly, exhausted to my core.

"You are not a victim. It's OK to tell someone to stop hurting you," she says, like of course it is. I stare at her blankly; I didn't even know that was an option.

The air shifts. I don't know how exactly, just that something is different. Like that moment before lightning strikes, the hum and sulfur in the air.

RC sits up a little straighter in her chair and gives me a hard stare. "You are going to have to talk about it. The thing you don't want to talk about."

I recoil like she slapped me, my body cringing and shaking, replying automatically, "I don't want to talk about it."

"I know. But you are gonna have to. It's coming up, it's oozing around the steel door you built to encase it, and if you don't let it out it's going to explode," she says like the lion trainers at the zoo—authoritative, calm and steady.

The girl behind the door screams.

* * *

In my mind, there is a beautiful library tower. Similar to the one in a gothic castle, its towering height is marked by twisting staircases and beautiful tall windows where rain patters softly. It's where I store memories, knowledge, feelings as books—organized and accessible. There are places to research and remember, study and review. All structured and neatly created for study and improvement.

A year ago I accidentally took too much pain medication during a recovery from knee surgery. The medicine opened my mind's library more broadly, where I discovered two doors I had never noticed before.

Behind the first door is a boardroom. The boardroom has lots of versions of me, sitting around a large oval table with a glass partition in the middle, meeting and discussing strategy for career moves and long-term planning. Mentors of my past sit on the other side, offering insight though they are not allowed in decision-making. The other me's look up and welcome me into the planning, but insist on my silence because they operate at a higher level than I am able to understand right now. They are kind and smart, listening to and dismissing the smoky figures behind the glass.

The second door leads to a basement. This first time visiting, I make the mistake of being curious and wandering directly down the stairs and into the basement center. It's a large, blank cement room with dark shadows and corners. There is no light except the small rectangle that filters down from the open door, casting a weak gloom over the front half of the room.

As I creep forward, there are big eyes of little girls that shine in the dark, sad and watery but not scary. They sit in the shadows like little

bunnies frozen by a predator's gaze. They don't say anything, the silence hanging heavy as the darkness.

The walls have huge cracks like earthquakes, deep enough to stick my arm in if I were not too afraid to go near them. They loom open and yawning, terror residing in their deep black fissures.

On the furthest wall of the basement, there is one more door just visible in the gloom. A girl is behind the door—screaming, kicking and howling, trying to get out. It is slightly ajar, something wedged in the bottom of the door to keep her locked away from the rest. I turn and run.

I have been back to the boardroom and the basement since, during self-guided meditations. Curiosity sometimes drives my mind to open the door. Sometimes the basement sucks me in when an old wound I have forced myself to forget erupts and demands attention.

Never do I visit the basement voluntarily; never do I try to talk to the girl behind the door. I give the cracks and little sad eyes repair when they demand it, but always just enough to move on and forget again.

RC is asking what's behind that door. What does that screaming girl want to say? What is the worst memory I have never spoken of to anyone? She wants to hear it right now.

"But I'm not ready, I don't want to talk about it. I don't know what you want me to talk about." I jumble the words because they are thick on my tongue, too awkward for my mouth.

Logically, I know this is the lowest I have ever been in my life. I have never felt this awful about myself. I am unemployed, hated by those who I thought loved me. I spend hours on the couch, terrified I will fail and my life will crumble around me. All I have built. All I have suffered so much to achieve.

RC sits in silence, waiting. She knows this is the moment. Felt it many times before as a professional, completely new to me. She is patient as I wiggle and adjust, willing myself to muster some courage.

If I am going to have a total breakdown, I guess this is the best place to do it. I trust RC completely, a decision that has served me well over the years. She is intelligent and knowledgeable at what she does. She has put in the work to be able to say these things to me and have me listen.

I have a loving husband and beautiful son at home. I have enough money to last another month or two with some careful budgeting. I trust RC, and if she says this is it, I have to do my part and trust that if I do what I don't want to, if I tell her the stories I have hidden for so long, it will not destroy me. I guess if I break my brain now, it might help me get where I want to go quicker.

"Tell me about the screaming girl behind the door in the basement," she says quietly through the heavy silence. "What do you remember about her? What do you see?"

I look up into her eyes, and steel my resolve. I pull all the courage I have inside together into my mind and close my eyes and concentrate. "I see… a mop and bucket…"

AGE 4 THE JANITOR

CHAPTER EIGHT

I go to preschool at Undercroft Montessori. I love being there, all the clean tables and shiny new art supplies. Those are my favorite—the paints, crayons, and clay. So many colors and so clean and nice. It is one of my favorite places.

I skip into school in my uniform. I am here early because my daddy dropped me off before work so no other kids are here yet. I take a deep breath of the crisp autumn air and open the big glass door by myself.

The Mother made me wear the dress I wore yesterday, the one with the sticky stain on the front. She says I deserve to go to school smelling like the little slut that I am. I don't know what a slut is, but my tongue and knees still sting so much from last night's punishment I don't even bother to argue. My dress is not that sticky. I scrape and pick at the stain until it's just an old spot on the hem.

I like school. I am always eager to escape to my friends and the beautiful art supplies in our class. So it's normal for me to be the first kid in the class for the day. Ms. Lindsey welcomes me with a warm smile and hello. She knows I like to have a little time to myself in the activity center in the mornings if I am early. It is a time that is calm and soft and all for me. I like that.

I stand near the apple-carving station, thinking it might be nice to cut up some slices for a morning snack. I ask Ms. Lindsey if I "may" (not can) cut the morning snack, and she smiles and nods.

"That sounds nice. Be extra careful with the knife. I am going to step out here for a moment and speak to Ms. Flowers, OK?" she says over her shoulder as she steps into the quiet hallway.

I turn to the chopping table and select a nice red apple with no bad spots on it. I center it on the board and carefully balance the point of my blade on the tip before pressing down firmly and continuously until I reach the bottom. I am very pleased with myself to have completed this task correctly and continue to repeat the procedure until I am suddenly bumped from behind.

The knife slips and slices my hand. It begins to bleed. I stand staring at the red line growing on my finger before dropping the knife and reaching for a towel. I wrap my hand in a paper towel from the nearby stand, watching with gathering concern as the white towel turns red. I hold my hand to my chest and huff and puff, turning finally to see what is behind me.

I turn to see Mr. Turner standing there with his bucket and mop. Mr. Turner is the school janitor. He stares at me like he is waiting for me to finish my project so he can mop. I quickly step aside from the cutting board and the small crimson drops on the floor so he can mop the entire activity center where I am standing.

But instead of beginning to mop, his stands still, eyes staring down at the stain on my dress. Just a few dribbles of crusty white gook I missed, heat rising up my neck as I look down at the stain, embarrassed. I only have one hand, and I have to hold it because it hurts so I wiggle from foot to foot, trying to make my dress swing and cover the stain.

He gives a quick glance to the door and then stoops down to my eye level. "What's on your dress there?" he asks, sniffing the air. "You smell like sex."

He sniffs again, wiping his finger on my dress to smell it as I look around, embarrassed. I sniff the air, confused. What is sex? I don't smell anything.

My eyes start darting around the room, looking for the teacher who may be able to hear. I don't want Ms. Lindsey to know that my dress is stinky. My eyes settle on the tall mop handle gripped tight in his hand. Pinpricks of fear creep up my spine—is he going to hit me with the mop handle for having a dirty dress? Am I in trouble?

"Come with me. Let's put a bandage on that finger," he says as he turns, heading to the back of the room where the janitor's closet sits discreetly.

I look down surprised at my bleeding hand, a little relieved. "It's not my finger—it's my hand. And it's OK. I'll just wait for Ms. Lindsey," I chirp. She has smiley face Band-Aids.

"Get over here," he demands gruffly, and I jump right out of my skin, walking hurriedly with my head bowed.

He opens the door and guides me into the janitor's closet. It smells like lemon Pine Sol and is filled with brooms, an upside-down bucket, brushes, and cleaning supplies hanging over a small work bench. A long tall window gives gentle morning sunlight just starting to peek over the horizon, little paper cut-outs pasted on it for the holidays throwing cute shadows on the floor. I can see the circle drive for parent drop-off being set up with little orange cones, Ms. Lindsey laughing with Ms. Flowers as they prepare for the morning routine.

The janitor closes the door and begins fumbling with his belt. He wears a long striped shirt that is wrinkled where it's tucked into his pants that falls to his knees when his pants puddle on the floor. It is a tight

squeeze for both of us to fit in the tiny closet so my face is close to his crotch as I turn away, embarrassed. Anything I can look at to avoid seeing the snake under the shirt.

"You know what to do," he says as he pushes me down on my sore knees, my hand dropping its bloody binding as the other hand reaches to the floor to ease my descent. I settle my knees on the floor tenderly and open my mouth; I do know what to do.

As The Janitor pushes and grunts, I send my mind away to avoid looking at the black curls tickling my nose. I stare out the window, concentrating on the mommies and daddies beginning to arrive in their cars, giving kisses and love as my classmates jump out of the car for school.

Kids wave hi, carrying lunch sacks and backpacks in fun cheery colors as I hold my breath and wish for it to be over soon. My daddy drops me off at school like that sometimes, when he is in town and doesn't have to go into work early. But that isn't very often.

He continues to grunt and pump, but I make sure he doesn't go too far again by pushing my tongue to the roof of my mouth. I don't know if he will remember to pull out in time for the goo. I don't want to accidentally swallow it. It smells bad, and I don't want to. I don't really trust Mr. Turner very much.

As I suspected, he doesn't know when to go and spurts creamy snotty yellow in my mouth, making me spit and gag like when I get a big gulp of the ocean. A little dribbles down my chin to my dress, landing next to the other stain that got me into this mess. I heave a big sigh and grab up my injured hand, standing without help to wipe my face and dress the best I can with my good hand.

I turn away and keep licking my sleeve to get the taste out as he wipes off his pee-pee. He mumbles about how it's not right to get spit up on his pecker. But I just couldn't stop it; a little just came up before I could get his pee-pee out. Maybe now he won't do that again.

He pulls up his pants and leans down close to my face, grabs the front of my uniform. "If you ever tell anyone about this, I'll slit your throat, " he spits in my face. His breath is stinky and hot; I turn my head so I don't throw up again.

I nod, and he lets go. He zips up his pants, finishes tucking in his shirt. The janitor shoos me out the door, wiping a stray strand of vomit from my hair and wiping it on my dress as I leave.

I never did like Mr. Turner very much. Now I wonder where I can get a band-aid.

CHAPTER NINE

RC slowly comes back into focus, both of our faces shining with glossy tears. She sniffs, reaches for the tissue box on the tiny table, and offers it to me.

"So he made you give him oral sex," she clarifies with a steady voice, wiping her face quietly to keep us both from breaking into a million pieces.

My face wiggles and sags, and my body shakes, but I nod.

"You have to say it," she commands gently. "It's important to your healing."

"Yes. He made me lick and suck it while I stared out the window at the other kids hugging their mommies goodbye," I say shakily, like admitting it will require severe punishment.

"Yes, it did happen. And you are OK now. You got out of there. He will never touch you again," she says, equally commanding. She knows I don't quite believe myself so I have to say it. She has to make sure I see that she believes me.

I stare blankly and nod obediently. I can't believe I just told that story. I have never told anyone about that… I didn't really even remember it. The girl behind the door cries; the blackness beyond the now-open door yawns to infinity. I mentally rush back up the stairs.

"What are your weekend plans?" she asks as she glances at the clock on the desk. "You are hurting, and I want to make sure you can be somewhere safe to process this. If you need me to arrange something for you, I can,

like an inpatient or something." I can see the concern and kindness on her face. That's good enough to get me through the weekend.

"Nah, I'm OK. My daddy and stepmom are coming to town tonight to see Jack's play. I will keep it lowkey with them and just stick around the house. I will text you if it gets bad, OK?" I smile weakly and try to reassure her. As long as I have resources, I can make sure I use them.

"Ok, please do. I am always available for you, OK?" She is worried, but she knows I am being honest. I trust her enough to call before I do something potentially stupid.

"Thank you." I give her a hug and head out the door.

* * *

It's always a joyous occasion when my dad and his wife come to visit. Daddy is old and crotchety now, in his 70s and a staunch Republican, but he loves me fiercely, and that makes it all better. Nanny (aka Mother of my Heart, my stepmom) is always a flutter of fun with prizes, snacks, hugs, and lovin's. She is like warm yellow sunshine after walking out of August air conditioning, melting worries and momma bear vibes. A perfect setting to heal from this awful tale.

I drive home on autopilot, lost in thought over the words that just came out of my mouth. I have never told anyone that story before, not even to myself. I am shocked to hear the details and names so effortlessly flow into a cohesive narrative. I am sad that it happened, sad for the little girl inside, but it isn't devastating like I thought it would be.

With the pain and terror of recounting the event, there follows a certain peace. A releasing of emotion whose tide leaves a cleansed beach

in its wake. Though it's barren and lonely, it's also light and airy. The levity comes from being heard for the first time, I think.

Telling a story like this, even to yourself, is awful. It's the hardest thing I have ever done voluntarily in my life. The disbelief that these events, hidden so long and so deep, are actually true. Confusion at the small voice coming out of my mouth, recounting details I couldn't remember until this moment. The shaking of my body, draining every ounce of strength I have to focus on getting this story out. The overwhelming despair as a mother, hearing a story from a child, even when the child is me.

That is the hardest part, hearing this story as a mother. My mind is so terrified it violently rejects any flash of my sweet little boy, Jack, being forced to live something like that. Thinking of what I would do if I found out my darling child was treated that way, and asking myself why I was.

I stare through the traffic, not noticing the crazy Dallas drivers zipping around me. That's a dark thought, looming over the cleansed landscape of my memory—why? Why was I treated like this?

Did The Mother not know? Did I ever tell?

Wait, why did that man tell me my dress smelled like sex? How would a four-year-old even know what that means?

The grey, gloomy fog gathers in my mind, threatening and crackling like a building thunderstorm. Questions and more questions bubbling up more upon reflection as the buildings streak by unnoticed on my drive home.

Why did I know to put my tongue back?

Why did The Mother send me to school in a dirty dress?

It gets so dark my vision begins to darken, taking all my concentration to focus on taking the exit from the highway. I pull through the tall oak trees in our neighborhood, frantically searching in the background for something good to focus on until I get home. I need to drive safely and just get home.

As I look up at the top of the windshield, at the same time trying to focus on the beautiful trees and keep my vision from swimming out of control, I feel a small glimmer of hope. A tiny shimmer, really, not much in the bleak darkness, but there is always something good that comes out of bad.

A new feeling of telling a story—my story—to someone and having them believe me instantly. What's more, she was upset for me. She cried because it was so bad. It was so bad she said it was OK to be upset. She didn't call me a liar, didn't question my details or observations. She believed me and agreed that it was bad. An absolutely and wholly new experience for me.

I pull into our driveway at last, the familiar aging hybrid already parked in the driveway. Nanny picking at the front porch plants and their tiny Yorke puppies yapping excitedly.

"Hello-ooooo!" she sings in her raspy smoker's voice with arms raised high for a big welcome hug as she steps into the garage to meet me. She wraps me up in a tight squeeze and pats my back with an extra thump. "It's so good to see you!" she coos.

"It's good to see you too, Nanny," I reply. "I am so glad you are here."

She pulls back and holds me at arm's length to get a good look at my face.. "What's wrong, honey?" Concern creases the corners of her mouth in tight lines.

"I just had a really rough therapy session today," I minimize. "With all this other stuff, I am just exhausted," I say as I turn to give my daddy a hug.

"Hey, sweetie pie." His familiar warmth slows the storm in my brain a little. "You doing OK?" he says with concern, his big blue eyes more weathered than in my memories, but still the kindest color I know.

"Yeah, just, you know, a lot going on that's not great." I carefully choose to diffuse his concern and move things into a safer space. "You guys have any issues with traffic?"

"Ah hell, it was backed up for miles around that construction…" He gets going as I let the rant flow harmlessly around me.

* * *

My daddy married Nanny the same year Jack was born. It was a difficult time for us all. Dave and I barely made enough money to feed a cat at that time, and my daddy was still recovering from the vile divorce from The Mother, but bringing Nanny into the family was a highlight for us all.

Nanny is a hard woman, self-sufficient and always on duty. If there is a dish to be washed or a blanket out of place, she will ensure everything is shipshape. She ain't gonna cry, and she ain't no pussy, so everyone just puts on their big boy pants and gets to it when Nanny is around. Her greatest ambition is to finally make the news for a Walmart-centered drama while pretending she has wandered away from the nursing home. She voraciously devours murder shows and instigated our traditional SPAM-carving contest at Christmas. Always throwing wicked dance moves to '70s disco tunes as she cooks, proudly embarrassing her grandkids as she

sings off-key to Tina Turner. She has taught me how to laugh at accidents and have fun on holidays. She keeps my daddy in line, and she keeps him happy, which means a lot. She loves us all like we are her own and treats us like the kind of grandparents you only see in movies. She's an excellent addition to our little family, even more now that the relationship with The Mother has ceased.

She flutters around the house upon arrival, ensuring the tidiness is up to her standards, my daddy promptly taking all the dogs outside to enjoy a cigarette. He knows better than to get in Nanny's way when she is doing her thing.

Once the house meets her cleanliness standards, she joins us on the patio, and the chatter stays light as the sun fades. I am quiet, listening more than I talk. I don't feel like I have much to say to elevate the conversation, and I don't want to bring everyone down into the memory fresh in my mind. I listen and nod as the elders lament cataract surgery and relay detailed conversations with urologists. It's easy to listen and keep the conversation off yourself—just continue to ask more questions than you answer.

Dave comes home from work, and dinner is a simple affair, four adults enjoying a meal on the patio in the spring sunset. It's a gentle sort of meal, nothing memorable yet nostalgic.

Jack returns home from rehearsal late with a "thank you" to Charlie's mom as he slams the minivan door shut. He bounds into the house, brimming with excitement over his new theater show's opening night success. Excitedly hugging the grandparents, he tells us all how the show is better than they thought it would be and all the little tics that no

one noticed. As quick as he arrived, he stuffs a burger in his mouth and quickly sprints upstairs to jump online with his friends. Teenagers.

His sweet energy is a soft balm that fades too quickly, leaving the bleeding wound in my mind welling with renewed hurt. How could anyone make a little child do something like that?

"You know, it's been a long day. I think I am going to lie in bed and read my book," I say carefully to the group. There are general nods and groans as everyone eases out of their comfy chairs to head into nightly routines.

Tonight, it's a treat to have Nanny walk with me around the yard, the dogs carefully giving the yard one last inspection of the evening. I am finally treating myself to a few hits of my THC pen; it helps calm the shaking and helps me to eat.

Since things have fallen apart, I am doing anything I can do keep my head above water. Every morning for two years, I practice yoga and listen to a guided meditation first thing in the morning. I take walks outside. I visit my primary care physician for anxiety. I attend therapy religiously, pushing hard to listen and use those discussions to heal as quickly as possible. I read inspiring books, follow micro-learning therapists on social media. I connect with old friends, spend time with my family. And when it's still too much, when I am full to the brim with good coping activities and I still feel like giving up, I take THC.

Never in my younger years did I indulge in drugs. I was a DARE kid from the '80s; "just say no" was stamped into my brain. But last year I had knee surgery and really struggled being able to eat. I lost close to 40 pounds over a four-month period because I couldn't eat. My daddy was concerned so he brought me a THC pen, said it worked for cancer patients

so maybe it would help me. Since marijuana is legal in Oklahoma, the THC came in a small discreet vape pen inside a professionally packaged box with ingredients, warnings, and labeling. Granted, I have never taken medicine called Purple Passion with a tongue hanging out on it, but two hits of that pen had me eating within minutes. It also has the added benefit of relieving some stress and lifting my mood. It was a delightful surprise, and I have since done my research about risks and best practices. It is a medicine, like my others. I use it when I am sick. All my doctors even agree.

I am definitely sick today, I think as I pull one last hit before heading inside. Three is a lot for me usually, but it's been a very hard day. I took a sleeping pill too; I don't want my brain wandering as I try to sleep tonight. Rest is the best thing for me right now. I am exhausted.

I close my eyes and soak in the songs of the night as I let the vapor exhale into the sky—the hooting, croaking and babbling of the backyard, the sounds of a lovely life that I have built for myself and my family. A life worth fighting for. And I am a fighter, so I will survive this.

Within a few minutes, I begin to feel a soft relief creep through my body as I leave the scene to head into bed. My favorite part of the day, climbing into bed. Our soft too-expensive sheets, the heaps of down feather pillows, the billowy comforter—my bed is my sanctuary. The quiet moments before sleep, when I can lie down and relax and not have to think about anyone or anything. The THC allows me to relax. So pissed the '80s scared me to waiting fucking 30 years to try the damn stuff. It's some of the best medicine I have ever had. Hopefully, it will soften the edges enough for me to sleep as I snuggle up tight with my old book buddies and relax.

CHAPTER TEN

Hours later, I lie in bed shivering. My teeth clack, and my body jerks, I don't understand why I feel like this. I mean, logically, that bad thing happened a long time ago. I survived, and it didn't really bother me until now. I will get another job and make money and be just fine. This is so silly to be acting this way about some stupid memory from 40 years ago.

I take deep breaths.

I take an extra anti-anxiety pill. I take another sleeping pill.

I stare at the green numbers on my watch lying on my nightstand as they tick by.

I close my eyes and I see the mop handle. The window with the smiling kids. The stain on my dress. I avoid looking at his face. His face is close to mine. Over mine. I look up—and it's not the janitor anymore. It's The Grandfather's face I see.

My body lets out a ferocious spasm that feels like someone hit me in the gut. Like there is an invisible string at the top of my tummy that someone yanked and won't stop pulling until my insides come out my mouth.

I climb out of bed like a wounded animal, clutching my insides to keep them from burning out of my skin. I pull on my robe, wrapping the heavy fabric around my spasming limbs. My favorite one that's like a big hoodie, given to me by my dearest friend. I'll sit outside in nature for a bit, see if the stars can calm me. That's a healthy coping mechanism.

I sit on the edge of the padded patio chair, doubled over, trying to keep the vomit rising in my throat at bay. I shake so violently the metal chair rattles against the patio, and my teeth chatter until they hurt. How could I think something like that?

Something is trying to break out of me. The girls in the basement stare with big eyes from the dark that gathers like a hurricane, ready to sweep it all away. I could let the storm take me, let it carry me out to sea and never come back. Or I can stay and fight to stay adrift as the storm destroys all that I have built.

It is only moments, but they stretch forever, staring at the possibilities in front of me. The Grandfather's face flashes in my vision again, then my son's, then my sister's, then my own.

I can break the cycle. I don't have to shield those I love from the terrible damage inside.

Thoughts bubble up from the deep… I don't understand what's happening.

Images trying to surface push the storm into terrible violence, turning and striking with flashes of images so horrible they can't possibly be real.

Is this the time? Will I be able to survive this now?

I retch again as The Grandfather's face appears in my mind, lips tightly pulled back over beard and teeth like a predator about to pounce. Spittle drips from my lips as I pant over my knees.

I pick up my phone and write out a text to RC with trembling hands:

Me → It was my grandpa

I cry like a mother who has lost her child, and maybe in a weird way I have. I feel so awful for saying something like that. The Grandfather loves me of course. How could I say such a horrible thing?

84

RC → I have suspected

I stare at the little words on the screen, rereading them over and over and over and over.

Nanny steps casually out the patio door, pausing to let the late-night puppies out for one last snoop. It's late night-early morning, quiet and still in our North Texas suburb. She turns as she taps a last twilight cigarette from the case and startles as she sees me sitting on the deck.

"Oh! Honey! You startled me!" she exclaims with a smile. But as her eyes adjust to the dim light and she sees the terror on my face, she freezes like her pups at the sight of danger ahead.

"Are you OK, honey?" she inquires as she frowns and squints to get a better view.

I look up and realize I am going to break. I am going to split at the core, just like an extinction event on the Nature Channel, the montage of the volcano erupting, earthquakes splitting vast chasms, a storm raging and waves crashing over barriers. The world inside me is on the precipice of Armageddon, so I must choose to let it take me or to forge ahead.

"I'm not OK I'm not OK I'm not OK I'm not OK.

I'm not OK. I'm not OK. I'm not OK. I'm not OK. I'm not OK. I'm not OK...." I plead as I stare wide-eyed at her.

I know what I am really asking—I am asking if she really wants to know if I am OK because I am NOT OK, but if she sits down, she is gonna see it all. That it's all not OK and it's a lot and it's more horrible than she can imagine and that it's going to be awful. She can see it in my eyes, on my face, in the tremor of my hands.

"I'm right here, honey. You just let it out," The Mother of my Heart says as she swoops over to the small cushion in front of me without a moment's hesitation.

"It's my grandfather It's my grandfather It's my grandfather," I spew and retch. I shake and my teeth chatter and I am going to throw up and it can't be true. Why would I say something like that? He would never do anything like that.

"Your grandfather hurt you?" she gently asks. I am a blubbering mess, barely coherent.

I need to breathe. I need to breathe. *To breathe, you need to sit up*, a small voice in my head whispers. I faintly realize that she is right, and I sit up a bit to catch my breath. I stare down at my hands, knuckles white in the moonlight, fiercely gripped by Nanny's soft, kindly hands to share her strength. It gives me the courage to lift my gaze just a peek, to see if there is a chance she isn't about to chastise me and tell me what a naughty girl I am. Just a peek.

"Yes. It was The Grandfather," I say, quiet but still the same words. And then the stories come….

AGE 4 THE BLUE DRESS

CHAPTER ELEVEN

My mom says we're going on a plane to California. It's going to be a really big deal. We have to dress up real nice and hope we get seats on Aunt Ivy's special plane pass. She works at American Airlines and gets family tickets to share. That's good because we couldn't afford the plane tickets at full price. We don't have money like that, The Mother says. But that means we have to dress up, just in case we get in First Class and have to sit next to rich people. They don't want to be seen sitting next to some street urchin, now do they?

We walk into the plane station, and it's really busy. It smells like farts and lemon cleaner, kind of like a hospital. People are walking fast and carrying bags that bang around me so that I have to watch my head not to get hit. I don't have a suitcase; Mom packed my clothes in her bag. I am too short to see much more than legs and bags and flapping tickets so I hold tight to The Mother's hand.

We are going to Semi Valley, CA to my Aunt Robin's house. She used to live in Tulsa too, but then my Uncle Brad made her move back to California to be near his parents and his fancy job. That made me sad because my cousin Rick was my age, and he was my friend. We got to play together at The Grandmother's house. He was kind of weird, always wanting to play Star Wars and Legos, never the games I wanted to play. But at least he was a friend.

I was extra sad when they moved away last year because they just had a baby girl named Charlotte. My Aunt Robin, she couldn't have children. Something was wrong with her insides. So God just sent her a little girl

like me! A new friend who may want to play some girl games for once. But her daddy made her move away when she was just a baby, so no friends for me.

The Mother drags me through the lines at the airport, squeezing my hand too tight. I can't walk that fast. Someone turns and gives my mom a dirty look as she gives a rough jerk to my arm for not paying attention to when the line moves. But I don't cry. I know better.

Aunt Ivy is going on the plane with me and The Mother. She says she is going to get married in California and that we need to look extra special on her extra-special day. I can't wait to wear the beautiful new blue dress The Mother got me to wear to the wedding.

My Aunt Ivy is The Mother's little sister. She doesn't have any kids yet, but she is still fun. She likes to color and paint with me, or sing songs and dance around the house like rock stars. Her house is always warm and soft, no shouting or hitting. She is one of my favorite people, so looking extra special for her extra-special day is important.

I walk through the big empty door scanning me for metal. Not sure if they think I am a robot or if they just want my mood ring, but they don't stop me. No beeping, the uniform guy smiles at me and says, "Enjoy your trip."

I smile back, the big one I use to help adults see what a cute good girl I am, and reply, "I will! I am going to California."

A quick yank of my arm and The Mother hisses, "Come on." My Aunt Ivy, The Mother, and I hurry to walk down the long path to get to our plane.

The floor is kind of sticky; my nice shoes are making a wet, sucking sound when I walk. But I don't look down because there is too much

to see. We are going to fly in a plane! In the sky! I see them lined up at different doors with people exiting and entering in lines. I just need to be quiet and good, and The Mother says she will get me some pilot wings. It's all so exciting!

As we pass the nice lady our ticket, Aunt Ivy leans over and whispers, "Tell me about your dress for the wedding."

"I have a new blue dress!" I exclaim, "It's blue checked with puff sleeves and white lace just like Alice in Wonderland. I have new white socks with the frilly lace on the turn-down and black shiny shoes to match. Mom is going to wrap my hair in curlers tonight to make it curly like Shirley Temple."

And we can put a little bit of makeup on the bruises on my arms and legs so I look perfect.

I only think that last part because perfect is the most important thing, and not everyone can know how to do it. If you're perfect, no one gets mad.

"Ooooh… I can't wait to see it!" She gives me a wink and falls into line behind me as we walk down the tunnel to the plane.

We find our seats, walking down the long narrow aisle of the plane. I sit in the middle between The Mother and Aunt Ivy. The Mother leans over and loudly says, "You can lean over me and watch us take off if you want, but I need to sit in the window, or I'll get motion sick." She needs a story to explain why she took the window seat. It's OK; I understand. She needs special things.

We go faster and faster, and I can actually feel the plane lift off the ground. It's a heavy weight in my tummy, but different from when you know something bad is coming. It is lighter, an exciting feeling. I

lean over and stare out the window as much as I dare, in love with the beautiful clouds. You think that we are going so fast they would be racing by, but they are drifting so slowly. It's like what you see in the cartoons. It's wonderful.

"OK, Lucky Girl, that's enough. I need to be able to breathe!" The Mother huffs at me as I quickly jump back into my seat and sit up straight quick.

"Oh, Pam, let her look. It's not every day you get to see the world from above the clouds," Aunt Ivy says with a smile and a wink at me. She understands how much I like soft beautiful things and sometimes pokes The Mother about being too strict. She and my daddy are the best at taking my side against The Mother; I wish they were around more often.

We fly in the air for a long time. The Mother and Aunt Ivy talk about flowers and other wedding stuff the whole time. But it's OK because I get to color in the sky. The plane ladies bring me tiny snacks and orange juice and tell me what nice manners I have. The Mother smiles and acts like she is very proud. Like I don't mess up and make her mad and have to be punished. But we are sitting on a plane with respectable people so we have to be on our extra-good behavior. That means do all the things extra right and no telling fibs.

Sure hope I don't mess it up. This is already such a big adventure!

* * *

California is just like the movies—everything is gold with sunshine, even the grass and palm trees. There are cars and clothes that no respectable people would buy. The people are loud and flashy and vulgar.

The air smells of sun tan oil, fresh lettuce, and something like the binding of an old book, musty and leather. I love it instantly.

I almost lose my arm to the tugging talons dragging me off the plane and down to get our bags. It's crowded, with lots of lines and groups of people that don't look where they step. I am still small; I can't always get out of the way on time.

Uncle Brad and Aunt Robin are waiting to take us to their house outside in their minivan. Uncle Brad helps us to the car and goes back for our bags. The backseat is squished with Aunt Ivy, The Mother, and me. But Charlotte and Rick have their new car seats. They need to stay safe in the captain seats so we three have to squeeze in tight.

I don't need a car seat; I am the oldest. Four is a very big-girl age.

It's kind of hot and stuffy as we rock and sway to Uncle Brad's jerky driving. Traffic is a bad thing, I guess. But Aunt Robin keeps promising it's better outside of the city.

She is right! The little window that is too low to be of any use to The Mother is open so I can see (and get some air). The bright colors of the people and the buildings turns into mountains and valleys, just like in the picture books. They really are craggy and huge! And the valleys have trees and meadows and tiny houses.

And then the mountains open and I can see the ocean. The stinging air is salty like tears, but without crying. The blue is bigger than I have ever seen, like the sky but more solid. I can hear the waves crashing under the car noise, and I close my eyes for a second and breathe—salty and delicious. Unlike food and toys, memories can never be taken from me. They are shining golden moments I can pull out in my mind anytime I am feeling low, small comforts in the dark that no one can see but me.

So I do my best to take a picture with my brain, capture the sounds and smells and soft touch of the ocean breeze to pull out later when I need a light in the dark.

After hours of driving, we FINALLY get to Aunt Robin's house. It is big and all spread out, no second floor like The Grandfather's. We pile out, and I rush into the living room. I had heard but didn't want to believe it… they have a POOL! We are gonna get to go swimming in the middle of winter, and it won't even be cold. I allow a quick moment of excitement before I fix my face. This is gonna be so much fun!

* * *

The afternoon is filled with Uncle Brad in the pool with us kids as we splash and play. The sunshine is warm, but not stinging like in the summer. Their pool is super fancy; it is in the ground with a waterfall and everything. No one really watches me since Uncle Brad has the two babies, so I can go underwater and do fishy swims all I want.

Too soon, my Aunt Ivy comes to wrap me in a towel and take me in for a bath. Aunt Ivy always knows how to make things a little extra wonderful. She wraps me tight in the big fluffy towel, then wraps her arms around me and squeezes me tight to lift me off the ground. She gives me kisses and snuggles, and I feel buzzy and warm.

She plops me down in a bathtub filled with bubbles, and then Rick runs into the room naked. Aunt Ivy gives a "Whoop!" of surprise to see his bare bottom streak by and barely turns in time to miss getting a bath splash on her face. It is a brave move; I would be too scared she would get mad. But I guess since it's Aunt Ivy, she never seems to get too mad at things that are silly and not on purpose. She laughs and splashes us back,

and we make a mess! That is another nice thing I like about her—she laughs at messes.

Rick and I sit in the tub and play battle boats and Star Wars. Since he's the boy, he is always in charge and chooses the games. I get mad when he demands to be the winner too; he doesn't get to cheat. Being a boy doesn't mean you can cheat to win. It just means you get to choose the game and make the rules. But if I am good enough to win your game with your rules, I get to win even if it hurts your feelings.

Aunt Ivy washes us both as we blow the bubbles off our hands like wishes, singing ducky songs. She is extra gentle on my ouchies and private parts, which is nice. I like soft things. She always has the extra-fluffy towels that smell clean and are not damp. Aunt Robin swoops up Rick, and Aunt Ivy guides me into the guest room where we are sharing with The Mother. Aunt Ivy invites me to sit on the bed and helps The Mother curl my hair for the big day. The Mother wraps my hair tight on the pink foam rollers, pulling and tugging a bit extra for fun. Aunt Ivy gives her a look, but The Mother just says, "What? She keeps moving."

I can't ever seem to sit still enough.

I climb like a little bear to the top of the covers and snuggle under the soft worn sheets. I lose my head in pillows as big as clouds. Even with the little pokes and presses from my curlers, it's heaven. Tomorrow is going to be a special day, and I can't wait.

CHAPTER TWELVE

I knew four was a big-girl age, but I didn't know what being a big girl meant.

The Grandfather shakes my shoulder to wake me up—he needs my help. I am really tired so I don't get up right away. The wedding party was so busy. There was a lot of sitting and being quiet and standing still. The part where we had food was even kind of boring, no other kids to play with but Rick, and he was busy being with the grownups.

I rub the sleepy in my eyes and blink up at him, confused. Why would The Grandfather need my help?

"I need your help. Come on. Be a big girl now and come quick," he whispers. The Grandfather is always quiet, not loud like me.

I slip from under the warm covers and slide out of the bed on my tummy. My toes touch the soft carpet, and I tiptoe to the door. The Grandfather is waiting for me. He takes my hand and leads me down the hallway to a room on the left. I know this room, because it's Uncle Brad's office. We aren't allowed to go in there. It's big and brown, and it is cold. There is a big desk with some shelves behind it and a plant in the corner. There are some chairs with maroon cushions turned the wrong way, away from the boss at the desk. Uncle Brad sits in one chair, with some blue shorts on under a white t-shirt, his blue cotton robe hanging open.

Something is wrong. Uncle Brad isn't supposed to be showing his body to anyone that way; he usually has special temple garments on. He has a poked-up pee-pee making his blue shorts stick up like a tent. I immediately look away so I don't get in trouble.

It's silent, but I can feel The Grandfather behind me. He steps around me and sits in the other seat next to Uncle Brad. He is quiet for a long time.

I slowly lift my eyes to The Grandfather's face. I have seen those eyes before, but not this close. They are black, and tight around the edges. Little wrinkles around the sides that tighten when his nose flares or mouth twitches. His mouth chews like he is eating something bad.

Gently, so gently, he turns me away from him and gives me a little push to walk to the blank wall opposite the desk. I take a few steps and turn around on their command. Uncle Brad clicks on a flashlight like a Scooby Doo gotcha. I freeze. A doll on a stage.

"Did you see the way this little slut pranced around all day?" asks Uncle Brad. "Flashing those chubby little thighs at us, trying to tempt us?" He laughs as he reaches for my thigh and gives it a quick twist. White pain flashes through me, sharp and crisp. It's tinged with black fear—the start of something I don't understand and don't know why it's happening. I was extra good just like they asked.

The Grandfather chuckles and sits back in his chair, casually crossing his ankle over his leg. He puts his hands together like he does when he is thinking.

"Yes, I did. Quite the vain little vixen, aren't you," he teases. He can see in my face that I have no idea what he is talking about… and he likes my confusion. He drinks it like sugary soda, getting all hyped up and making him jiggle his foot… and then he shifts his position to stop it after he sees me noticing.

"Do you think she did it on purpose?" The Grandfather asks with a glance back over his shoulder to Brad. It's a game they have played

before, but I don't know the rules or how to play. My brain is screaming at me, trying to think of what a slut or a vixen might be or what I did on purpose.

I start to get wiggly and need to pee. I don't know if I can go.

"Let's see what she's hiding under there," Brad leers as he reaches in to pinch again, just inside my left thigh. White fireworks burst in my vision again, this time with a little throw-up in the back of my throat. The Mother says nobody should ever touch me there except for a doctor. I cross my legs and begin shivering.

"Come now, honey, go ahead and take off your nightgown." The Grandfather makes it sound like a request… but I know it's not. This is the voice he uses when he tells Aunt Ivy she cannot have what she wants. It is low and hard, and it makes my hands start shaking.

I guess since they are family, these boys are OK to see my underpants. I wiggle around to take off my dress without showing any skin if I can. Then I cup my suddenly too-little hands around my boobies so they can't see those. I shake from head to toe, but maybe if I am real good, they will see I am a good clean girl and let me go.

Uncle Brad brings the flashlight closer so he can see every inch of my skin. He attacks like a snake, fast and hard. He twists and pinches my skin between his giant hairy fingers, his gold ring catching me sometimes in an extra-stinging scrape. He targets my boobies, then my tummy. My thigh, then the top of my private place. Tears roll down my face, but I stay quiet. Maybe that's the game. Am I strong enough to pass the test?

The Uncle stands to tower over me and quietly yells about what a little slut I am. He is disgusted with my wanton regard for men's appetites and my girlish cuteness that tempts him when he is a chaste and righteous

man. How I have been teasing him and The Grandfather all day trying to make them break their vows to God. Figures since I am my mother's daughter—she is a filthy slut too.

The Grandfather sits silently, leaning forward, elbows on knees, listening intently. He doesn't yell like The Uncle, but his silence is louder. He has made this happen; he is happy with the result… but why?

I know he likes to look at my bruises—maybe he is mad I used makeup to cover them? But how else could I have looked perfect when people asked questions?

The Uncle continues to spit out his angry words, talking about my daddy not deserving his success because he is a backwoods hillbilly piece of trash and how The Uncle deserves to have his golf career because he DESERVES it.

Is The Grandfather mad at me because I wore the blue dress? Is it too vulgar?

The Uncle is starting to sweat, taking off his shirt that has circles on it like my dad after racquetball. But I am really surprised when he takes off his blue shorts. He is really tall, and I am small, so I have been trying hard not to stare at the tiny buttons on the flap of his shorts as it bounces around. As long as that stays closed, I figure I'll have time to move if he reaches to undo them. But I am totally unprepared for him to drop them to the floor, and quickly crouch to avoid bonking heads as he pushes them down.

I peek up at him from my side crouch and see his floppy pee-pee wiggling below his big fat hairy belly. He stares at me hard, at the blooming purple and red welts on my butt and legs. He licks his lips and quiets to a mumble about how he is gonna teach me and he is in control,

rubbing his hand up and down his pee-pee till he throws his head back and lets out a big grunt. White goo drips out the hole on the end of his private parts. It smells stinky.

The Grandfather doesn't look like he approves, but he doesn't interfere. He is above people like that, but he understands their impulses are not as tightly controlled as his own. He is exceptional.

The Uncle moves to the desk to grab a few tissues to wipe up his mess. He throws on his discarded robe and casually walks out of the room and closes the door.

I am frozen in a crouch, staring at the drops of goo drying on the floor. I am not sure what to do. The Grandfather still sits in the burgundy chair facing me, hands resting on the arm rests, feet flat on the floor. He looks like a judge, making an important decision.

"Do you understand why we asked you here tonight?" he asks with a small tilt of his head. He is interested in the answer; I can tell. That's how you know, when he tilts his head like a cat.

I shake my head no, too scared to speak. Safer to be silent.

"You will be groomed to be a lady. You will be educated and indoctrinated in the teachings of our lord and savior Jesus Christ. You will be prepared to support a man of faith who follows His original teachings, ALL of his original teachings. That includes the obedience and subservience of you as a woman to men of the priesthood.

"You did very well tonight. I think you will do quite nicely. However, I worry about your intellect and willful nature. It will be hard for you to accept this calling. You might not like what is required of you or what you are asked to endure.

"If you ever feel like you can't take it or you want to strike back, do not act. Your mother lives at home with you and your father. She will be my eyes and ears. If you strike out at her, you are striking at me. If you tell on her, you are telling on me.

"And if I ever find out that you do tell your precious father or any of those backwoods rednecks he calls family, I will find them all and slice them up, one by one, until you have nothing left. So just remember that."

He sits back in the chair a bit—I didn't even notice he had leaned forward to hover over me. I am trying to make myself as small as possible, crouching and shaking in only my panties and bruises. I feel the putrid purple goop of shame ooze down my tummy. I don't have enough hands or arms or legs to cover it all under his watchful eye.

I don't trust myself to not break into a million pieces if I move so I sit still and silent. Sometimes that's enough.

He nods, slowly stands, and wipes the wrinkles away from his striped PJ bottoms. His bright white T-shirt is still spotless as he walks out the door, leaving me shaking and alone.

* * *

Sometime a lot later, I roll onto my butt and reach out a shaky hand to grab my nightgown. My legs are sore and creaky, so it's easier to sit on my butt as I carefully and quietly slip it over my head and curl into a ball on the floor.

I close my eyes tight and wish it didn't happen. I let the tears leak down my cheeks; I can allow that as long as I keep quiet. The tiny pinches of skin have begun to bubble and color, screaming a deep fiery-red lullaby.

I dream someone finds me and picks me up. She is soft and warm and gentle, oh so gentle. She carries me against her chest, humming a song that's familiar but no words. She sits in a rocking chair and cradles me in her lap, rocking and petting my hair to quiet the shaking. She smells like expensive lotion, and her hair is black like Snow White. She hums and it's warm and she whispers, "I'm so sorry. I wish I could do more. I'll always rock you, just please don't tell."

* * *

I wake up in bed with The Mother. For just a moment, before the wave of pain and fear drowns everything else, I think it may have been a dream. My family loves me: they would never hurt me.

But then the pain comes, and with it the first drips of black shame in my little heart. What have I done wrong? Why are they doing those things to me?

The Mother is already out of bed and dressed. She stares down at me like she has a big surprise that I am not gonna like, like going to get a shot at the doctor.

"Time to go home. You need to get up and get dressed, lazy bones," she laughs as she grabs the top corner of the covers and yanks them back to expose my little body. My legs are covered in bruises and welts; it looks like I was wrestling with the boys. But her eyes focus on the collar bone and shoulder.

"He wasn't supposed to leave any marks where your dad can see. I can use makeup on some, but those are awful. Nothing is going to cover that. Goddamn it," she swears as she stomps out the door.

As I look down at all the colors on my body and slowly roll out of bed, I know this is not something I can pretend away. No way would The Mother approve of them showing me their pee-pee. If I don't say something, they might want to do it again. But can she stop The Grandfather?

My brain is so swirly all the way home I don't even look at the clouds.

CHAPTER THIRTEEN

All the traveling and thinking has made me sleepy. I snooze against the scratchy car door as we head home from the airport.

"Did you have fun in California?" The Mother asks in her too-happy voice. "It's a special privilege to get to fly on a plane like that. When I was your age, only really wealthy people got to fly on planes."

I peek with one eye, slowly opening my lashes just enough to see her face. Yup, it felt like she was laying a trap. She likes to do that, say something to get me in trouble. But I am not sure… is she going to talk about The Uncle and The Grandfather? Does she know?

"Yes, I did. I like seeing my cousins," I say carefully. I look at her and add an extra smile. The smile that says I really do like whatever she thinks I don't. But this one is so bad she knows I can't like how they treated me.

Ah. So, this is what we are going to talk about. Be careful.

"Did anything bad happen while you were there?" She stares at the road and keeps her face still, flipping on the blinker to turn the car.

"Yes," I say softly, "The Grandfather and The Uncle weren't nice to me."

"Oh really? That doesn't sound like them. Are you sure? What did they do? Maybe you just didn't understand," she teases. She likes to remind me I am a little girl and don't know what grownups do. It makes her feel smart.

Careful.

"Well…" I speak slowly, unsure if she really wants to know or if she just wants me to say it. "The Uncle likes to pinch real hard. See all these ouchies," I say as I lift up my skirt to show my thigh.

She has already seen my arms of course—we traveled all day together—but she frequently pinches and squeezes my arms so she can't remember which bruises are hers.

"Hmmm… what did you do? Did you do something wrong and make him mad?" she asks. A little twitch at the corner of her mouth tells me she knows that's not it. Great.

"I didn't do anything. The Grandfather came to get me out of bed and took me to The Uncle's office. He saw The Uncle do it, and he watched," I say in a rush. I can't stop myself. I didn't do anything wrong, and she has to believe me.

"He pinched and hit and told me I was a dirty little slut. And The Grandfather said I might get a calling, but it might not be good, and I don't know if I want that," I finish in a huff. The bright fuchsia of panic fades as I stop talking and refocus on The Mother.

She has calmly pulled over on the side of the road. It looks like our neighborhood, but I can't be sure. I am not allowed to walk alone so I don't pay much attention to where I go because I rarely get to choose.

My eyes widen when she leans over me and opens the metal door with a creak. She leans in real close to my face, her stinky breath snaking up my nose, her mean blue eyes staring real hard like she will set me on fire.

"How could you say that? He is a member of the church. If he says you have a calling, you should be grateful. Maybe you need to think about your story and realize what a blessing it is to be in this family." She pauses her angry words to sit back and take a deep breath. Ladies don't lose their temper.

"Get out," she says, like she is saying no to candy at the store.

I just stare at her. I don't know where I am, and I know I am not supposed to be alone by myself. What if somebody takes me for their little girl like that kid on the news?

"Get. out. NOW." Mother is using the quiet anger voice. I know that sour yellow stench of her stubbornness when she decides she is right. There is no arguing with her without hitting. I have already lost.

I take a big breath and step out onto the curb. As soon as I am free of the door, she leans over and pulls it shut hard. Then she drives down the road and around the corner out of sight. I don't know exactly where I am, but I start walking to have something to do.

As I am walking, I start worrying about all those kids who got kidnapped at bus stops and at parks. They had parents who cared and loved them, kept an eye on them like my daddy does for me when he is around. They had moms that made them treats and held them when they cried.

And it still wasn't enough to keep them safe.

And here I am, walking down the road by myself, and if anyone decided to pick me up, the only person who would really be sad is my daddy.

I get a little shaky, and my legs feel like jelly. I stop and sit on the curb, staring at the leaves flapping in the running gutter. Sometimes you can find interesting feathers or rocks in the gutter. That would be nice.

* * *

A car beep startles me. My daddy's Beetle Bug, my favorite two things in the world. A smile breaks my face in half as I run to him, tears leaking down my face even though I don't want to cry.

"Honey! What are you doing out here all by yourself?!" he stammers. I jump into his arms, and he holds me so tight I can't fall apart. My daddy gives the best hugs. He wraps me up and squeezes all the crumbly pieces back together again.

I can't talk. I just bury my face in his pokey neck and breathe in the starchy smell of his white dress shirt and let him pet my hair.

When we get home, Daddy stomps into the house real mad with me snuggled tight against his chest. Nothing bad can happen to me when Daddy holds me; he isn't like the others.

"WHAT THE HELL DO YOU THINK YOU ARE DOING?!" he screams at The Mother as he storms through the front room into the main living area.

My daddy's temper is just like matches. He gets real mad and hot and big at first; you can't touch or talk because the heat fries his brain. But if you let him burn for a little while, he is soft and kind and talks gentle again. That's my favorite. I don't mind the screaming; he never hits, and he doesn't say things that hurt, just angry sometimes.

But I hope this match burns so bright it lights them all on fire and frees us of their meanness. I hope he sees that she will hurt me again.

The Mother pokes her head back from washing dishes in the kitchen. "Well did you ask her what she did? Or did you just swoop in and save her like you always do?" she throws over her shoulder, disgusted.

The heat flares in my daddy's neck, and I hold tighter to the warmth. It's for me, and I can't get enough. Like the best hot cocoa warming up my frozen bones, it feels so delicious. But I know it won't last. And the tears begin to leak down my cheeks again.

"You left our four-year-old by herself in the middle of the street! What the fuck were you thinking?!" he demands. But he has lost some steam. He doesn't know what a good parent is supposed to do either.

"Oh, calm down. It was in our neighborhood just a few blocks away. Didn't you ever wander off when you were her age and some neighbor brought you back?" she explains calmly while she wipes her hands on a dish towel.

"She was just fine. And she learned a valuable lesson, right, honey?" she coos. She expects me to super big smile and thank her for the lesson.

"Yes, Mother," I say softly into the rumpled and soggy fabric of my daddy's shirt.

"Don't do it again," he throws at her and plops down on the recliner with the remote, me snuggled in his lap.

I venture a quick peek over his shoulder to see if the Mother is going to let it go. She gives me a low sneaky smile, like the Cheshire Cat, and then turns to continue doing the dishes.

AGE 45 CRACK

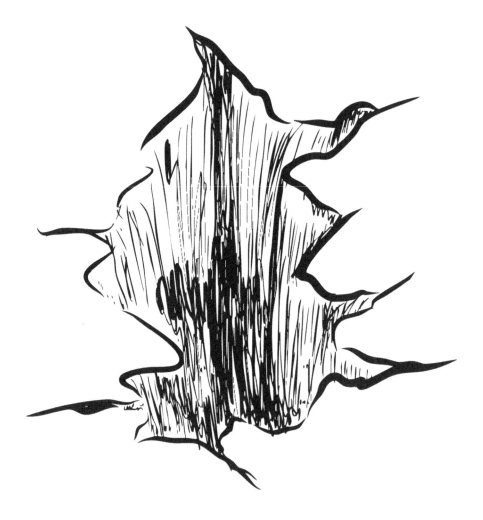

I sit with my arms crossed tightly about my chest, hugging my sides to keep me from breaking apart. The tension sits like a Goliath on my shoulders and neck. I shake violently, uncontrollably, teeth chattering and eyes squeezed shut. The violence of the river of memories rushing out of my body is ebbing to give me a breath.

I can't believe the words that are coming out of my mouth. It's like having amnesia and remembering an entire life lived all at once. A whole other life of terror and abuse I managed separate from my "real" life. I feel like I thought I was standing in a dark room that was small and manageable, but someone turned on the lights, and I am actually standing in the heart of a football stadium filled with awful memories waiting for their turn to be heard. It's overwhelming. It's the true feeling of despair.

The night air is cool, a few hours away before dawn still. The crickets and frogs continue to chirp as we sit in stunned silence.

Nanny never falters. Her hands are still tightly clenched in mine, tears streaming down her face. She pats my hand and says, "I'm here, honey, I am here. You are safe. I love you," over and over and over. It will never be enough.

I have never said these words before. I can't believe I just said those things about The Grandfather and The Mother. Uncle Brad has always been a mean bastard, so I don't feel as bad about that.

The Grandfather hurt me? *The Grandfather hurt me.* The Mother hurt me?

You know she did, the little girls in my mind whisper back.

My insides crack even more, and new horrors tumble out of my mouth.

AGE 4 BITE

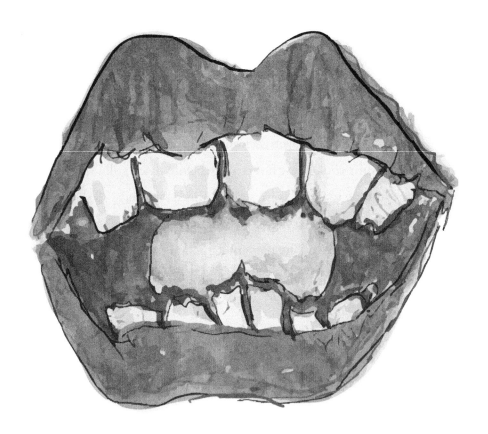

CHAPTER FOURTEEN

I will be turning five soon. That means I can start school. This is very important because The Grandmother says that an education is a treasure that can never be taken away from me. I like that idea.

The Mother is taking me to a super-fancy dress store. The Grandmother says Utica Square is the best place to be seen. We should wear our Sunday best when going there and stroll through the shops like we have money to spend.

The dress shop, Marge McNearney, is the best in town. All the best little-girl dresses come from here. We don't usually have this kind of money to spend on a dress, but they are having a big sale, and it's a special occasion. My fifth birthday is just 10 days away, and it's on Thanksgiving this year. I need to look extra nice.

We get to the store really early, and there is a loooooooooooong line. There are lots of moms in their Sunday best with crying and sleeping and staring kids clutching their hands.

The Mother lets out a disgusted grunt and mumbles about all these people, and we march to the back of the line. Not sure who "these people" are; they all look normal to me. Some smile, and others just ignore us as she grabs my hand this time, a rare treat but only for show. Sometimes people get prickly when she pulls me too hard with her long nails digging into my upper arm; people can see. So she chooses the safe look rather than her secret punishments today, and I'm grateful.

We stand in the cold and wait for the clock to tick by the time. It's not too bad; I am very good at standing for a long time. The Mother trains

me sometimes, having me stand for hours with a book on my head. I need to have good posture. It's important for a young lady. She shifts from foot to foot grumbling and giving me orders about what to do once we are inside.

"Now when we get inside, it's going to be a zoo. You hold my hand, and you don't let go, you understand? You are to stay with me the entire time, OK." It's not really a question, but I nod anyway.

"Can I pick out my dress? Can it be pink this time?" I ask excitedly.

"No, we are only looking for a blue dress," she spits on my head carelessly as she lifts up on tiptoes to see over the people's heads in the line to see if we are moving yet.

The line starts to move as the feet in front of me shuffle forward. The Mother clutches my hand, squeezing the fingers so tight my bones creak. We move past the shop girl and into the store.

It is bright and sunny, with lace and ribbons and bows in every direction. There are dresses that poof out like Shirley Temple and dresses that sway like Sleeping Beauty. They are up high and down low, racks of sale items surrounding the store like cowboys in a corral.

The Mother is frantically searching through the dresses, being rude to other moms desperate to find the perfect dress. There are kids abandoned behind their mothers' butts as they all lean over one another and grab the velvet and smocked creations.

Dresses fall to the floor and are draped over racks, so I stoop to pick one up. It's a pink dress with yellow flowers on the top. It has puff sleeves and lace on the collar. It's beautiful. It's perfect for my birthday.

"Mom!" I exclaim, tugging her arm hard enough that she turns in the madness, annoyed at the interruption. "Look at this one. I love pink.

Can I have this one for my birthday? Please?" I meekly trail off as I see the curl of her annoyance get longer.

"No, it must be blue. The Grandfather is paying for this dress, and it will be what he wants. Not you. Now put it back and help me find one he will like," she says with finality.

Throw-up rises in my throat, and my heart starts racing. It feels like a big wrecking ball came down from the tower building across the street and knocked me full in the chest. It is going to happen again. It took me a long time to stop shaking at night after California. The bruises were everywhere so I had to wear tights and turtlenecks, not my favorite. Daddy might notice if I have to do it again.

I turn to the rack and gently put the pink dress back hanging up. At least I can be kind to it, even if The Mother doesn't see how pretty it is. Maybe someday I can choose my own dress.

* * *

We slowly make our way around the store, pushing and shoving with those silly ladies who are just now arriving after all the good dresses are gone. The Mother clicks her tongue in disgust as she hugs the mountain of dresses in her arms a bit closer.

She finally feels satisfied that she has snatched the best of the remaining dresses and makes her way to the dressing room with me in tow.

Of course, there is a line snaking around the back of the store to try on dresses with moms sitting on the floor next to mountains of discarded dresses and tiny dancing shoes being lifted off their feet by quick pulls of garments over their heads.

The Mother is already pissed we had to wait in line to get in. Another line is not going to help. My breath starts to get short like when I am running. What will she do with so many people around? Is there enough to watch and protect me? Not when we get home I know.

"Goddammit!" she says, not so quiet, and throws the dresses on the floor. "You know, you are only four. No one here cares. Here…" She grabs my hand and takes me and a dress and positions me between two tall racks of dresses.

"Strip," she commands, like this is just as good as a dressing room.

Behind me, I can feel the wind of the door opening and closing, letting in a draft with each mother that walks out with her new dresses. I can hear women behind me complaining about it. And these are little-girl dresses, so the racks on either side of me only come down to my shoulders. Some of them are so tiny they are above my head. If I strip here, everyone will see my panties and my boobies and my ouchies. They are never supposed to see my ouchies or they will take me away.

I stand shivering, not knowing what to do. She thrusts the dress at me again, a baby-blue velvet with a white collar and puff sleeves. Different from the last one because it's softer and heavier. The room starts getting smaller, like *Alice in Wonderland* when she eats the cake. But there isn't a White Rabbit peeking out to show me a secret tunnel to escape.

I look around wide-eyed. Would anyone be upset if they see me naked? Will they yell at The Mother? I don't want to undress in front of the little boy staring at me across the room clutching his mom's skirt.

The Mother reaches forward like she has a hundred times before and grabs the hem of my dress to force it up over my head, but I can't do it HERE. I hit.

I hit. And I hit again.

And then I scream.

And I cry.

I throw a big fit.

I can't stop myself—I am screaming and crying, and don't want anyone to make me be naked in the store. I hit anyone who comes near me and snap my teeth and scream for someone to help.

The little boy I was staring out runs over and tries to tell me to stop being a bad girl, and I grab his arm and bite him. Hard. The Mother grabs me around the middle and screams at me to let go while she slaps my face. I let go, and my body feels like humming jelly. The room goes a bit fuzzy. I see all the faces staring, horrified at my behavior, but not one of them comes to help.

They are all looking at the little boy's arm that is now bleeding while he howls in pain.

A woman who works at the store rushes up to The Mother and asks that she politely take her child outside. She clamps her hand over my mouth, whispers harshly that I better not bite her, and she rushes to the front of the store with the dress still in hand. She throws some money at the protesting clerk and hurries out the door, carrying me like a sack of potatoes.

"There. Glad we got one He will like, because He is NOT going to like to hear about your behavior today. At least you will look pretty before," she says with a Cheshire smile.

I am not stupid; I know what that means. It means I fought, and I lost. And losers must be punished.

CHAPTER FIFTEEN

We get in the car, and she throws the dress at my face. "Ooooh, girl, you are gonna get it," she mumbles with a whistle and a smirk. She settles in her seat and slams the car door. Turns on the car and backs away from the store.

"I'm sorry. I was angry, and sometimes my temper is hot like Daddy's, and I can't remember what to say." We drive in silence for a while. I sit in the front seat looking out the window with the new dress clutched in my lap. It's a cloudy day, just like my mood. I am sad and afraid.

"Where are we going?" I whisper. It feels like we are going to the doctor's to get a shot. Heavy dark slime creeps down my insides, and my body goes even stiffer. The wrecking ball hitting my chest thumps a big one when we pull into The Grandfather's driveway. Oh, this is bad. I look at her in alarm.

We pull up and park in the driveway. She slams the car into park and gives me a hard look. "Get out. It's time to tell The Grandfather what you have done."

I am not sure if I can move, I feel glued to the seat. I slowly move my hand to the metal handle, and she—quick as a snake—leans over and pulls it for me, pushing the door wide and shoving me to topple out onto the driveway. The pavement is wet from the rain last night, the clouds still heavy. I can smell the sharp scent of the leaves and dirt wet on the ground.

The Mother leans back and opens her own door to get out, casually walking around the front of the car toward the pathway to the front

door, and stares at me splayed on the ground like a bunny caught in a flashlight.

"Well, aren't you coming?" she says with a sigh. I stand up and try to wipe the leaves off my dress. I carefully put the new blue dress back in the car and start to shut the door.

"Oh nooooo. What are you doing? You have to bring the dress in. It's too important now." She beams. Making The Grandfather happy makes her smile the dirty smile, the one that says I am going to hurt and it's not her turn anymore.

She is excited about the dress-store incident and begins spilling out the story as soon as The Grandfather comes to the door. He tells her to calm down and wait to talk until we are inside. He holds the door open for me as I slink in behind her. Since California, I have stayed away as much as possible, but his looming presence is never far. He enjoys looking down at me as I walk down the hall to the kitchen where The Mother sits fuming.

The Grandparents' house is big and fancy. I walk straight past the no-touch room down the hall to the kitchen. I see my reflection in the mirror at the end of the hall. My sad eyes staring back at me makes me feel worse. My pretty dress is crooked and still has a bit of dirt on the white pinafore. My beautiful curls are all messy. My ruffled sock has ripped on one side, and I have a scuff on my shoe. It feels even scarier knowing that the dark shadow behind me can see all this too. Being untidy is not allowed.

I pause at the entry of the kitchen. Maybe if I just wish hard enough, this will all go away. I squeeze my eyes closed, standing as still as I can

so maybe they will just forget I am here. The Grandfather's hand gently guides me through the door and into the kitchen.

* * *

The Mother begins telling the story as soon as The Grandfather sits down at the old kitchen table. The fancy dining table is only for holidays and special occasions; family business is conducted at the kitchen table. I stand over by the stove, silent and still, as her side of the story pours out.

How she was taking me out for a lovely treat to get a new dress for my birthday. How I was an ungrateful little brat who threw a fit because she couldn't get the dress SHE wanted. How I screamed and kicked and BIT someone.

"And THEN she THREATENED to tell her father if we made her wear the blue dress again," she adds at the end. I gasp and give her a hard look; I don't remember saying that. But I don't say anything. No one would listen anyway. She looks down at her hands and glances up at The Grandfather to see how he listens to that news. She is focused on what he wants to say. He just sits there like a snake, waiting.

"I don't know how to keep him from finding out. I mean, I can manage the bite, but if she decides to tell…" The Mother looks sad. "It could mean trouble like last time."

The Grandfather assures her that they took care of it before and they could again if they needed to, but let's not jump to conclusions.

The Mother is crying now, her weepy cry that means she doesn't want to get in trouble. I think she is worried that my daddy won't love her anymore if he finds out. I hope she's right.

The Grandfather says, "Oh, good grief, we got rid of your first husband, and we can get rid of this one too. Quit being so dramatic now and tell me what's really wrong," he chides, trying to coax out the real story.

"I am worried those people at the store saw her bruises," she whispers. "What if they think I am a bad mother?" She sniffs and huffs in the quiet, tears dripping down her saggy face.

"Nobody thinks you're a bad mother," he says but it's not the truth. It is silent for a while except for The Mother's sniffs.

The Grandfather finally slowly turns to look at me and says, "Telling her dad would be an issue, though." It's the first time anyone has spoked directly to me a in a long time, and I flinch a little at being addressed.

I stare straight ahead, staying perfectly still like that girl robot on TV. When she shuts down to charge, everyone forgets she is in the room. Maybe I can be real still and they will think I just shut down. I don't know what to say and I am scared.

"If you tell your dad about your calling, we would have to kill him. He doesn't have the priesthood so he doesn't get access to our divine gifts from God. I would have to cut him up into little pieces to make sure he didn't tell any of God's secrets, maybe put them in your food to punish you for making me have to do that," he says, real soft and sad, like it's something he doesn't want to do, but I could make him do it.

"Wait!" I plead before I even know what is bubbling out of my chest. "Please don't hurt my daddy. I won't tell. I'll do whatever you want—just please don't hurt my daddy."

I don't mean to speak, but I don't take it back. Wearing a blue dress and getting pinched doesn't seem that bad if I can save my daddy. He is

my favorite person; I need him. I stare right at The Grandfather's eyes and show him that I am telling the truth.

"It would be really easy to make him disappear, you know," he says casually, sitting back and putting on his thinking face. Hope starts to shine like a tiny light in my heart. Maybe I can save my daddy.

"Your mother could cover it long enough to hide the evidence, and then no one would ever know," he says and then pauses. "We can get rid of anyone, really, who causes us problems," he finishes with a little tiny smile.

I have made a mistake, but I don't know what it is. The hope flicks out with a wink, leaving the darkness yawning wide to swallow me.

The Grandfather likes puzzles. He likes that I am smart, and he can tell me little riddles like this and I can solve them. He watches my face as I try to work out what he is really saying.

He sees in my face when I work out the puzzle. The Mother sits, stupid.

He wants me to never tell about anything. Because there is more. I can see it in his eyes—there is so much more.

And I begin to shake.

CHAPTER SIXTEEN

I don't have a lot of experience with big decisions. Still, at almost five years old, I know what a hero would do—save her daddy. Though I don't know that I have many examples of little girls rescuing their parents, I have a way of taking a story's general good idea and putting it to good use. Here comes Snow White to save HeMan.

So I take a big gulp of air, lift my head, and say, "I understand."

With a gleam in his eye, The Grandfather smiles the Grinch smile. He has yellow crooked teeth that are really stinky so he doesn't show them off very much. Kind of looks like the Grinch cartoon, without the slimy bugs (sometimes I liked to pretend them).

"Oh really?" he almost purrs and gets up to walk to the phone hanging on the cabinet near the window. He pushes the buttons and waits. He talks real soft into the phone so I can't hear. He hangs up the phone and leaves the room.

The Mother and I stay still and silent, her occasionally hiccupping and sniffing. We both nearly jump out of our skin when the doorbell rings some time later—BING BONG.

The Grandfather passes by the kitchen on the way through to the front door, where I hear him greet Brother V and invite him to come inside. I hear The Grandmother come downstairs in her quilted bathrobe. It's turquoise with fancy peacocks on it and sticks out a little at the bottom like a princess dress. She is always perfectly pretty, no matter the occasion.

I hear her steps and see the hem of her gown pass the kitchen doorway, followed by two sets of men's shoes and pants. I don't have the courage to look up yet to see faces; I am saving my strength.

"Honey, can you come in the living room for a minute?" The Grandfather calls like it's a regular day and there are no bad feelings scattered around at all.

I glance at The Mother. He eyes are not mad anymore; they are sad. She looks like she doesn't want to go into the living room either. I wonder if she will get in trouble too. I carefully walk past her chair, and I hear her chair scrape across the floor.

I tiptoe like ballet class into the living room to see The Grandfather. He and Brother V stand shoulder-to-shoulder like come over red rover. The Mother comes up behind me and pushes me forward with a hand on the small of my back. I didn't even realized I had stopped. She is never this gentle unless it's about to be worse so I begin to drag my feet and go slow.

"Now you haven't changed your mind, have you?" asks The Grandfather, wide-eyed. "I thought this was what you wanted, to save your *daddy*. But if you don't and you would rather not, then…" He gestures to Brother V's pants, but his pants are around his feet, and his big pee-pee is hanging down but twitching. Brother V gives The Grandfather a knowing look and bends down to grab his pants to pull them up.

The throw-up is in my throat again, but I swallow it and step forward, gritting my teeth. I can do anything for my daddy.

"OK, OK!" I pant as I prepare to obey. I can't breathe. I feel really shaky. I close my eyes and take a deep breath. "What do I have to do?"

"Well, now you have made poor Brother V here wait. I think he deserves a little extra for that discomfort, don't you?" he says to make sure I know that he wants to see all of the fire in my eyes gone.

"I understand," I reply meekly, shutting the screaming girl in the basement in my mind.

The Grandfather asks The Mother to get a dish towel and soak it with water and bring it back. She jumps to do his wish, in a hurry to get out of the room with the crying girl and the big pee-pee hanging down. He then asks that we all move to the hallway in front of the mirror, away from the large windows.

The Mother returns with the tea towel, and The Grandfather gently folds it into a little pillow. He lays it down on the tile where it will be easy to clean up The Grandmother's floors. He gestures for me to come on the side in front of the door with him, Brother V following me, dragging his pants around his feet.

The Grandfather and I stand on one side of the wet tea towel, Brother V facing us on the other. The mirror gives me a view of the group without looking up, The Mother and Grandmother smiling wickedly, like cartoon bad cats waiting for the mouse circus.

I am not as stupid as they think so I don't protest when The Grandfather gently pushes me down to my knees on the tea towel. I thought it would be soft, but it begins to hurt pretty fast. The wet towel feels like little needles in my knees against the hard tile. It makes me wiggle and dance from one side to the other, the adults laughing as I try to do so without making contact with the pee-pee in front of my face.

Brother V isn't supposed to show me his privates. His temple garments are sticking out right there under his shirt. He is supposed to be modest. I don't like looking at it, but it's not so bad. Is this going to keep my daddy safe?

Then The Grandfather firmly pushes my face to Brother V's pee-pee, where it's standing up and he is rubbing it. It is dark purple and blue and black and pink in some places, a nest of curly black hairs all around it. Brother V leans down to stick his thumb in my mouth and open it wide and says, "Don't bite. You understand."

It is a command I have to obey. This is the deal.

"Ey ubba-spnaa," I spit around his thumb as he opens it wide again and lays his pee-pee in my mouth.

It's slippery and smooth, with little folds on my tongue. I am not sure what I am supposed to do so I sit quietly with my screaming knees and focus on breathing through the tiny airway between the roof of my mouth and my tongue.

To my surprise, Brother V lets out a big ol' "EhhhhhhhAhhhhhhhhh!" with a smile on his face and grabs the back of my head to push it down further on his pee-pee.

I panic; there isn't enough room. My throat hurts, and I see black-and-white tiny fireworks until I can figure out how to breathe through my nose and the panic lessens a little. My eyes pop open at the shock of fresh air when he pulls it out after a few pushes, shocked as the sticky goo spurts out, not dribbly like Uncle Brad.

I look down at my dress and my hands, just a little bit of sticky creamy icing that smells of lemons and ocean. I look up, confused, at all the adults laughing at me. Brother V bends down and takes a finger through the icing and wipes it on my cheek, boops my nose. More laughing. I try not to let the tears go, but one slips silently down my cheek anyway. I just want to get off this tea towel and know if my daddy is going to be OK.

My knees feel like little needles are poking them, fiery pain shooting up the back of my legs where I am working hard to keep from falling over. But I stay bent like saying a prayer, hoping that if I am good, it's the end.

I take a chance and risk a look up at The Grandfather, who gives me a small hand wave to get up. I carefully roll back on my heels. The relief is quickly followed by a red-hot pain as I slowly stand on wobbly knees. I don't say anything. I study the grey-and-white marble tiles on the floor. I want to ask if it's over, but I don't trust the girl in my mind screaming behind the door I am holding closed.

After a few moments, I say softly but firmly, "Was that good enough?"

"For now," The Grandfather replies and gives me a pat on the back. "Take her home, Pam," he says and she reaches to grab her purse.

Quick as a snake, he reaches out to snag her hand, and she turns quick with terror in her eyes (she knows The Grandfather is not nice too). "Make sure her daddy doesn't find out about today," he growls. Always quiet, never yelling, but still scary.

He turns his head to look at me, squeezing The Mother's arm, making white knuckles so I know it hurts. "If you tell your daddy about this, he'll never love you again. They don't like black men in the South. They especially don't like little white girl sluts who use their mouths to please black men," he sneers. The Grandfather doesn't mingle with such trash, I know. "So you better keep your mouth shut about the things we are doing to prepare you for celestial marriage. Do you understand?"

I nod silently. I am scared so I hope it's the right thing to do because I can't think of anything else.

I know my daddy. He is from Alabama, and that's in the South; that's true. Sometimes he lets me say Damn Yankees, which is a bad word, but Daddy says it's OK for fun. But he says he doesn't hate anyone for their skin.

Sometimes he takes me to Alabama where he grew up. Sometimes, it's just him and me on an adventure. It's a whole weekend of hanging out with his friends, being silly and dirty and sharing tickles. There is no Mother and no punishments. They call me little sis, and I like it. Those are some of the golden memories I keep in a safe place in my brain for the bad times—like now, when it gives me a little firefly of light to think about.

I know The Grandfather is lying. My daddy loves me no matter what. He tells me that, and he tells the truth. But The Grandfather and The Mother, they will hurt him just to see me die inside.

So I meekly stand still while he eases his hand off The Mother's arm, leaving bright brick-red marks. She pulls her purse to her chest and sticks out her hand to me, which I take without question, and we walk down the hall and out of the heavy oak door, closing it softly behind us.

We didn't even get hugs goodbye.

CHAPTER SEVENTEEN

We drive home in silence. I stare at the blue dress in my lap, delicately fingering the lace stitched so perfectly on the collar. It really is a beautiful dress, just not the one I wanted.

My knees hurt, my throat hurts, my brain feels full of cotton. When we get home, I drag up the steps like Elmo going to the doctor. I wish I had someone to hold my hand too.

As we walk into the kitchen from the garage, the Mother commands, "Sit," as she slaps her hand on the kitchen counter next to the sink.

I walk slowly through the kitchen and pull over the dining room chair so I can climb on the counter. I sit next to the sugar and the flour containers, dreading what comes next. It's already been a horrible day. I'm really tired; I would even take a nap without complaining.

The Mother smiles as she reaches across the kitchen counter for the black pepper, bringing her shiny face close enough for her to give me a little peck on my cheek (not the sticky one; that's gross) before pulling the shaker closer to her to twist it open.

She picks up the pepper shaker and lifts up one eyebrow and looks at me. *You know what comes next,* she says with her eyes. I take a deep breath, sit up straight, and stick out my tongue. The Mother pours out black pepper on the middle of my tongue. I am grateful for every little pebble that bounces and falls into my lap—one more that won't hurt me. But she puts an extra lot on this time, including the dry powder in the bottom.

After a long time and a lot of pepper on my lap, she stands back and says, "Now close your mouth."

I can't freak out. If I lose my focus, I could breathe it in, and that STINGS. Real bad. And you can't cough it out without coughing more in. So I shut my eyes, carefully hold my breath, and pull my tongue inside the biggest cave my mouth can make. It hovers there like an alien in space, deadly to move in any direction. I control my breath by pretending I can see the air in my mind, getting from my nose to my lungs and back without touching the pepper. It's really hard. The pepper feels like it's burning my tongue, and the little powder puffs sometimes block my throat.

"Don't move," she warns as she grabs her purse and grabs the garage door handle.

"If I come back and you don't have just the right amount of pepper on your tongue, we will have to start alllllllll over again," she almost sings as she closes the door behind her, making me jump and choke a little.

Hold still and calm down. I can sit; I can just sit here real still until she comes back.

* * *

I jerk upright and almost upset my breath when I hear the garage opening that evening. My back hurts from sitting straight for so long. I don't know how to read time yet, but I watched the sunbeams travel across the floor, making rainbows and changing colors as it got later, so I know it's been a while.

I kept wishing Daddy would get home from work first. He would save me if she didn't clean me up before he saw. But The Mother walks in with a sigh, slinging her purse on the bar, and turns at last to see if I am still there. She smiles when she sees me wobbling a little. I am trying to sit up

straight, but it's hard to focus this hard and be so scared to move because I might not be able to breathe. She claps her hands, and I jump, barely remembering to push out breath. Now the pepper is clumpy and not so powdery, but I still have to be careful.

She doesn't say a word as she walks into the living room and set down her things. She lazily comes over to the sink and pulls on her yellow dish gloves, turns on the water. The pepper burned and numbed my tongue a while ago, so it's not that bad when she washes out my mouth with the dish soap by sticking her rubber-gloved fingers into my mouth and scraping the inside.

Everything must be clean, clean, clean.

The Mother wipes my mouth with a towel, gently getting the corners last. Then she stands and takes my hand to walk down the hallway to my bedroom. A white room, a bed, a few books. The books are my favorite.

She goes over to my white dresser with the gold trim and pulls out a play outfit, some pants and a shirt. She pulls my soiled dress over my head and dresses me in clean clothes, brushing my hair into a neat ponytail.

To my surprise, she neatly lays the dirty dress on top of the dresser. "Naughty girls deserve to be dirty. You can wear this soiled dress tomorrow to school, let everyone know what a filthy little slut you are," says The Mother.

I blink at her, confused. I thought we weren't supposed to tell. Will my teacher get angry that I have icing on my dress at school? Maybe she can help me get it out. Maybe she will give me a hug and tell me it's OK. Sometimes she does that; I really like it.

* * *

The front door opens, and we hear my daddy. "I'm home. Anyone here?"

"Daddy!" I yell as I dart around The Mother's legs and run down the hall. She won't hurt me in front of Daddy. The Mother and I both love my daddy. She doesn't hurt me in front of my daddy; I don't tell my daddy she hurts me. I guess today just made it bigger, because now The Grandfather is going to hurt me too. But I can take it—I can stay quiet if it protects my daddy. But I will need to get better at protecting my brain.

"There's my cutie pie!" he exclaims. My daddy is in a good mood, swinging me up in his arms and giving me kisses all over my face. That's my favorite, soft kisses on my head and cheeks with my favorite person.

"How's my little Lucky Girl today?" he asks as he gives me a squeeze, "Did you get a dress at the fancy store?"

I put on my happy face, the one I save just for my daddy, and give him a big sunshine smile and nod my head.

"Yup, a beautiful blue one. Mommy picked it out for me. It's just perfect for my birthday party!" I exclaim overexcitedly. I need to be extra sweet if I want to be extra sure he is safe.

"Ahhh, I am glad, punkin." He smiles with his eyes and laughs as he puts me gently down on the floor. "Let's go sit down and we can have a fashion show, honey," he suggests as he undoes his tie and walks back to his bedroom to change. "And, hey, I thought you wanted to go to Oxley Nature Center for your birthday. You can't wear a fancy dress there," he shouts from the bedroom closet.

I stand frozen in the front room, exactly where my daddy set me down. I am facing the kitchen where The Mother has gone to prepare dinner. I see her go still as a statue too, and she only turns her head to

see me out of the corner of her eye. I am paralyzed with fear. She pushes her lips together and stares real hard at me like she is sending me a secret message with her eyes, and slowly, she shakes her head. That dress is only for The Grandfather.

"Oh yeah! I forgot about Oxley, I didn't know if we could go. But that's what I want to do. I'll wear that dress to my family birthday dinner," I say in my cheeriest happy-girl voice as The Mother stares real hard into my eyes. I am a liar, but so are those child actors at Disney. And this is more important than remembering lines.

She dips her chin just a little to let me know that the danger has passed and goes back to what she was doing. I sigh in relief and go to my room to sit on my bed. I sit in the corner, facing my bookshelves and pretty white bedroom set and closet full of lovely things, but I can't see any of them. I just feel fuzzy.

I lied to my daddy. No. I had to lie to my daddy. To protect him. And that makes it OK. That makes it OK. That makes it OK. That makes it OK.

AGE 45 GOOD JOB

I shake with the remembered stress of sitting, tight and still on the countertop with the pepper on my tongue. The relief of my daddy coming home and the renewed fear of realizing that the dress was meant for something worse.

"I had to protect him. That makes it OK to lie," I say in a small child's voice, in between gasps and sobs. A little girl trying to cover getting caught.

"So your dad didn't know?" Nanny asks, relief and disbelief coloring her words with the unsteady blue and midnight of hope shimmering in the air between us.

"No. I did a really good job keeping it from him." I shake even harder as the words bubble up and continue to spill out without control. "They told me they would cut him up into little pieces and cook him in my food if I told. So I was a super-good girl so I could protect my daddy."

I sound more confident than I feel, proud of my accomplishments but horrified that I was doing that subconsciously for decades and never admitted it to myself. How did I hide these stories from my own mind? It's like waking up one day and realizing that you have been living a whole other life while sleeping. Having memories of things I have done with my face and my mind but locked in a child's perspective.

Nanny stares at me, crying silently with granite-hard eyes. She is mad. That makes me feel better. No one ever got angry for me, only at me.

"And your mom was helping him? She was doing this to her own child?" Sparks fly from her eyes. "What was the blue dress for?" she finally whispers like a kid watching a horror movie who knows the killer is about to murder the innocent girl and feels helpless to stop it.

The acid bile of terror rises in the back of my throat, and I open my mouth to vomit more horror.

AGE 4 PICNIC

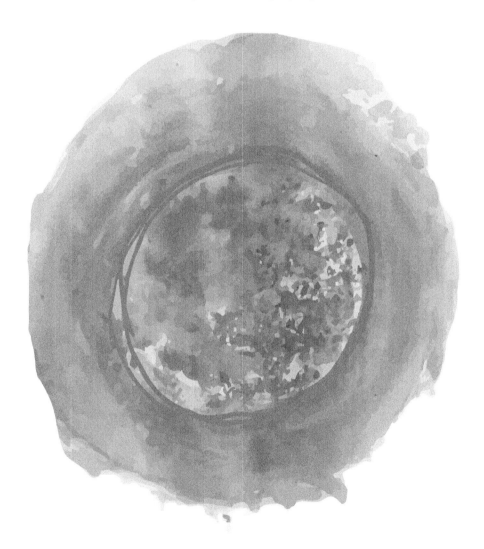

CHAPTER EIGHTEEN

My five-year-old birthday is on Thanksgiving day this year so my daddy said we can celebrate early. Our school went on a class trip to Oxley Nature Center last year, and I am dying to go back. A special day is planned—my daddy is even off of work for it! The Mother, my daddy, and me are all going to my favorite place for my birthday.

Oxley Nature Center is a special place where people can learn about the animals and plants in the forest. There are all kinds of birds, insects, and animals that live in the forest that help us learn more about how to protect them and their environment. I like the idea of protecting the little animals that can't protect themselves from humans.

There are nature trails in the forest behind the building to explore; that's where I want to go most. We only got to try two paths last time. I want to try more. Be an explorer! You won't get lost if you stick to the path. That's my favorite part.

"Are you ready for your big adventure today, birthday girl?!" my daddy says as he ruffles my hair and drops a kiss on my forehead. Those are my favorite kisses. Forehead kisses are the best.

"Yup! Now you need to wear good walking shoes and bring a jacket just in case," I tell him like a school teacher. I have been to Oxley before so I know what to do. He smiles and gives me a soldier salute as he wheels back on his heel and walks back into the bedroom to get dressed.

It is a special treat to go to Oxley, and I am going to make it great. I bounce in my seat as we enter the parking lot, passing the other people entering the buildings to the zoo nearby. I liked the zoo a lot, but I love

Oxley Nature Center. I love that the animals are free, and I get to see them being happy.

The Mother is wearing her smiley-mommy face and pretending that we are a perfect family. She calls me precious and sweetie and holds hands in the nice way. It's nice. I know it's just for my daddy, so he doesn't ask questions, but I also know better than to fall for her tricks. I put on my big-girl-smile for her and do as she asks, but delight when Daddy swings me up on his shoulders. "Birthday girls get to sit up high!"

I giggle and laugh as I clutch tight to his head without wiggling his glasses. I love my daddy; I always give him the special sunshine smile. It's not even hard.

* * *

We look at each exhibit in the Nature Center, pulling my daddy's hand from delicate butterflies pinned on a board to small aquariums with little lizards. My daddy smiles and asks me silly questions, even though I know he is a grownup and probably already knows most of this stuff. I am just a kid; I am still learning.

I love learning. Like my dance class, learning new things is something that you can never have someone reach in your brain and pull out. I can lock it in safe deep in my brain and pull it out in the dark times and make stories to keep me company.

Though I like the exhibits, I race to get through so we can go outside. I can see the start of the nature trails through the large glass door in the back. There is a wide concrete ramp with wooden rails on the sides leading straight down a large path to the forest. Once you get to the trees, there are THREE trails to choose from.

Last time, our teacher got to choose the path so we only took one and all had to stay together. This time, we are trying something new, and I get to choose. I feel so smart and big. My belly bubbles with delight.

The Mother lags behind as my daddy and I skip-walk to the bottom of the ramp.

"Come here, cutie pie, hop on," he says as he bends down and lets me climb on his back. I love piggyback rides; it's like walking in a hug. It's my favorite.

"Just point to tell me where you want to go. Birthday girl gets to decide today!" he declares as we march toward the three paths.

"Well…" I say thoughtfully, "I went on that path with our teacher because it's the shortest and easiest, but I would like to try this path because it has more flowers on it."

Even though it's my birthday and it's my choice, that last part comes out a tiny bit like a question. I just don't know if that's an OK path, and I need him to agree.

"I like that one too," he agrees easily, and I beam, snuggling my face on his neck for just a quick moment for being on my side.

"It looks awful rocky. Are you sure that's the path you want to take? I heard the lady say she saw s`ome squirrels on the middle path this morning. Wouldn't you rather see those and take this path?" The Mother decides as she walks forward onto the center path.

I can feel my daddy take a deep breath and the heat that is rising on his neck. He doesn't like it when The Mother makes decisions for me when it's my turn, but I know he wants today to be fun so he doesn't start a fight. He does little things like that for me.

My daddy eventually swings me down from his back, and we all walk for a while, pointing out small wonders and little sights, and it's nice. We walk really far into the trees, surrounding ourselves with bird calls and windy branches. No one yells, and The Mother only trips a few times, so no fights yet.

The afternoon passes, and my tummy growls loudly. I am not sure I ate much this morning because I was too excited. Stupid me. My daddy laughs, "Getting hungry? Me too. Let's start heading back and get some lunch, huh?" he says as he looks back at The Mother to see if she agrees.

She looks at her watch and at the sun and agrees it's time to head back that way.

We are a little quieter on the way back, me thinking about the bright blue blue jay we saw. The Mother says blue jays are mean.

I look up to see we have come to a choice of new path. One path is straighter, the Oxley building up above the trees that way. The other path has a log down across it, but is clear beyond as it disappears into the dark trees.

"You should go that way, and we should go this way," The Mother says. I turn to her in surprise. I am never encouraged to be alone.

"That doesn't seem smart," says my daddy, surprised. "We don't know where that path goes, and she shouldn't be by herself in the woods."

The Mother gives him the look that says he is a stupid daddy. "Oh really?! Come on. She is five years old now. You have to stop being so protective and give her some independence sometime. The Nature Center is right there," she says, pointing to the building roof peeking over the trees a little ways away. "She can find her way there without a path."

I stare in disbelief. The path does look dark and mysterious with the soft shadows of the leaves dancing over the smooth dirt. It looks like an amazing adventure.

"I can do it, Daddy!" I encourage excitedly. "I am a big girl now, and I have been here before. I will follow the path and not even step one foot off of it and meet you at the center. OK?" I say with my secret sly smile and eye twinkle. I know my daddy can't resist me when I really want something, and this is something I want real bad.

He heaves a big sigh and bends down to a crouch to look me in the eye. "You be careful and stay on the path. If it ends or you get scared, you just follow the path back. If you get lost, STAY PUT. I will come find you, and it's easier if you aren't moving around. Got it?" he says with the little wrinkle between his eyebrows that says he is worried.

"I will, Daddy," I say with a huge sunshine smile. "You can trust me."

And as he raises up and wipes the wrinkles out of his pants, my eyes slide over to The Mother, and my insides turn to ice. The Mother is smiling the scary smile. The smile that says I just walked into a trap.

CHAPTER NINETEEN

Too late to back out now. I take a deep breath and set out over the fallen log and down the path without looking back. Maybe she thinks I will get lost. I will show her; I will stay on the path no matter what.

I walk as quietly as I can, enjoying the softness of the woods: bird chirps and fiddle bugs, rustling leaves. It's peaceful, and I slow down a little. I stop to look at weird footprints in the mud, a gross worm in the grass.

After a while, I look up to see the path looks like it ends ahead. I can't be sure, but it looks like it stops at some trees around a circle of sunshine. I start walking faster. Maybe a unicorn or fairy will be in the circle of light like in the storybooks. I reach the end of the path and there are no fairies. Instead, I see the edge of a white-and-blue blanket on the ground.

Why is there a blanket in the woods?

I get nervous. I keep walking, all the way to the end, because I don't know what else to do. I stop, confused, staring at the corner of the blanket.

Then my eyes creep up to the man sitting on the blanket, The Grandfather sitting with a picnic basket—it looks like a page from my *Dick and Jane* books. But this doesn't feel like a happy afternoon picnic.

I stare at his shirt, stiff white that sticks out from his body like it doesn't want to touch him either. He is getting wrinkles in his pants and grass on his shiny shoes, The Grandmother will not be pleased. My eyes creep up to his gold-rimmed glasses reflecting the sun into my eyes in a wink that makes me look away quickly.

"Happy birthday, honey," he says quietly, like the snake in *The Jungle Book* with swirly eyes trying to get me closer before he eats me.

"Come sit next to me here. I made you a lovely birthday picnic," he says as he pats the blanket in front of him.

I don't want to go, I want to turn around and run and run and hide in the forest forever. *Could there really be good forest fairies that will come out and save me if I got lost?* I think in a panic.

My feet know it will be worse if I take too long so they start walking while my brain tries to figure out what to do. Walking slowly but not too slowly over to the blanket to take a seat.

"I notice you are not wearing the blue dress today. I'm disappointed," chides The Grandfather, reaching into the basket for some green grapes, my favorite.

"It's not appropriate for a nature walk. I need sturdy shoes," I say softly, picking at a loose blue thread on the quilt.

"Yes, I suppose so," he chuckles, which makes me squeeze my eyes tight for a moment. That's not a happy laugh; he is not happy about the blue dress.

"So now that you are a big girl, I will need to have frequent inspections of your body to make sure you are developing and keeping yourself chaste. You haven't been touching any other boys or letting them touch you again, have you?" he says like a question, but I know it's not. I know I can't ever again after playing doctor that one time with the neighbor kids and getting caught.

He looks at me out of the corner of his eye as he is bent over the basket getting napkins and adds, "Those jeans are going to be more difficult."

I don't know what that means. My daddy said they would protect my legs from sticks and chiggers.

The Grandfather lays down a single napkin and folds his hands in front of him, "Now please take off your jeans and underwear and lie down on your back," he orders softly, which means it's not my choice.

I slip off my sneakers and stand to unbutton my jeans, shivering in the sudden cool autumn breeze. "Panties too," he reminds me as he watches every move.

I reluctantly slide them down my thighs until they make a puddle on the blanket. I stand there shaking in the cold, my face burning. I can't remember what I am supposed to do next.

"Lie down," he says, getting angry. "I don't have all day."

I gently bend forward, trying to cover myself but exposing my butthole to the wind so I finish lying down quickly. I lie stiff and shaking with the hum of fear.

I stare at the light pink flowers on the white cotton of my undies lying under my leg as he carefully selects a grape. I need to pee. I squeeze my naked legs together as hard as I can.

I don't stop staring at that spot as he parts my legs and sticks the grape inside my vagina. It's cool and slippery and pops right in.

My eyes snap up to the sky, and I inhale a quick breath and hold it. I didn't know things went in there; I am not supposed to touch it or let anyone else touch it but my doctor and The Mother. Panic rises burning my throat and back of my teeth. Stay quiet. Stay quiet.

"Now I am going to get it out of there, and we will see what it tells us about your insides." He tries to soothe me as he slips two fingers inside my hole. He wiggles them around a little. It makes me feel sick

and squirm. Then he hooks his fingers around the grape and pulls it out with a pop. I gag and almost throw up, turn it quick to a cough. Keep it down. Keep it down. Throwing up is going to make a mess and make The Grandfather angry.

I don't dare move; I just lie straight and squeeze my legs tight.

He looks at the grape, examining it in the sun, then pops it in his mouth like he is testing the ingredients in potato salad.

"Very good," he decides and begins packing up the picnic. Maybe that means it's almost over. I squeeze my eyes shut.

"You can go." He dismisses me like I have come to ask a question of a teacher at lunch.

I quickly get up and pull on my undies and jeans. I sit to lace up my shoes and have trouble with the rabbit ears because my hands are shaking. Finally, they loop around and go into the hole like they are supposed to, and I stand up, waiting.

"You better get going. They are probably worried about you," he says as he packs up the napkin and pulls out his hanky to blow his nose. "Tell your mother she did a good job today."

I stand still. Go in the woods, by myself again. I suddenly don't feel like a big girl anymore. The trees are dark, and the sun is going down. I am not sure I want to go on the path by myself again.

"I'm not taking you." He shoos, "Go!" so I turn and run into the woods.

CHAPTER TWENTY

I don't how long I have been running. I don't know where I am going. I don't know where I am. All I know is I am running away. Away from The Grandfather.

I run through bushes and around trees. I trip in animal holes and scare pecking birds. Every time I stop to breathe, a loud snap or moving leaves and I am off again, anywhere but here.

* * *

The sun is almost gone now. The shadows are long and scary. I don't have the energy to run anymore, but I keep walking. I know my daddy said to stay put, but he thought I would be on a path. How will I ever explain why I went off the path? He will be so disappointed… if I ever see him again.

I stop and take a break, look around for the millionth time. I think I can hear kids. I walk to where the trees are lighter, and I can see people sitting at picnic tables outside the trees. Maybe those people will help me. The icy grip of fear on my spine begins to melt. I made it.

I start getting excited and run until I reach where the trees stop. There are picnic tables and a few families eating the last of their dinner. I stay hidden behind the shadows of the trees and slump down with my back scraping against the bark. I think I know what safe people look like—I study them a lot at school—but I am not sure. If I talk to a stranger, it has to be an emergency, and I think a bad stranger wouldn't have kids with them.

I look for a family that has some smiley kids and a dad that doesn't look like he hits. A little ways away, there is a mom giving her kids snack cakes and laughing at their animal impressions. I like the impressions too. They make me laugh a little, and then I begin to cry. It comes up like a bubble of warm milk, thick and sour, and pours out of my heart through my mouth. Why can't The Mother and Grandfather just like me as I am? Why do I have to be chosen?

CHAPTER TWENTY-ONE

I sit watching the family, sniffling. I see those kinds of families at school. The happy moms who give kisses and snack cakes. No bruises or callings.

I wait until they are finished eating and begin to pack up before I step out of the woods and say, "Excuse me," in the tiniest voice.

The dad is packing and laughing with the son, but the mom turns her head right away and sees me

standing there. I know I look messy, hair falling out of my ponytail, dirt on my knees, snail tracks of tears on my face.

"Oh honey, are you lost?!" she exclaims as she puts down the ketchup bottle and rushes toward me.

I take a step back. I don't know if she is going to be mad.

"Yes, I lost my way. Can you take me back to the nature center, please?" I ask politely, using my best manners.

"Oh, of course, honey," she says with a wide-eyed glance over shoulder at the dad. "Did you get separated from your parents?" she continues as she squats in front of me, reaching to wipe a tear away and then stopping right before she gets to my cheek. I flinch on accident; I never know if it will be a hit or nice in time.

"I won't hurt you," she says like I am a lost kitty. "Let's just get you a cold cloth and something to drink, OK?"

I nod, and she leaves me standing there while she looks through their cooler. She comes back with a paper towel dipped in cooler water and a can of soda. It's not the caffeine-free kind, so I can't drink it, but the cold

cloth feels nice. She gently presses it to my face and places my hand on top so she doesn't have to be too close for too long. I think she knows sometimes it hurts more to be touched when you are hurting.

* * *

The nice family absorbs me into their nice tan minivan with brown seats and air conditioning in the back. They talk about cheery things to try and help me smile. I like that they try; it's a kind thing to do.

We pull up at the center, and I jump out of the van. I shoot like a rocket to the front of the building as my daddy comes busting out of the glass doors. I meet him halfway and launch into his arms, squeezing him like a little monkey, belly to belly, arms and legs wrapped tightly around the middle. I dip my head into his neck and breathe in his sweat and worry like the smell of something baking. He waited for me, he worried about me, and that's all that matters.

"Oh, punkin, don't ever worry me like that again!" he says sternly, and my eyes sting with tears as I squeeze him tight.

"I didn't mean to get lost. I won't do it again—I promise," I plead as I shake and leak in his arms.

"Of course you didn't, baby. It's OK. You are safe now," he soothes as he rocks side to side and rubs little circles on my back. I am still leaky, but I am starting to feel better now that I am back with my daddy.

I finally turn my head and rest it on my daddy's shoulder, opening my eyes and blinking at the brightness of the sun's last rays.

I see The Mother step into a sunbeam as my daddy leans to talk to the nice family. She has that sneaky smile on her face, the sideways one that means she wants something. She jerks her chin and turns to walk

down a small hallway inside the doors that says "Restroom" over the top in blue letters.

"Daddy, I need to go to the bathroom, " I say with a sink of my tummy and slide down his warm body to stand on my own feet again.

"OK, baby, let me know if you need anything," he says with a kiss on the head and a small pat on my back as he continues to deal with the nature center people and the nice family. My knees wobble as I walk up the ramp I'm so tired I could fall asleep right here, but whatever happens… my daddy loves me.

* * *

I walk into the bathroom and move real fast past the mirrors over the sink. I don't need to see my messy appearance. I choose the middle toilet and turn to lock the door behind me. I can hear The Mother peeing in the handicap stall. She likes it because it's bigger.

For a second time, I unbutton my pants and peel them down my legs… but this time there are tiny pricks of blood all over them. Blood-red dots are oozing trails of pink swirls down my legs where they have joined with the sweat like paint running down the easel.

I begin shaking and crying; I can't stop. It comes up like a wave and won't go back down. The blood and the running and the sweat and the burrs in my socks and The Grandfather and the grapes and the

BANG BANG BANG

The Mother slaps her hand against the door and asks, "What's all the fuss about? Open the door and let me see."

I stand as still as I can as the shaking starts in my knees and works up to my lip. I carefully reach out and slide the lock out of the door and let

it squeak open. She stands there like any normal day, no worry or sweat or snail marks on her face.

"What's wrong?" Now she can't quite stop the smile creeping over her lips. She wants the news, and she isn't patient.

"The Grandfather said you did really good," I say to my puddled pants, wishing I could melt on the floor and escape through the little silver drain behind my heel.

"Good. You almost ruined it by taking off into the woods like that. What were you thinking?! You should have just taken the same damn path you came in on, stupid," she chides with her hands on her hips and a smirk twitching her lips. She likes it when she is smarter than me.

"But you found a way back so no harm done. You were smart not to tell the nice family where you were—that could have been real trouble," she warns with a sharp eye on my face. "You better never tell anyone about the preparations. That goes against what the heavenly father and Jesus Christ want for you, and you wouldn't want that, now would you?"

I keep my head down and say a quiet, "No, Mother," as she nods and moves toward the door, checking her hair as she grabs the handle and swings it open.

"Now you hurry up in there. We are already going to be late getting home," she says as the door slowly closes behind her.

Chapter Twenty-One

AGE 5 INSPECTION DAY

CHAPTER TWENTY-TWO

My daddy says my birthday is my special day. This year is extra special because it's on Thanksgiving. That means our whole family will go to The Grandparents' house to celebrate with a turkey dinner AND birthday cake! Chocolate cake with fudge icing, my favorite. And the best part—my daddy is off work for four days! He said we will celebrate all day long.

So I jump out of bed as soon as I wake up on Thanksgiving morning and run across the hall to my daddy's room. I quietly open the door—The Mother is a light sleeper and doesn't like to be disturbed—and tiptoe around the bed to where my daddy is snoring.

He snores so loud sometimes I can hear it in my room. The Mother hates it. Sometimes she sleeps on the couch just to get away from the noise. It doesn't bother me that much; it is a reminder he is there.

I lift the corner of the blanket and squeeze into the bed next to my daddy. I curl into a little ball, snuggling tight into his warmth as I arrange the blankets carefully back over us. He grunts and wiggles and wraps his arms around me tight, pulling me in close to his belly as he rolls over and almost squishes me.

"EEEeeee!" I squeal with delight. His warm tummy with his hairy arms and smelly morning breath on my head, the best present I will get all day.

"What's this little birthday girl doing up this early?" he asks sleepily. He is teasing, I can tell.

"It's my birthday, and it's Thanksgiving.. I couldn't sleep!" I explain. I'm not worried he is mad, which is almost as good as the tickles that come next.

We tickle and snuggle until The Mother gets upset. "Uh, you two! I have a lot of work to do today. Would have been nice to get some sleep," she complains as she sits up on the side of the bed.

They have a waterbed so it wobbles and wiggles her head as she turns to look at us laughing and smiling and gives a little smile. She loves my daddy too, and she likes it when he smiles. It's the one thing I can do better than her.

"Come on then, birthday girl, let's go put that Sara Lee coffee cake in the oven," she says as she bends over and stands up to put on her house coat.

"Are you going to have coffee cake with us, Daddy?" I ask with a sideways glance. Daddy doesn't usually eat breakfast. He likes black coffee. Yuck.

"I might have a piece, if you save any for me, you little piggy girl," he teases as he tickles my tummy.

"I won't eat it all, Dad," I joke as I roll off the bed and my daddy sits up to put on his glasses.

* * *

I have a big family. There is The Grandfather and The Grandmother, Aunt Robin and Uncle Brad and cousin Rick, Aunt Ivy and new Uncle Anton. Plus The Mother and my daddy and me. That's a lot of people so family dinner is always a busy day, but holidays are even busier. All the mommas run around the kitchen and yell at each other, cooking and

stirring. The Grandmother sits in the chair and tells the Aunties and The Mother what to do, sometimes tasting or poking at the dishes to give directions.

It smells wonderful in The Grandmother's kitchen, like potatoes and bread and gravy, but I do my best to stay out of sight. No momma is ever in a good mood in a family dinner kitchen. If you are close by, you get asked to help and then yelled at for doing it wrong and ruining everything. If you don't help, you get yelled at for being lazy and ungrateful.

So I find the best thing to do is to play upstairs away from the grownups. Cousin Rick brought his Star Wars Legos from California so we have some toys to play with. IF he shares. I never have toys to share so I can only play with what he says. We'll see what kind of mood he is in today.

* * *

After our big meal, the boys all watch football on the TV in the living room while the mommas clean and put away food. I am about to make a sneaky exit to the stairs when The Grandfather grabs my arm and guides me into the hallway bathroom.

My breath rushes out, and I can't breathe. I squeeze into the tiny powder room with The Grandfather, looking hard at the floor to avoid any unnecessary contact. The tea towel and the icing flash in my brain as I look down at my blue dress and try to get my breath. I had almost forgotten who bought this dress and why.

"After the game, your mother and I are going to take you to the Church for Inspection. If your dad asks, you need to make sure you tell him you want to go—is that clear?" he says softly. "Or if you don't want

to protect him anymore, you can just scream right now," he says as he slips his hand down under my white ruffles and into my panties.

I almost can't stop the panic from bursting out of my mouth. I can hear my daddy clapping and cheering for the game in the living room. I know he would come; he would take me away.

But they would find me and cut him up. The Mother knows everything. She would find out.

I stand really still, trying to focus just on the white button of his shirt as he wiggles and gives a little pinch as he pulls his fingers out.

"Good girl. To be continued this afternoon," he says with an ugly smile.

I can't leave the bathroom for a long time. I can't seem to get the pee to come out.

CHAPTER TWENTY-THREE

A few hours later, the Mother and I follow The Grandfather into the back entrance of the New Haven LDS church. The Grandfather is a member of the High Council, an important man, so he has a set of keys. I go to another ward by our house, not as fancy as this one. It is in a pretty neighborhood with lots of old trees, but The Grandfather likes to be with his ward.

We walk down the orangy-brown hallway where the Bishop's office is. I usually go down the other hall with the Primary classrooms so this area is new to me. I know the building is a big square. The other side is the gym and the chapel, so maybe we are going there?

The Grandfather stops abruptly, and The Mother pulls my arm back to keep me from bumping into him. He turns in the middle of the hall to put a key in a small silver keyhole above my head. It clicks, and he pushes the wall, opening a panel door in the wall, like The Secret Garden opening like magic with the key.

A heavy door that looks like the wall opens, and inside is dark until The Grandfather snaps on the lights on an all-white room. There are white walls with white curtains, white carpet, and a little white bed high on a platform in the middle. Not a bed so much as a couch without the sides and back. Slick and shiny leather with metal bars on the bottom sticking out like maybe a seat is missing.

The room is cold. I don't want to go inside. I might get something dirty.

* * *

The Grandfather takes off his coat and hangs it on the wall. The Mother closes the door and takes a seat in a chair in the corner. She doesn't take off her coat; she is always cold.

The Grandfather stoops down to undo the buttons of my coat, removing my hat and gloves as well. He lets them drop to the floor, so I automatically bend to pick them up, but he catches my hand. I look up at his hard blue eyes and puffy wrinkly face, and he commands, "Stand up."

I'm scared. I don't know what I am doing wrong. I didn't tell—why do I feel like I am about to be punished?

He removes my panties but leaves on my dress and picks me up under the arms like a wet dog. He carries me over to the platform and lays me down on the little bed. He goes to the end by my feet and pulls them both to slide me down so my butt is on the edge. He places my feet by my butt, opening my legs, and tears start to leak down my cheeks as I stare at the ceiling.

I can't help it. I am so afraid, and I don't know what is going to happen. I can hear The Mother breathing real fast in the chair behind my head. She doesn't give me any hope that she will help me out, but I give her a quick look anyway. She is smiling. The scary one, that always feels like it's more bad than good.

I close my eyes and try to drift away in my mind. Picture paintings and puzzles and fairytale

stories, anything to survive the poking in my butthole, the burning of my privates with little matches, the giggles when I scream and then don't say another word.

* * *

"We'll need to do this often," I hear The Grandfather tell The Mother through a sweaty exhausted haze a long time later. "She needs to be prepared. With her intellect and grooming, she could end up being a candidate," he says as he finishes wiping off his hands.

I don't know how long I have been here; it feels like a long time. My brain is all fuzzy. The fire and pain are too loud.

I don't open my eyes even when I start to wake up. I am not sure how I get in the car; I must have fallen asleep. The Mother is angry.

"Little Ms. Perfect. Had to stay still and quiet on your first time. Of fucking course." She is talking at me, but I don't open my eyes yet. "Well, there are only so many times I will go over and help him with that sort of thing so he better be grateful."

I just pretend to sleep all the way home. I don't really know what to say anyway.

CHAPTER TWENTY-FOUR

I admit I had hoped that maybe my daddy would see the pain and know what had happened. That it wouldn't be my fault—it would just be too much that he would see.

But when we finally get home, my body is screaming with ouchies and yuckys and burns. The Mother tells my daddy to get me out of the car. I tired myself out playing with the other kids at church. I let her tell the lies and wait eagerly for my daddy's arms.

He comes to pick me up gently and carries me into my bed. My daddy lays me down softly with a kiss on the forehead.

"Let her just sleep. She's exhausted," I hear my daddy say to The Mother who has just walked into the bathroom. I hear the squeak of the water tap and the rush of bathwater.

"She's filthy, been running around all day. I'll give her a nice warm bubble bath and then put her to bed. She'll be fine," The Mother replies.

My daddy lets out a sigh, and I open my eyes to see him shaking his head as he walks away.

* * *

I drag myself off the bed and strip down naked, walking to the bathroom. I like bubble baths. I am tired, but it does sound nice.

I step around The Mother into the soapy warm water of the tub. It's only up to my ankles so I squat down into the growing bubbles to get warm.

"Eyeeeeee!" I scream as I shoot straight up, almost slipping, clutching my privates.

"What's the matter?" The Mother stares at me.

"I sat in the bubbles, and my privates sting where they touch because of the burns." I gulp as fresh tears stream down my face. A burn just like the matches over and over with each tiny bubble. How will I sit in the water? Will the water hurt too?

"Oh, you've always had sensitive skin. Quit being such a baby and sit down. It'll hurt less if you go fast," she tells me with her hands on her hips and her hard blue eyes.

I stand holding my crotch, turning around and around, staring at the water for a place to sit down that won't hurt too much. I can tell she is getting angry, can feel her eyes burning my skin.

So I take a deep breath and sit down. It is a shooting of fire from my crotch out to the ends of my hair. I can only see black. I stop breathing. But I sit.

"There now, isn't that nice." The Mother smiles her Cheshire smile and folds a washcloth to give me a good scrub.

CHAPTER TWENTY-FIVE

The next day, I wake up later than usual. The sun is already peeking through my window. My body is sweaty and shivering at the same time. I don't remember falling asleep, just the pain going on and on. It's still there; I don't want to move. But I have to pee.

I can barely push my legs over the side of the bed without collapsing from pain. How am I going to hide this? It hurts to sit; it hurts to lie down. My tummy feels like it's going to make me throw up. I can be a little quiet if I say I have a tummy ache.

Slowly, carefully, I stand up a little and waddle into the bathroom. I cry as much as I pee. It feels like the matches burning over and over again. I pat, pat, pat at the fiery-red skin. I look under the counter and find the cream for sunburns and put it softly on my privates. The cream is cold and feels nice. Better not let The Mother catch me touching myself—she says it's what dirty girls do.

The Mother will be happy if I wear a dress over to The Grandparents'. Maybe I can find some panties that aren't too tight. I waddle over to my dresser and choose a dress. Of course The Mother will make me wear tights, but I can pull them down low if I walk careful.

I don't know how I am I going to smile all day while I am around the adults. I wipe sweat and tears off my face and lie face down on the bed to save myself the trouble of wiping more away as they leak into my pillow.

* * *

I try to be extra invisible at The Grandparents' house. I give all the important hugs and kisses hello. Say extra thank-yous for the birthday presents that I don't remember opening.

I don't really remember any of my birthday party after we came home from The Church. I know I had a cake with pink icing, a party hat, and everyone sang. I smiled like I was supposed to, but my brain was all fuzzy. Everything was too bright and happy when my privates hurt so bad I had to try real hard to breathe.

I had to push the chocolate cake down my throat so The Mother wouldn't think that it wasn't good enough. Her sisters always think they are so much better at cooking than her. She needs a lot of words from me to help her feel better.

The cake is still in my tummy. It hurts too much to let the poop out. I am squeezing it in, which makes my tummy hurt more. I feel full and hungry at the same time.

But I don't want to eat or drink anything. Even if I am hungry, the smell of food is making me stick. I don't want to do anything but put on more sunburn cream and cry. Instead, I find a small corner of the room behind the big chairs and look at my new unicorn book. A place where no one is crying or burning.

"Hey, hunny bunny," says a sweet high voice as Aunt Ivy's face peeks around the chair down at me in my corner, "wanna go get a treat?!"

She smiles her big warm smile, always sunny fun times with Aunt Ivy. I try and give her a smile too, but it comes out a little bit wiggly. I take a big gulp to steady my voice as I think of something to say.

"Oh, yeah, that would be nice, but what about Rick? He should be here soon, and he will be upset if he misses the treat," I say without

crying. I really want to go for a treat, anything to get out of this house, but I don't know if I can sit through another car ride. I already have to sit through the ride home.

"Nah. It'll be a girls-only kind of treat. Sound good." She moves away from the chair to go get our coats from the hall closet. Well… I guess a treat is worth the struggle.

I sigh and stand slowly, carefully tucking my unicorn book under my arm. Once I feel like I can move a little, I walk like a tippy-toe cat to the door before anyone sees me moving weird. I am sweating as she bends to bundle me up with a hat.

"Are you OK, honey? You're looking kind of green," Aunt Ivy asks with concern. She puts the back of her hand on my forehead. "Doesn't feel like you are running a fever."

"I just have a bit of a tummy ache," I whisper softly, so no one else hears in the kitchen.

"OK, we can just grab a treat, and then I can take you home. You can rest with your dad. He should be there. Sound like a plan?" she says with a conspirator's smile and takes my hand to walk me out to the car.

"What's your favorite drink?" she asks once we back out of the driveway.

"Strawberry pop," I reply automatically. "Mom says I am allergic so I can't have it."

I wiggle around until I find a way to sit on my hands so that it doesn't hurt so much sitting in the car seat. Now I can focus on getting a treat and realize my mistake. "Sometimes she lets me have a little because it's my favorite."

"I've never heard of anyone being allergic to pop before. She doesn't know what she is talking about. She always thinks she knows about medical stuff because she was in nursing school for a little bit," Aunt Ivy says as she rolls her eyes. "Good grief, that girl always has to have something wrong."

I don't say anything else. It's nice to stare out the window and listen to the radio.

Aunt Ivy pulls into the drive-thru and orders us two strawberry pops and fries. We sing songs real loud and eat in the car!

She drops me off a little bit later, watching me walk slowly up my front steps to the door.

"Now don't get sick and get me in trouble, OK," she yells with a smile in her voice, "Love you, sweet girl," and she drives away. I smile and wave as she drives away

Before I go in, I walk around the end of the front porch and hide the drink cup in the bushes with a final slurp. I'll need to remember to throw it away later, but right now, I am too tired. My whole body throbs, and my breathing is raspy.

I open the door and limp inside, my daddy asleep in his chair snoring loudly. I want to give him a kiss, but I can't make myself go that far. I cat-walk down the hallway and drop on my bed.

Wiggle on my back to get off my stupid tights. Take off my stupid dress. Crawl under my blanket and go to the unicorn picture in my brain.

* * *

The next day is Saturday. It's appropriate to spend the day in my room. Being still and reading books, playing with my stickers, coloring. I am

lying on the floor on my tummy (the best position so the floor doesn't touch my ouchies) and I hear The Mother coming down the hallway. Her heavy, lumbering footfalls are much slower than my daddy's.

"Do you want to tell me what this is?" she asks as she holds up the strawberry pop cup.

Oops. I stare in horror at the pop cup I hid in the bushes. I was going to get it this morning, but I forgot. I stay silent. It doesn't matter what I say; she is already mad.

"Who got you strawberry pop?" She is getting louder, angry.

I just stare as I slowly sit up. If she is gonna jerk me up by my arm, I need to be up so it doesn't pop out of joint.

"Your aunt?" she spits. "She doesn't care if you are allergic. She doesn't have kids. She doesn't understand how to take care of you."

She reaches down and grabs my arm, but I am already getting up so her nails don't dig in too much. She marches me down the hall into the kitchen and pushes me down to sit in a chair at the table.

The Mother walks over to the cabinet and gets a cup, slams it down on the counter. Trudges to the fridge and gets a tall red pop bottle in the back with no label. It bubbles a little on the top, making floating white clouds. She pours the pop in the cup, filling it almost to the brim. Then she slams the pop bottle down and brings the cup over to the table.

She sets the cup down carefully in front of me, not spilling a single drop. I can see the little bubbles inside climbing up the walls of the glass. There are still white little clouds on top, but they look kind of sticky.

"Well, drink up. You like strawberry pop so much—don't care if you get sick and I have to take care of you—so just drink it up."

She stands over me with her hands on her hips, breathing fire. I stare into the red drink, afraid.

"But I didn't get sick," I whisper. I can't help it; I am confused. I didn't get sick so I don't understand why she is upset.

"Then why are you not drinking this one? If you love strawberry pop so much and you are so sure it doesn't make you sick, then why not just drink it?" she asks with the sly mean sideways smile, words thrown like knives.

I sigh, take a drink. It's sticky and sweet, thicker than the crisp, bubbly soda I had from the hamburger restaurant.

"Drink it all. You deserve extra-special treats, don't you, birthday girl," she says as she sits in the chair next to mine, fire turning to sweet syrupy words.

I want to believe that she is being nice. That she feels bad because she knows my privates are hurting. Maybe she doesn't know it will make me pee and that it hurts. Maybe she really does think I can drink it now that I am five. Maybe this drink is the same and won't make me throw up.

I take another drink, and she tips the bottom of the cup with her finger, forcing me to drink more. I gulp and gulp until it's just a red gritty goo at the bottom.

She takes the cup as I gasp for breath, washing it in the sink and putting it away. I sit listening to the red liquid gurgling in my tummy, already fizzing acid in the back of my throat. I am gonna be sick.

I look up at her standing by the sink, shocked as my tummy gurgles so loud she can hear it. "Maybe you are allergic after all," she says with a lift of her eyebrows and a sigh.

I run to the toilet and barely make it over the bowl before I barf up red splatter. I cough and heave; I can't get it out fast enough. The floor is sticky from the spit and sweat dripping off my face when I get a short rest. Then I puke some more, red and pink and then yellowy green.

When my tummy is done heaving, I am a puddle on the floor. I hurt in so many places I can't move anymore. I have vomit on my front and in my hair, spit hanging out of my mouth, and I don't care. I just want to stop feeling.

At some point my daddy comes home. I can hear The Mother telling him Aunt Ivy got me a strawberry soda when she told her I was allergic, and this is what happens. She throws her arms up and tells him what an awful day it's been, how her sisters always act like she is stupid and don't treat her like she is a good mother. My daddy pats her back and tells her it isn't true as he heads down the hallway to see me.

I can't even manage to lift my head to look up at him. I don't have anything left in me.

"Oh, punkin, you feeling rotten? I'm so sorry, hunny," he coos as he sticks his arms under me and lifts me off the floor. He carries me into my bed and lays me down softly, covering me up with my blanket. He takes a corner of the sheet and wipes my mouth and hair where there is still a little sick.

"Oh, just let her be." The Mother orders, "I'll go get her some ginger ale. It should calm her stomach down."

My daddy leans down to give me a kiss on the forehead and tells me to get some rest. I am ready to fall asleep and not feel anything in the blackness.

AGE 45 WAKE UP

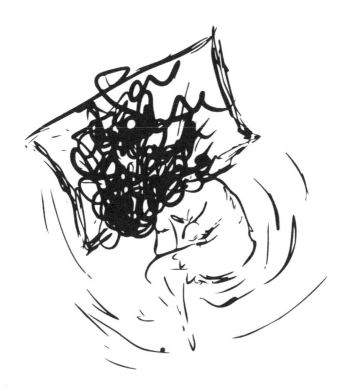

CHAPTER TWENTY-SIX

"Well, she's a fucking bitch," The Nanny proclaims as the flood of memories ebbs again and I stop to sob.

I almost muster a smirk, but it doesn't quite make it to my face. I appreciate the support. But I feel the most pressing need to say it. The words coming out of my mouth are so unbelievable. Inconceivable. They cannot possibly be true. Why am I making up such things? I look at her tear-streaked face and ask in the tiniest, five-year-old voice, "Do you believe me?" It's an honest question, and I tremble as I wait for her to recover her voice.

"Of course I do!" she exclaims with a few other choice words tacked on that do manage to make me crack a small grin. "That woman is a fucking bitch. She led you like the lamb to the slaughter. How could anyone do that to their own child?!" Tears stream down her face, and I stare in wonder. Nanny never cries. It scares me almost more than the stories I am telling.

We sit for a time, just crying quietly and listening to the night sounds of the backyard.

"I think it's time for me to wake up Dave," I say tonelessly. I hate to wake him; he has work in the morning. Someone in this family has to keep a job. Logically, I know that's not the most important thing, but it also kind of is.

"OK, honey," she replies sadly with a soft squeeze of my hand before releasing me. I can see the exhaustion sitting in the deep lines around her eyes, the worry pulled tight across her mouth. She pats my hands for good measure and says, "I love you," as I rise with aching knees.

Sitting in the night air, vomiting traumatic memories, and fearing for my life is not great for my joints. I gingerly take a few steps toward the patio door and gently ease it open.

This door opens directly to our bedroom, with the path leading around the king-size bed and past the large armoire into the primary bathroom. I take a quick moment to relieve my aching bladder and splash some water on my face. I look into the mirror in the dark. I look… destroyed. I hardly recognize the girl staring back at me. The night has not been kind to my complexion. My eyes burn bright with trauma and fear. I have never told these stories to anyone. Never spoken of them in 40 years. It's wild to hear them out loud for the first time.

I quietly reenter the bedroom and sit next to Dave on the bed. I gently touch his shoulder, and his eyes spring open.

"What's wrong?" he asks, looking around. He sits up on one elbow and reaches for his glasses. Now that he can see me better, I watch as the concern blooms across his face like a hideous flower and feel a small pang for the moment. The last moment he will ever see me this way.

Bittersweet but inevitable, I suppose.

"Come," I say softly, "I need to tell you some things."

* * *

"So your grandfather hurt you and your mom knew about it?" Dave asks lamely, shock and

fatigue stealing the color from his voice. He blinks and sits unnaturally still, unsure of how to react or what to do after hearing these stories for the first time. Disbelief that so much was happening under the surface.

"Yes," I say timidly.

178

Nanny gives a sigh and pats my hand. "Darlin', since Dave is here, I am going to go to bed. I am exhausted. That OK?" She gets up from her chair with a squeak and leans over to hug me. I squeeze her tight, laying my ear on her shoulder.

"Thank you, Nanny," I whisper as fresh tears leak into her nightshirt.

"I love you, you hear me?" She barks it like an order. "And those people are assholes."

I give her a weak smile as I sit down, watching her go back into the warm glow of the kitchen. The screen door snaps shut behind her.

I turn my gaze back to Dave. He is sitting oddly straight, fidgeting with his beard, looking pensively around as he tries to absorb the news.

"I have been hiding it from everyone for years. I am so sorry I lied to you." I look at him through the waves of guilt swimming in my eyes, trembling with the stress of searching for any clue about how he will respond.

I lied. I lied a lot.

The thought comes crashing in, a powerful gust of fear stirring the abating storm anew. I lied about so many things—how will he ever forgive me? I lied about my virginity. I lied about my family's happy perfection. I lied about why I did so many things, trying to protect him, but lies just the same.

I put our son in danger.

It is the aftershock of the earthquake breaking the foundation of my life even deeper, ripping my insides further still. I pretended everything was OK. I thought I could manage to keep them all safe. I feel pretty certain that they never hurt him. He is a boy, and boys are different. But I put him in danger. I put us all in danger time and time again.

Destiny. Oh god, Destiny.

Her face appears in front of my mind, her big brown eyes searching mine for understanding. She tried to ask me, tried to talk to me about it once, and I stared at her blankly. I pretended that I didn't know, that it wasn't me. Or that she shouldn't talk about those things because they are not safe.

The guilt and shame are buckets of scalding self-loathing being poured into my heart over and over again. I tried so hard to do the right thing, to take care of my family and protect them. I did the best I could. It wasn't enough.

Tears slip down his cheek, falling into the rivets still sunk in his skin from his pillow. He wipes his face with his hands and sits forward a bit, grabs my hands.

"Honey, I am so sorry. I am so sorry they did that to you." His blue eyes swim in the moonlight, pain and shock dancing across his features as he tries to grip on to this terrible truth.

HIs wife has been leading a double life, has been lying for years, put his son and himself in danger. I understand there are consequences for my actions. I took the risk knowing full well what the consequences would be when this moment came. It's a risk I decided to take twenty years ago when this sweet man told me he would wait for me until I was ready to get married.

Marriage is a weird concept that I never really understood or thought about seriously. The people in my life who were married, preaching monogamy and honesty as requirements, were contradicting themselves from the moment they tried to teach me their importance.

The Grandfather was praised by our community for being a loving and devoted husband, but those same people would indulge in the pleasure of others hours after their sermons. The Mother was always demanding the truth, but her truth changes with the wind.

I had no intention of being married; it seemed like a big hassle for nothing. I was content to live my life by my own rules, enjoying companionship when it came along until it ended or I decided to go my own way. I didn't want anyone owning me with a piece of paper, telling me what I could and couldn't do. Once I got free, I was never going to be under the control of a man again.

But Dave proposed and assured me he would wait until I was ready. It took me two years to set up the stories and justifications I would need, weeks of careful planning, of subverting The Grandfather and The Mother's panic at losing me. To them, I was a celestial bride who couldn't be married to any other man because I was already a heavenly bride.

In the end, I outsmarted them all. Getting married in a secret ceremony at the courthouse the day before my wedding. Another secret in my arsenal, but this time I had an accomplice. I knew Dave was special when he didn't mind at all, just easily going along with a wild and skittish bride's weird plans. He just accepted my stories and married me at the courthouse, repeating the charade the next day with the same smile.

And now he knows why.

"I lied to you. I lied to you a lot," I say boldly, steeling myself for my punishment. "You didn't sign up for this. I know this is a lot of awful stuff. I put us all at risk, but I promise I did it only to protect you." I am pleading with him now, begging him with my eyes to look past the betrayal into the motives.

"I never wanted to hurt you. I love you—I have always loved you. I did it to protect you." The power of words too often unspoken have a brittle bite. The three big words are not ones I use very often—repeated into meaninglessness over years of misuse by my family. Like so many other terms regular people learn so early in life, those never really had much meaning for me. The Grandfather and Mother spent decades contradicting themselves with "I Love You" being the reason for hurting me.

"I love you too. I'm not mad. I am just stunned," he says slowly, always a man of few words.

"Do you think we can go rest now? I am tired, and I'll need to get up early to call in for work tomorrow. I think I need to stay home."

"Oh yeah, right, good idea," I say quickly, anything to talk about something else. "I just need to check my phone for a message from RC. I told her it was my grandpa, and she said, 'I suspected'… so I need to let her know I am OK. I think I need to have an emergency session with her tomorrow," I finish sleepily. Like flipping a switch, my mind focuses sharply on being polite and fulfilling my responsibilities to take care of myself.

"Oh. She knew?" he asks, surprised.

"No, she suspected. I guess she started figuring out something was wrong, but I know she didn't see this coming. No one could ever know this much—it's too much for even me," I say woodenly, the muffled cotton of exhaustion beginning to envelop my head.

I swipe up my home screen to check my messages as Dave ducks through the bedroom door.

RC → Remember that none of this changes who you are. But the truth takes away his power over you and puts the power with you.

The little grey bubble stares up at me, immediately after the "I suspected" reply, but I can't quite understand the words. They get all jumbled up in my brain when I try to read them.

Me → Can you squeeze me in anywhere in your schedule? I think I need to tell you some things.

RC → I can do a quick virtual at 8 a.m. tomorrow. I'll send you a link. Try to rest. Keep breathing.

CHAPTER TWENTY-SEVEN

Rest is restless. Moments filled with dreams or memories, pressing fear of the past and the future. I sit cradling my phone at 7:30 a.m. watching the sunrise over the trees. Patience has never been my easiest virtue, but now I know it's one I have mastered.

I click the little blue button the moment it turns from red, connecting the physician's video chat through the little blinking dots. RC's face pops up after a few seconds, still midmorning routine.

"Hey, what happened?" she says without preamble. This is serious, and she knows we have a lot to cover. She sits more comfortably at her table, using her laptop instead of her phone so her hands are free to clasp under her chin. Undivided attention. Concern etched in her face.

I give her the rundown of the events that led to the most heartbreaking moment of my life. A jumbled telling of flashes of The Grandfather's face. The Mother's nails digging into my skin.

The screaming girl behind the door bursting forth wearing a blue dress and gnashing her teeth. Of the woods and inspections. Strawberry pop and sensitive skin.

The stories are flashes, a few moments, then gone. No details or specific events, just accusations and denials. A story told in flashbacks, like ghosts in *The Sixth Sense*, lurking and flickering until I have enough strength to really sit with each one and listen.

"So your grandmother and mother knew," she prods. Tears drip off her lashes, and she wipes them with a tissue carelessly. It's an odd first question, which is why I adore her so much as a professional. Sometimes it's easier to engage my logical brain than my emotional feelings.

I stare at her blankly; I had never thought about it that way. Confusion lines my face more as she clarifies, "You said your mom held you down? And your grandmother watched some of it?"

Flashes of eyes looking at me hard, willing me to understand their intensity. *This will not be easy, but you must survive it,* I hear The Grandmother's voice say in my mind.

"Yes. They knew." I feel guilty for admitting it. Like I am letting them down. And then I'm lost to a new memory of The Grandmother's face.

AGE 5 THE OTHER GRANDMA

CHAPTER TWENTY-EIGHT

My daddy is from Alabama. It is a long way from Oklahoma, where we live. Sometimes, my daddy goes to Alabama for the weekend, and The Mother doesn't like to go. She doesn't like the long drive just to be at his mother's house for a day. These are my favorite times, when it's just my daddy and me driving to the Other Grandma's house.

My other grandma, Grandma G, is so different from The Grandmother. Her house is simple; I can touch and look at anything I want. She has little figurines on shelves instead of behind glass, comfy soft pillows instead of hard velvet. She buys my favorite things, green grapes and Apple Jacks cereal, and we eat them real early in the morning while we watch cartoons together quietly so Daddy can sleep. It's heaven.

So I am excited when my daddy wakes me up early to tell me he has to go to Alabama. "Can I come too?" I ask sleepily as I sit up in bed and wipe the eye bugs away.

"No, honey, not this time. Something has happened," he says in a cracking voice, his eyes watery and blue. "Grandma G had a stroke and has died."

I blink up at him, not sure what to say.

"I need to go down there and take care of the arrangements. We will be gone for a few days," he says softly as he sniffles and wiggles. I am not quite sure what he means. I have never seen my daddy sad before. It's scary. I don't know what to do or to say to make it better.

"Can I come too? Maybe I can help Grandma G feel better," I say hopefully. But in my tummy I feel like something is not quite right.

"No, baby, Grandma G has passed. She has gone up to heaven. We are going down to bury her," he says with a tear in his eye, almost ready to run down his face. Now I am getting more scared. My daddy never cries. My Grandma G is gone to heaven. She is one of my favorite people, and she left me. My eyes start stinging too, but I am a big girl so I won't cry.

He continues, "Your mother and grandmother seem to think you are too young to go since it's in another state. They say it's inappropriate. Anyway, we will be gone a few days, and you don't want to miss too much school, right?"

Now I am really scared. If I have to stay by myself, I might do something wrong and burn down the house. Or let in a stranger.

"I can help, Daddy! Please let me go. I want to see Grandma G." I trail off as the tears escape my eyes and fall even though I am trying real hard to keep them in.

"It's OK, honey. It's better if you stay anyways. I want you to remember your grandma as she was when she was alive," he replies as he lets me crawl into his lap and get tears all over his white shirt.

"We will be gone a few days so you are going to stay at your grandparents' house. Won't that be fun?" He says it like it's a treat, but we both know it's not. That house is stuffy and old and boring, and he doesn't know about the bathroom checks and the inspections. I start to shake and cry more into his shirt as he holds me tight and lets the tears cry themselves out.

* * *

"Don't look so down, cutie pie. It's only for a few days," says my daddy as he gives me one last hug goodbye.

190

I stand on the stairs in The Grandparents' house, watching my toes make dents in the beige carpet. I can feel The Grandmother standing behind me, keeping her icy stare on The Mother, to make sure she keeps her composure.

The Grandfather gives my daddy a handshake. "Sorry for your loss. At least she is with our heavenly father now," he says importantly. Like he talks to the other men at church.

My daddy shakes his hand but doesn't say anything. I think he's trying to hold it in still. No one wants to cry in front of The Grandparents.

"We will be back in a few days," The Mother says to The Grandmother over my head. "I'll call you when we get there."

"And you be a good girl while we are gone, you understand me?" The Mother says to me with an evil glare. "Don't cause any trouble for your grandmother."

I can't smile. It's hard enough just to keep the tears in my eyes, so I look up and nod at her glare so she can see that I understand. Being good means doing what you are told. Obey.

CHAPTER TWENTY-NINE

"I don't understand what all the fuss is about," says The Grandmother coldly from behind my tight back. "I am the only grandmother that matters," she finishes as we listen to the car pull out of the driveway outside.

My chin slowly turns to look up at her standing on the stairs above me, her eyes staring hard at mine as they meet. I feel a heavy black goo leak into my heart, and my back gets tight as my body freezes. The look in her eyes says I am doing something wrong, but I don't know what I did.

"Come," she commands as she turns and heads up the stairs. I follow like a good girl.

As I climb to the second floor, I look at the pictures proudly displayed on the walls of the staircase. A baby picture of me. Aunt Ivy and Uncle Anton smiling at their wedding in California. Aunt Robin and Uncle Brad with baby cousin Rick in his blue sailor jumper. Smiling, smiling, smiling.

At the top of the stairs, I follow The Grandmother past her sewing room down the hall toward her bedroom. I am not allowed to go in here without The Grandparents' permission so I am curious to see.

The Grandmother stops halfway down the hall, in front of her closet door. I am not allowed in there. She has very expensive things in there, so I usually forget it's there. She delicately turns the knob and opens the door like she is opening the door to Narnia.

"In," she says simply, sweeping her hand to give me a little push on my back as I walk slowly to obey. I walk straight into the center of the small room and try not to touch anything. Maybe she is going to show me something new, but I need to be careful not to touch.

She holds out her hand. "Give me your dress," she says. I slip it over my head and hand over the blue dress. I have a lot of blue dresses now; they are The Grandfather's favorite. I wonder if he will be angry The Grandmother took it.

"I think you need some time to think about what really matters in this life," she says, a little loudly. "Not everyone is so lucky to have people looking out for them the way you do. You need to think about what family really means to you."

I stand there in my underpants, socks, and shoes, hugging myself around my boobies to keep from shivering. It's not very cold up here, but I am scared of having so much skin on display.

She squats down in front of me, bringing us eye to eye—every gray hair in perfectly in place, skin precisely smooth, in-the-lines lipstick, and hard blue eyes.

"This will be hard, but you will get through it, you understand me?" she says softly, staring into my eyes, telling the words to the back of my brain. "I will make sure of it."

Then she stands up and closes the door, her denim skirt and soft tennis shoes swishing as she walks away and leaves me in the dark.

* * *

The first few hours, I am scared to move. I stand like a dummy and try not to touch anything. But then I sit down (crisscross applesauce is my favorite), but I have to pull my knees up to keep warm.

I listen to the creaks and groans of the old house around me. I watch the sunshine sliver from under the door creep across the floor and change from yellow to orange. I play with the dust motes in the sunshine, pretending they are magical fairies come to keep me company.

When the sun disappears and I can hear The Grandparents getting ready for bed, I listen hard to hear if they will come get me. But it feels like they forgot I am here. No knock on the door.

I jump when The Grandmother opens the door and the light blinds my eyes.

"Come use the bathroom and brush your teeth," she says. I scramble to get up. My legs are like wooden sticks from sitting tight so long.

I go to the potty, wash my hands, and brush my teeth in the bubble-blue tile bathroom. The Grandmother's face creams and lotions are lined up like a fashion show. All the beautiful potions smell lovely, but I don't dare touch them.

The Grandmother knocks hard on the door, and I open it at once. My break is over, I guess.

On the way back to the closet, my tummy makes an awful growling noise. I clutch my tummy and look up with big puppy eyes. I am really hungry, but I am too afraid to ask for food.

"Hmmmm…" she says with a grin. "Maybe next time you will be grateful for the food you have and not sad for missing green grapes and sugar cereal."

I lower my head and slump back into the closet without a word.

CHAPTER THIRTY

Once the lights go out and it's quiet for a long time, I decide it's time for a blanket. I stand up and look around at what's available, but it's so black I can't see anything. The moonlight coming from under the door is no help at all, and I have to be super careful not to make any noise.

So I use my other senses, like we learned in school—touching, smelling, listening (don't think taste will help this time). It's a game, like being blindfolded, and having to figure out what things are. The crisp folds of The Grandfather's suits, his stink mixed with starch and aftershave. The light soft waves of The Grandmother's skirts smelling of face cream and rose-scented lotion. The warm scent of leather and the gentle rustle of taffeta. It sparks a soft light in me, a glow-in-the-dark of the black goo, the love of the clothing and fabrics in the dark.

I decide to wear a fuzzy soft sweater that is big enough to go over my knees. I can use some shoes with a bag on it for a pillow, easy to put back in a hurry. I lie down to sleep.

* * *

The Grandfather takes a walk at 5:30 every morning. He keeps his walking shoes and jacket in the chair by the window so he doesn't have to open the closet. I hear him use the bathroom, brush his teeth, and change his clothes, walking quietly down the hall past me on his way out. I don't move a muscle. Maybe he forgot I am here.

The hallway door creaks open just a little. It's too late to put back the sweater. I lie there huddled inside the cashmere with my eyes squeezed shut pretending to sleep. It's all I can think to do.

He chuckles softly and bends down in a squat. He reaches out his hand to my leg and slides his hand up the inside of my thigh. The sweater climbs up to my panties, and I start to shiver, but I don't move. He slides his fingers up and down my private parts over my panties. I feel like an icicle, cold and hard, preparing for pain.

But he surprises me with a soft pat on the leg and stands to ease the door shut. No pinches, no hitting. I breathe a sigh of relief and nestle back into the makeshift pillow to maybe rest a little more, but The Grandmother flings open the door just after I hear the front door close.

She kicks me hard in the hip with her slipper. "Get up. I will make you an egg and toast, but you have to eat it before The Grandfather gets back," she says as she turns to walk briskly downstairs.

It takes me a minute to stand up, as my body feels like a stick puppet. But I don't know if she wants me to follow her or if she will bring it here. I think I better not take a chance, so I just stand.

Soon enough, she comes up the stairs with a silver tray. An egg, a piece of toast cut into two triangles, a glass of milk. She sets it down on the floor and says, "Eat."

I am so hungry it's hard to chew. I eat as fast as I can and even drink the milk, which I hate. It feels full and warm in my tummy, helping my body relax just a little.

The Grandmother picks up the napkin, harshly wipes my face, and then bends to take the tray. "Thank you," I say with a big ol' smile, to show her I really am happy with the food.

She doesn't even look at me as she kicks the door closed and heads off down the hall.

CHAPTER THIRTY-ONE

I count three sunny days and four moonlit nights. I use the sun under the door to keep track of the sun and the moon. The moonlight is my favorite. It's when it's time to play the blind game with the clothes. I can guess almost all of the different kinds of clothes and fabrics now.

I don't go to school. I worry because I think I missed a day, but I can't be sure. I can't keep track of the weekdays because I haven't mastered those yet. We are still working on time counting at school.

Every morning, The Grandfather does his inspection, and The Grandmother gives me a quick secret breakfast. Every night, I get to pee and brush my teeth. Then I am alone until the morning.

It isn't so bad, really. I can sing any song I like in my mind, remember stories I have read. I can make up new stories using all the different clothes and senses to create new characters and adventures.

Nighttime is hard because I get hungry. And sometimes I feel like I need to pee and have to hold it and that stings. And sometimes The Grandmother gives an extra kick if I look like I am having too good of a time. So I try to look extra sleepy when The Grandmother gets up after The Grandfather leaves for his walk.

On the fourth morning, I am sitting quietly waiting for my secret food tray when The Grandmother opens the door and says, "Get up and take off that sweater. You are taking a bath."

The bath feels like a warm hug. No bubbles at The Grandmother's— that's too indulgent—but I don't mind. The water softens my stiffness, and I melt like warm butter. The Grandmother scrubs every inch of my

body with a washcloth and soap, making sure I am clean, clean, clean. We even wash my long brown hair, dunking my head under the water to wash off the soap. She is quiet except for the commands of direction, and soon the tub is filled with soap bubbles and bits of hair floating on the top.

"I hope this has been a valuable lesson for you, that you have learned to appreciate this family," she chides as she wraps me in an old blue towel that's a hundred years old. "You are lucky this punishment wasn't worse with your disgusting display of tears over that woman." She pauses, sitting on the down toilet seat to look me in the eye real hard. "You have to be stronger than this. You have to be stronger than us all. No one else matters—do you understand?"

I stare into her hard steel eyes and nod. I understand. I am lucky. I am chosen. I must endure.

* * *

"Daddy!" I scream and run out the door the moment I see the car pull into the driveway.

"Hey, cutie! Did you miss me?" he says with a laugh as he swoops me up into his arms. "I sure missed you," he says as he squeezes me tight. I bury my nose in his neck and hang on like a monkey. His warm chest and smokey smell help my whole body to rest at last.

"What, you didn't miss your momma?" snaps The Mother as she gets out of the car.

"I'm glad you're home too." I manage a smile from under my daddy's chin. No one here is fooled about who my favorite is.

"Did you have fun here all weekend?" he asks as he walks into the house.

"More fun than you, I'll wager," says The Grandfather with a gleam in his eye at me, making sure I don't forget to keep secrets.

"Yes, lots of fun. But can we go home now?" I whine. I am so hungry and tired. "I really want to see my kitty!" I finish so no one can get mad. I do miss my cat; she is my best resting friend.

AGE 45 PIECES

CHAPTER THIRTY-TWO

"Wow. That's a lot. I am so sad this happened to you." RC sniffs and waters a bit, but her voice is steady and strong. She knows I will believe her, even if I don't want to.

"Really?" I say, confused. "It's hard to believe that things that happened to me are *that bad*. We used to joke as a family about how I loved to be in The Grandmother's closet and play with her clothes when I was little. Everyone laughed about how I was a budding fashionista just like The Grandmother. I have lived my entire life with every person I know repeating the same story, that it's not *that bad*—that I liked it." I blink, confused.

All of these stories are ones I remember from family retellings, just twisted into jokes with me as the stupid little girl who overreacts to small slights. I hated to wear dresses because I was a rotten tomboy. I bit a kid because I was such a wild little brat. I got lost in the woods because I was headstrong and went my own way. Stories my family retold over and over again, shaping the narrative we would all believe. Never a denial that it happened, just that it wasn't *that bad*.

When I started therapy seven years ago, I made a decision. If I was going to pay someone for their expertise, I needed to listen. When my therapist started challenging me, saying things I didn't want to believe or found unbelievable, I had to listen. It's the only way I would see a return on the investment.

So when I made the decision to believe RC over my family, I had to resort to a logic tree when RC said something I wanted to believe but couldn't. For example:

Do I trust RC? → yes

Is RC knowledgeable in this subject? → yes

Does RC have a vested interest in the outcome beyond patient care? → no

Am I paying her for her professional opinion? → yes

Is there any logical reason to not believe what she is telling me? → no

It's a struggle to keep my thoughts straight, to see the logic. I look up from the small tissue I have shredded during the session, wide-eyed and curious.

"Do you believe me?" It's a younger girl who stares at RC and waits for her answer, a wizened elder presence collecting all the logic it can find and focusing it on this one answer. The one answer I have waited my entire life to hear.

"Yes. I believe every word of it," she says calmly but sternly. "You have no reason to make this up. I don't think you could if you tried," she finishes bluntly with a small lift of a lopsided smile.

"This is some crazy stuff. This is some Tara Westover-like stuff," she says, trying to drive home how big this is to my little tiny brain by comparing it to the story of one of my favorite authors.

Tara Westover's *Educated* is one of my favorite books. Her incredible story was the first I ever saw that had even a glimmer of what I had experienced in the Mormon church. Seeing her horrific, honest account of the abuse she suffered in the name of Joseph Smith was jaw-dropping. The LDS church protects its beliefs and practices ruthlessly. I couldn't believe a woman had the courage to bring to light those practices with no physical evidence. She set the abuse bar when it came to our discussions

on the LDS's cult-like practices. Saying my story is as bad as Tara's is shocking.

I am speechless so I stay quiet. I feel so empty it's hard to find words. I can't quite believe her.

"OK, you need to take a break from this and just rest. I am going to block off a session for us tomorrow morning for two hours, and we will really talk through it, OK? Just go to Jack's show and be kind to yourself," she says with authority. A prescription of a band-aid for a massacre.

* * *

[12:15 p.m. same day]

ME → Just an update, the things pouring out are horrifying. It's a house of horrors.

ME → But I am breathing. My Apple Watch pings me when my heart rate is too high, and then I can slow myself down.

[2:26 p.m.]

ME → Don't reply. Just sending you a list of story pieces that have come up, to hold myself accountable. It's all coming up in bits and pieces. We can use these to puzzle out the full stories tomorrow.

The Blue

Dress Uncle Brad Pinches

Aunt Robin sang me to sleep

How could you say that

Dress shopping

Don't hurt my daddy

The Mother laughing

Black pepper

The Janitor isn't nice

Picnic The Woods

Birthday girl

Bubble bath

Strawberry pop

The Other grandma

Fashion feeds me

Bathroom checks

R → Yes my dear. Get some rest. Let it be a bit. Your body is reliving these memories as they come up. It's having a hard time keeping up with your brain, and it's important to be gentle with yourself and take some breaks along the way.

ME → Thanks for holding this. See ya tomorrow.

* * *

[7 a.m. the next morning]

ME → I am headed your way. I am not putting on makeup, feels like a waste of good product.

RC → I am very lowkey. That's fine.

ME → They keep coming. It's like a floodgate has been opened, and my brain is trying to remember everything all at once:

Sister

Soldier of God

The basketball

Tell the bishop

The White Room Poop

Baptism Ruined

Chapter Thirty-Two

The Queens and the lightning

The roses and the strawberries

RC → Let it all out. Get it out of you into a pile. Then we can sort through the pile and look at things as we need to. And at some point burn the motherfucker down. Once it's all out, the flood will slow down some.

ME → OK, headed your way.

CHAPTER THIRTY-THREE

We sit on her patio, and the horrors pour out into the morning sunshine. Her coffee cradled in her hands to keep them steady, my cup sitting on the table, forgotten. I heave and gag, choking on the toxic truths as they burn a new path through the carefully crafted stories of my life. I speak without analyzing or taking time to edit, words tripping and jumbling together to drip long-hidden sentences, confused and secret.

Silence has been a part of my life for so long; it's difficult to talk so much about such things. When anyone mentions sexual abuse, parental abuse, torturing children—people tend to quickly shut down the conversation and steer toward nicer things to talk about. I used to think it was because people didn't like to think about bad things happening to little children, but now I see it's because so many of us have suffered in silence. It's a secret language so many of us share, the warnings and connections that are beyond words and conveyed with a glance or a knowing nod.

I see the belief rise up RC's face. The honesty of these stories isn't in doubt. Tears instead of outrage about the blue dress. Pity instead of fear at my outburst in the dress store.

"Of course you would protest your abuse," she says to my dripping face as I try to collect myself for the millionth time. "I'm proud of you for fighting for yourself." She says it gently, with a small pat on the hand. I blink at her, confused; the words don't make any sense.

"Angry is a safe emotion. You have a right to be angry if someone hurts you." Now she is worried, the confusion on my face deepening at

her train of thought. Those words do not make sense, and yet they are totally logical.

I power on through the rest of my five-year-old birthday week—the worst week of my life. The dress shopping, the trip to the nature center, and the first inspection day rounding out those first awful memories to surface in the last 48 hours.

"You are the first person I have ever told any of these stories. I mean ever. I can't even believe the words that are coming out of my mouth." I slump, exhausted. I am horrified at the stories as they unfold.

RC is still sniffing and wiping her nose as she continues to keep strong eye contact with me. She won't break her silence until she is sure I am done talking. I suspect it's an important detail to her job, the listening through the pauses, but I am a child where long silences mean punishment.

"Do you believe me?" I ask timidly, staring steadfastly at the shaking hands in my lap, not daring to accidentally catch a flicker of doubt in her eyes.

"I absolutely believe you. Every word of it," she says quite sternly, grabbing my hands in her own. "These people are monsters. But you got out." She squeezes my hands and holds my gaze. "It's not happening anymore—you are just remembering." Another jumble of words in my brain I can't arrange in the right order.

I look up to see her staring at me with wonder. Her short cropped hair ruffling in the spring breeze, her face tilted in amazement. "You don't ever have to see those people ever again. You are an adult. You can make your own choices. They will never hurt you again."

The words don't fit together in my brain. I search her face for clues—what is she trying to say?

She squeezes my hands and tells me again, "They will never hurt you again. You are an adult. If they come near you again, you call the police."

Blink. Blink. Blink.

"But what if I made it all up? What if I am going crazy, and all of this is a big story my creative brain made up to get attention?" It's like the other words that have flown out of my mouth today, a long-dormant egg cracking open and releasing a wild bird of long-nurtured fear.

"Some of the details may move around and shift, but how could you make this up? Have you ever heard anything like this?" she asks logically.

"No," I say, a bit relieved. It's so odd, not knowing your own mind. It's difficult to know how to believe new stories instead of the old, safe versions. Seeing the truth through the shiny sparkle of lies I painted over them to make them palatable.

I see so many of my stories with a shiny glimmer on them, thousands sitting like little cloudy bubbles ready to rise up and burst their hidden poison. I feel full of them, an entire person's life I didn't know I was carrying inside me. That I lived and didn't acknowledge until now.

I look down at my body, my legs and arms I just described being so brutally treated. I don't even feel connected to that body, the little girl's parts that were so abused by others. The body I stare at is old and spasming violently at the trauma leaking from holding it all in too long.

Fresh tears renew the streaks that had begun to dry in the breeze. My vision blurring as overwhelming despair settles its heavy weight in my chest. I am a mess. How will I survive this?

"This happened. It's going to be hard to work through this, but you have already done a lot of the work. You already cut off contact with

them—that is usually the hardest part." She attempts a small smile as she catches my darting eyes.

I perk up a tiny bit. "That's true. Good thing you got me through that before all this. How did you do that?" I look up in awe. Seems like a wild bit of good luck for an unlucky girl like me.

"You did it. I just helped you get there," she says softly with a smile. The kind of smile I always wanted from a mother. The one that says, "You did a good job."

All I ever wanted was to do a good job. To be a good girl. For my family to be proud of me. But no matter how hard I try, I am always a disappointment. It feels nice to have RC believe me, say I did something right. It's just hard for the thing I did right to be the thing that makes The Family the most dangerous.

CHAPTER THIRTY-FOUR

I sit quietly empty as Dave drives me home from RC's house. I feel like I took the SAT, my brain so tired it's hard to process anything as the landscape whizzes by without focus. Dave is too stunned to speak, not knowing what to say anyway. Just gently holding my hand and making idle morning chatter.

Walking into the house, I realize I have one more story to tell today, to my daddy. He has watched us all, tear-streaked and weary, bustling around the house as we go our separate ways this morning, but now it's time he find out what the fuss is about.

Never one to shirk my responsibilities, I walk directly through the house and out to our patio into the May sunshine and my daddy smoking a cigarette.

"Hey, baby, how are you today?" he chirps as he gets up to give me a hug. But as he pulls back, he sees the storms in my eyes and, concerned, steps back into the sun.

"Daddy, I need to tell you something," I start timidly as I take the seat next to him. I glance back through the window to see Dave heading into the kitchen for coffee. My daddy and I are alone, the little waterfall babbling cheerily and the birds singing merrily. I sit for a moment, collecting my thoughts.

"What is it, baby?" he says, concerned, his blue eyes looking into mine, as kind and loving as I remember.

My eyes begin to water as I take a deep breath. "Daddy, The Grandfather and The Mother used to hurt me."

AGE 6 SISTER

CHAPTER THIRTY-FIVE

Life at my house is not like I read in the picture books. So many things are different. I think that's because we are a special celestial family. We have the church so we will be together forever. But sometimes I get hungry, and I don't know what food is OK to eat. Or The Mother forgets me in the closet and I have to figure out when it's safe to come out. I don't ever see those stories in my books, and I wonder why.

The Mother has been really sick a lot. Sometimes I see her with blood on her nightgown. She cries and cries, sometimes staying in bed all day or all week. It's OK. I like it because she doesn't yell or hit if I stay quiet. It gives me lots of time to read my books and climb the big apple tree in the backyard.

I love to climb my apple tree. I love feeling the strength of my muscles being able to pull and push me to the safety of the treetop. I can climb all the way to the top where I can see over all the houses to the Safeway down the block. I sit and feel the breeze on my face and the warmth of the sunshine soaking into my cheeks and feel happy.

Today is cold, not yet spring, so my nose and ears sting as the branches around me creak and moan. I don't mind because the sun is warm and The Mother is sleeping so it's quiet and calm. I am teaching myself to memorize little quiet moments and store them safely in my brain for when the bad times come. I can open it up like a jar of peanut butter and scoop out the delicious memory to help me lose focus on the bad things happening to my body. This memory will be light and crisp, like a candy cane, that I can enjoy slowly later when we go to The Grandparents' house.

My memory making is interrupted by the crunching tires pulling into the driveway; my daddy is home.

A big smile splits my face, and I scramble down the tree like a monkey, all wild swinging and feet gripping. Dropping at last into the bed of leaves below, I take off like a rocket across the yard to the back door. I slide open the glass and carefully close it before jumping into my daddy's arms.

"Well, hey, cutie pie, how's my little girl?" he says as he throws his coat across the back of the front room couch and bends to scoop me into his arms. "Did you miss me while I was gone?"

I nod vigorously into his neck, not trusting my voice to be cheery enough yet. It's been a tough week while my daddy was away on business. The Mother is getting fat again which always puts her in an extra-foul mood. She hasn't been cooking or cleaning at all so I have gotten sick a few times from eating rotten food. I am so happy he is home so we can get some good food. The Mother cooks when my daddy is home; it's her job.

"Ah, honey, I missed you too." He gives me an extra-tight squeeze and puts me down on my feet. "Gosh, you are getting to be a big girl, aren't ya?" he says with a twinkle in his eye that I don't quite understand. I am a big girl, but that's not news. I have been a big girl since I was four.

The Mother comes out of her room in her housecoat. She brushed her hair and her teeth and cleaned up a little so she doesn't look like a bad wife.

"How's my other girl?" he asks with one hand on The Mother's cheek for a kiss. The other hand rubs her belly.

"So far so good," The Mother says with a sigh. "I think it's time we have a talk with her," she says as she looks down at me. My stomach drops like an apple from the tree. Thud.

My daddy smiles and takes The Mother's hand, sits down on the couch and tugs The Mother to sit too. I can feel my smile falling down on the sides. I am trying to look happy, but more apples keep falling in my tummy, and I am getting worried by their changing faces.

"Honey, we have something to tell you." My daddy stoops down a little so he can look right into my eyes, my blue gaze a perfect match to his. "We are going to have another baby."

A freezing wind blows through my bones and is so loud I can't hear anything else. I see his smiling eyes, blue and sparkling, willing me to be happy too... but out of the side, I can see The Mother sitting with her arms protectively over her belly. He face is tight and drawn, like it's the worst job she's had in her life.

We learned about babies at school, how they grow in a woman's tummy. Carole's mommy is having a baby and brought a book for show-and-tell that had pictures of the baby inside the mommy's tummy. She was smiling and excited to be getting a new brother or sister. Her mommy is excited too; that's why she brought the book. I am confused... why does The Mother look so upset if she is supposed to be happy? It doesn't feel like a good sign.

But my daddy is waiting for me to be his sunny little girl so I mimic his exact face and say, "Oh goody! Can it please be a sister?" That's what Carole had said at school, and everyone had laughed so it seemed like the right thing to say.

CHAPTER THIRTY-SIX

As the weeks go by and the last day of school gets closer, The Mother starts getting real fat. Her tummy is so big, growing the baby inside, that she is slower and can't catch me as often. She is even nice when I get her things so she doesn't have to get up and walk around. Which is fine by me—I know how to stay out of reach when giving her stuff.

We don't know if the baby is going to be a boy or a girl, so we are picking out names for each.

William if it is a boy. Duh. I was named William until I was born. The Mother went into labor during Thanksgiving dinner and ruined the feast. I wasn't born until the next day AFTER the Alabama football game, just like my daddy wanted. They didn't have a girl name picked out so they copied my name from a little girl born down the hall.

So this time we are picking out a girl's name too, just in case. It's Rebecca. I got to choose between Rebecca and Susan. I chose Rebecca because The Mother wanted Susan, and I got to be the tie-breaker. It gave me a little zing inside to get to see The Mother pout about my decision. She isn't the best at playing the smart games unless The Grandfather tells her what to do.

At the library, I check out a book about mommies having babies. I want to understand what is happening inside that big belly. This book isn't as fancy as the one Carole had, but the pictures are pretty good. But I don't see anything about how to tell if it's a boy or a girl.

I had a bad thought on the last inspection day: what if The Mother has a girl? What if The Mother has another girl, and The Grandfather

wants her to prepare her for a celestial marriage too? I understand The Grandfather believes it's real important for my salvation, but I would rather risk eternal damnation and stop having inspection days. The Mother has started making me drink grape soda that makes me go diarrhea which is cleaner for inspection, but it really makes my butthole sore BEFORE The Grandfather puts his pee-pee and stuff in there. Sometimes I am so scared to poop after that I hold it in for days. Pooping out a sore butthole is the worst.

I had an idea that maybe there is a way I could help the baby be a boy, so then I wouldn't have to worry. Boys are sacred; they can hold the priesthood so they don't have inspection days. I look in all the books I can read, but there isn't much medical information at the school library. I'm running out of time, The Mother's due date is next week.

* * *

It's a sunny morning in May when I wake up to my daddy shaking my arm. "Wake up, punkin. Your mom's going into labor." He is whispering through his smile, but he is also a little sad in his eyes too.

"Oh, OK," I say, sleepy soft, "what do I need to do?" It's still early, too early for school yet. Will I have to miss school for this? I hope not. School is my favorite time of day.

"No. Your grandfather is going to come pick you up and take you to school. He will pick you up after and bring you to the hospital once the baby has been born." He strokes my hair and kisses my forehead. "I'll see ya later, OK, big sister?" he says with a wink as he closes the door shut tight behind him.

I lie in bed snuggled in the covers for just a few minutes more, thinking. Today is the last day it's going to be just me I worry about. It adds a heavy weight to the day as I drag myself out of bed to get ready for school.

Rebecca Sue is a tiny screaming human from the beginning. She screams in the hospital; she screams when she gets to her new home. She screams when she is hungry, when she is tired, and when she is wet. She screams in the middle of the night and early in the morning and after school.

I hold her. I feed her. I change her. I sing her songs. I read her stories. It's exhausting.

At night, I creep into her crib and stick my finger into her fist. Her tiny hands grasp my finger and hold tight, like she is pulling me into her misery. She is angry all the time. She doesn't care about making The Mother mad or waking everyone up on a school night. How will I ever protect her if she acts like this all the time?

Sometimes when she sleeps, I stare at her cherub lips and butterfly lashes and pretend she is my baby doll. My baby doll Victoria is a beautiful porcelain doll The Grandmother made me. She has real brown hair and a French lace dress. I am only allowed to touch her for photos or with The Grandmother's permission. Holding Rebecca is different, of course. She moves and screams, but she can be just as beautiful when she sleeps. I look at her tiny legs and wonder how long until they are too tempting for The Grandfather and The Uncle. A tear slips down my cheek. How will I ever protect her?

CHAPTER THIRTY-SEVEN

The Sunday before I start my first day in first grade, we are having family dinner at The Grandparents' house. The Mothers bustle around the kitchen cleaning up the afternoon meal of pot roast. They like cooking it because it's not a lot of cleanup, and it's good for leftovers. It's not my favorite.

I slip out of the kitchen under cover of all the dishes and chatter. The Grandfather is sitting in his chair watching golf alone, rocking softly in the tufted leather. The Grandfather always stays in his dress shirt and tie for Sunday dinner, so his shiny shoes creak softly with his rhythm. He glances at me and adjusts his gold-rimmed glasses as he sees my hesitation to enter the room.

This is the game we play now, kind of like chess but in real life. Who makes a move first is usually his decision, but he wasn't aware we were going to play a match today.

He waits patiently for me to speak, silently squinting his eyes and tilting his head to indicate he is listening and interested in playing my next move. We never finish the game; it's always playing. He likes when he can plan the big blows, see the traps as I walk into them. I am learning, but not fast enough.

I walk wordlessly across the room and kneel meekly at his feet, hands folded in my lap. My long, brown pigtails tangle with the green ribbon tied around them as they fall around my bowed face. Kermit the Frog's face peeks up at me from the apron on my dress under my trembling hands.

The Grandfather scoffs. This is new for me, so I hope he thinks I am learning good enough. I have a big favor to ask.

"Grandfather, I've been a good girl, right?" I say to the floor, not quite brave enough to look at more than a few quick glances to make sure he isn't going to hit me. "And Rebecca is such a bad girl. She cries so much and is always angry. You won't ever be able to make her a celestial bride, right?" I trail off a bit as I look up bravely to get a full view of his face. The Grandfather is like Gollum. He always talks in riddles. It's important I get as much information I can from his face.

"Oh, I think she will make a fine celestial bride one day. She will just need a strong hand to guide her," he says with his raspy softness, absolute confidence in his ability to make us all into celestial brides.

"A strong hand?" I wonder aloud on accident, staring at my own tiny hands that have been strong enough to carry her around and even lift her out of the tub. I think they are strong enough.

Too late I realize my mistake when I feel his gaze turn to laser beams on the bottom of my dress where my knees poke out. I hear him rock forward and stand up, adjusting his trousers while looming over my tiny kneeling form. The back of my neck feels exposed and cold as he shuffles around me, just barely nudging my shoulder with his leg.

"Get up," he says as he walks to the door that opens to the garage. He swings it open and gestures for me to step inside.

I roll back on my feet and up to standing like we do in ballet, using my toes in the carpet to take careful steps toward the black hole of the room beyond.

* * *

The Grandparents' garage is bigger than mine. They have enough room for two cars and a whole other garage for The Grandfather's woodworking. He makes all kinds of furniture and interesting objects out of wood with bright silver saws that sing real loud.

The Grandfather closes the door quietly and walks past me. He walks past the old 1950s refrigerator for soda and around the cars without opening the garage doors. That's weird. I follow because I don't know what else to do.

He walks over to his woodworking table past the big jagged saw. I stand on the edge of the space, dawdling by the rear bumper of The Grandmother's fancy car. Maybe he just wants to show me a project.

At the back of the garage are large storage areas that The Grandfather made himself. I think there are just old boxes and newspapers in there—I don't know. I am not allowed in there. The Grandfather reaches up into the bottom of one storage shelf to a spot I can't see and pulls out something shiny. It throws a bright star of light as he brings it over to the table saw, laying it down under his hand and commanding, "Come here."

I think all kids drag their feet when they don't want to do something, so it's extra hard to walk in the sawdust without him seeing me drag my feet. I pick them up slowly and put them down carefully, trying to focus on anything but the object lying on the table.

"Now, kneel down again," he says like he's about to give me a blessing. "You looked so sweet sitting there like that."

I look around at the sawdust and shavings on the floor. Some of them look pokey and splintered. I dance around a bit looking for the best spot and trying to cover my knees with my dress so they don't get splinters

in them. I settle as quick as I can, being as still as I can in the awkward kneeling position on my dress.

"You want to know what a strong hand is." His voice is low and scary, like a villain in a movie. It's dark in here with only the one yellow light above us. I can hear the mommies talking about the holidays, smell the roast beef still on my tongue. I look up, confused.

WHAM

The Grandfather slams the flat side of the gun into my head just above my temple with a big swing. My head whips to the side, splattering a few drops of blood on Kermit's face on my dress. My vision is black with a few little spots, and everything sounds really loud. I can hear The Grandfather talking, but I can't understand what he is saying. I stare at Kermit's bloody face as my vision clears, The Mother is going to be upset that I ruined this dress.

"You are a soldier of God," he says like a soldier on *GI Joe*. "You are in my army, and we leave no one behind. We will ensure all of us make it to the Celestial Kingdom. That is our duty—do you understand me?" He is raising his voice. I have never heard The Grandfather yell before.

I don't understand, and everything in my brain feels messy. There is a stomping on my brain that is hard to think through. I just want to go somewhere quiet and pretend I never had this idea. It's a puzzle. What's the best way to get out of this situation to rest?

I pick myself upright and lift my chin to look at him in the eye as blood drips down my cheek. "Yes, sir."

He looks over my face, his eyes bright with the fever of righteousness, and decides he has gotten through to me. He nods once and waves me away, as he turns to his work bench and lays the gun down. I take that

as my cue to slip away behind the cars and quietly back into the house. I creep past the kitchen without notice and crawl up the stairs to the closet. It's a risk to be in here, but I know I can steal a few minutes of quiet time before they find me. I find the blue cashmere sweater and bury my face in it to cry, careful to not to get any blood on the expensive fabric.

AGE 7 THE BISHOP

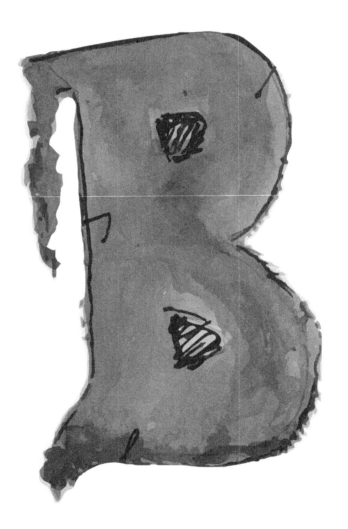

CHAPTER THIRTY-EIGHT

I stare down at the little stars covering my tap shoes as my daddy and I head home from dance class. Dance class is my favorite day of the week. On Wednesday nights, I have ballet and tap class at Hicks Recreation Park in my neighborhood. I have to wear a leotard, tights, and pink ballet shoes or black shiny tap shoes; that's the rules. You can only wear a skirt when you do tap class, because that's appropriate. I am not sure why a skirt is appropriate for tap and not ballet, but I don't argue.

We have an old lady who plays piano in the corner, nodding her head to keep the time. All of our classes are lead by Ms. Janice, a nice lady from the LDS church. She has long, brown hair and was a real ballerina before she had kids and moved to Tulsa. She is strict—it's important to mind the rules in class—but she is also nice when she smiles.

I have learned it's safe to like things that can't be taken away from you, like dancing. The Mother can hide my shoes and tear my tights, but she can't make me forget my dances. When she locks me in a closet or I have to hide for a while, I can practice each routine over and over in my head. I can listen real hard for the music and Ms. Janice's voice saying, "One, two, three, and breathe," and I can pretend I am far away dancing so I am not so sad.

At the end of every class, you get a star for your shoes if you are good and remember your steps. Gold is the best, then silver and green and then the worst is red. I have lots of gold stars on the top of my shoes, with just a few silvers and one green on the back. I am proud of all the golds and no reds. My friend Stacia has all gold and silver too; we are the best in class.

"Brad bragged at Christmas about all these connections he has with the LA Lakers. Said he could get me a signed ball," my daddy says as he puts on his blinker and turns into our neighborhood. "But here it is, nearly Easter, and he still hasn't gotten one for me," he grumbles as we head home.

I don't know what the LA Lakers are, but I know Uncle Brad, and he doesn't do nice things for people. He still likes to pinch and be mean. I don't like the idea of him not giving my daddy something he promised.

"I bet he doesn't even have any friends at the LA Lakers," my daddy muses and turns the car into the Hicks Park parking lot.

"Who are the LA Lakers?" I ask.

"A really famous basketball team in California where Uncle Brad lives. The team is having a superb year, and I would like to give your little brother a signed ball for his birthday," he explains with a sigh, "but not sure that's going to work out. He still hasn't gotten it to me and is dodging my calls."

Spring sunshine fades over the trees as they fly by, casting shadows over my daddy's face. A little wrinkle between his eyebrows deepens, and his lips get tight. He's been worried a lot about The Mother getting pregnant so quickly with another baby so soon after Rebecca was born. She is not even a year old yet, and The Mother is expecting to have another baby this summer. It's enough to worry us both. How will I ever take care of two kids? I just hope it's a boy, for my daddy and me.

"I bet I can help! I'll just tell The Uncle that you need the ball for the baby's birthday," I pipe up and sit to face him in the car, "But you don't know if it's going to be a boy," I tease with a smile.

My daddy smiles and reaches over to rub a thumb on my cheek (he knows not to mess up my ballet bun). "Ah, thanks, honey. I bet he would give you just about anything with a sweet request like that. Now go on. Turn us on some music," he says as he flips on the radio.

I punch the button for our favorite station with old rock music, the kind The Mother doesn't like. He smiles at the road and we both sing about a "Tiny Dancer" to the wind. Maybe I can fix this and help my daddy. I think The Uncle owes me at least that.

* * *

This idea keeps running round and round in my brain for a few days. It's like a puzzle, and it helps me focus on what matters and not my emotions. Logic puzzles are the best for thinking; they are my favorite. This idea needs to be a big one—it's a puzzle I can solve if I can figure out what the best move is. It's going to be tricky. I will need to plan.

First, I need to figure out how to make a long-distance call. Usually, I only talk to Uncle Brad on holidays when we all talk on The Grandparents' phone. They are rich and can afford the long-distance call. Our next family dinner is not until Sunday so I will have to be patient. How I will get Uncle Brad to agree without hurting his feelings, I don't know.

I know how sensitive Uncle Brad is about my daddy. He doesn't like trash like him being successful in business. I need to figure out how to get him to do something nice for my daddy. I figure I have two choices: offer something in return or threaten something if he doesn't. And since he is in California and I won't see him until maybe summer, there is not much I can offer him that he will want.

But if I tell him I could go to The Bishop—tell that Uncle Brad hurts me…

It is a big gamble. If The Uncle gets caught, he could turn on The Grandfather. But I think The Uncle is scared of The Grandfather too, so maybe not.

I will have to think about it. I have a few days. I suppose it's just a choice, which one is safest and has the highest chance of success.

CHAPTER THIRTY-NINE

Easter Sunday arrives cold and rainy. My blue Easter dress is hidden under a coat, and my fingers are cold. After the egg hunt (I got money in some of mine!) and ham for lunch, we all sit in the living room while the boys watch golf on TV. I like Easter; it's golf season. That means quiet afternoons when I lie on the floor and read with no yelling or jumping. Just have to be careful to not go to the bathroom during a busy time (to avoid The Grandfather's bathroom checks) and say "yes, ma'am" to any questions.

I sit lounging in the sun square on the floor like a kitty, warm and tight around my new adventure book. The adults are chatting and making polite talk about church and the weather when the phone in the kitchen begins to ring. It's long distance from California, calling to talk to everyone for the holiday. It's time to make my move.

I sit quietly, patiently waiting for everyone to pass around the phone and say awkward hellos and how are you doings. Usually I try to go in the middle, so I don't have to talk very long, but today I want to be last. I need some privacy. I am hoping they will not notice me if I leave the room as long as everyone else has already had a turn.

The Grandmother finishes her long turn on the phone and asks if there is anyone who wants to talk. I take a deep breath and get up, walking up to her. "Can I say hello before you hang up? I want to say hi to my cousins from California."

I give my big wide innocent eyes like princesses in cartoons, smiling like I really enjoy talking to Them.

She smiles and gives in. "Of course, just not too long, honey. It's expensive."

I take the phone and put it up to my ear, hearing a labored silence as I cheerily greet The Uncle. "Hey! How are you doing, Uncle Brad? It's so nice to talk to you," I lie as I hunch over the phone and creep into the hallway. Everyone else is either in the living room or the garden, so no one should be listening.

"Hello," The Uncle says dismissively. "Hold on. I'll get the kids—"

"So, my daddy said that you were going to get him a signed basketball game…" I venture bravely, shaking only a little inside my tummy. "Did you remember? Have you gotten it yet? He wants to give it to my new brother for his birthday." My voice rises a bit at the end, and I know it sounds whiny… but I can't help it. I'm nervous.

"Huh, yeah, fat chance I get anything for that guy. Come on," he scoffs. "Not like he can do anything for me. Now you on the other hand…" I can hear the dirty names on his lips, though he doesn't say them.

"Oh." I squirm and wiggle. I have to have courage for my daddy. "Well, if you don't get it… I can tell you hurt me."

I blurt it out before I can chicken out. My face goes hot pink and blotchy red all the way up my ears and down my chest. I remind myself he is in California and can't come punish me, not today anyway. So I need to be strong.

To my surprise, he just laughs. A big belly laugh, I can picture his fat hairy belly jiggling, and I shiver.

"Yeah, right, who you gonna tell?" he chides. It scares me that he is not afraid, sickly pea-green fear slithering up my insides.

"I'll tell The Bishop. He won't like you hurting and touching my private places." I feel bold as I throw the threat across the void. The power of the secret is strong, and I feel brave. It's the first person I can think to tell that isn't my daddy and might help me. I don't want to risk my daddy's safety.

"Ohhhh." He sounds amused. "Go right ahead, you talk to him—see how that goes," he says quite seriously, but I can smell the lie under his words through the phone. My little spark of light goes out, and the fear roars in my ears.

CHAPTER FORTY

My tummy is sick all week at school. I don't think my plan worked. Now I have a bigger problem. Do I try again or tell and get him in trouble? I am worried that if I tell, it might get everyone in trouble. But maybe it will stop The Uncle. Maybe it would stop it all—the pinching, the pee-pee rubbing—maybe even it could stop The Grandfather. The bathroom checks and inspection days are getting really bad. Sometimes I don't go to school because it hurts so bad.

I haven't ever considered telling anyone before, never felt like I could make it stop. Not since The Mother got angry at me for complaining to her about it and left me on the side of the road. I know it is my duty to be a good girl while they prepare me for celestial marriage, that it's important I be ready to be a good wife, but maybe I don't want to be a celestial wife.

By Sunday, I have convinced myself that this could be my chance to be saved. I could tell on The Uncle, he will get The Grandfather in trouble, and my daddy and me can live without them. I might not get the basketball; at least I could do this. As least I could try.

I wear my most responsible dress, the red one like Annie even though it is out of season. I wait patiently through the whole sacrament and testimonies and prayers. When we dismiss for Sunday School, I take off through the jostling crowd to catch the Bishop coming down from the stage. I know it is the only time I can catch him in person without others listening. I have seen people do that before.

"Bishop, can I talk to you about something? Serious," I say in a low voice, tugging him down a bit on his sleeve to make sure he looks at me.

"Serious, hm?" he says with a smile. "It must be important. Let's go to my office."

Relieved, I follow him around the legs and purses as those lingering in the sacrament hall offer their greetings. We walk out the open glass doors into the outer hall, stepping over to the leadership offices. The Bishop unlocks his office door and ushers me in, hauntingly similar to the gesture of The Grandfather as he leads me into the secret room down the hall. I avoid looking at the secret keyhole.

"This looks serious," he says, arranging his face from the smile he usually gives to the more serious one he uses for grownups as he settles behind his big desk.

"I need to talk to you about something important." I pant a bit; my palms are sweaty. Now that I am here, I am not sure exactly what to say. "The Uncle hurts me, and I don't like it," I say weakly. I didn't think it would be this hard to say out loud. I shuffle my feet and risk only peeks up at The Bishop, staring at his shoes instead.

"Hmmmm, yes, The Uncle did call and say that you were going through some things and there was an 'incident.' Do you want to talk more about that?" It sounds like a question, but I don't think it's what he is really asking. Maybe I should try different words. Sometimes grownups don't understand kids.

"The Uncle hurts me in my," I drop to a whisper, "private places." Not much louder, but I do manage to keep my voice sort of steady.

The Bishop sits back in the chair with his hands in a steeple in front of his mouth. He taps one finger on the other as he makes thinking tuts and snicks.

"Now I know Brother Brad, and he is a righteous man of the priesthood," he chides, as if I have said something unkind. "He and your grandparents have been good LDS families in this ward for years."

"I know," I say, confused. "That's why I am here—you have known me my whole life. I don't know what to do. It hurts." And the tears begin to fall. I am mad at myself for crying like a little kid, but can't stop them. I feel so red and helpless.

"When a member of the priesthood chooses you, you should be ready for him. If he touches you, that is blessed by God. If, for any reason, you feel uncomfortable or you want it to stop, you just need to say 'no.' But remember that his blessings will go with him if you turn him away." He walks around the desk slowly, sitting on the corner as he finishes talking. His crotch is right in front of my face. I drop my eyes to the floor to focus.

"I do say no," my teeny voice whimpers, "but he says it's my own fault. Which blessings will go away? Is it if I say no all the time or just sometimes? Sometimes it hurts and I don't like it and I cry," I say in a rising panic of confusion, snot starting to drip and shaking from head to toe.

I don't understand what is happening. At school, a police officer came to tell us that you should tell if someone touches you down there, only doctors. The Uncle is not a doctor so it's not OK…. right? Is it OK for anyone in the priesthood because The Grandfather says I am just for him but sometimes shares with others?

"Yes, but sometimes we are overcome by the spirit, and we weep in joy. Were you invoking the Holy Spirit like a good girl, praying for him to fill you with grace while you received your blessing from The Uncle?" The Bishop says as he stares over the rim of his glasses at me. He is giving me a lesson. This is something I am supposed to already know. He continues. "Good LDS girls do as they are told, so as long as you are doing it in service of our lord and savior Jesus Christ, is this maybe your calling?" he says with a smile, like it's an exciting gift and not a punishment.

"No!" I lose my temper, white hot like a match. "He pinches me and hurts, and he laughs while he shakes his pee-pee at me." My voice is getting stronger now as the anger fills me up with burning flames. This isn't how this is supposed to go. I am the brave hero, not the villain. I thought I was doing the right thing. I thought he would help me—I'm just a kid!

I take sharp breaths and shake while he stares down into my face for the first time. He has a kind face, with soft grey eyes and freckles on his nose. He has always been so nice. I don't know why he would think I would do something bad.

"You know this is a very serious accusation. It could really hurt Brother Brad. Are you sure that's what happened?" He looks at me real hard, like he is willing me to repeat his words so we can get out of here. "Are you sure he didn't just punish you for straying from the righteous path into sin?" He looks like The Grandmother after asking if I washed my hands when she knows I didn't.

"I didn't do anything wrong," I say in a whisper, breaking at last. "He and The Grandfather got me out of bed in the middle of the night and hurt me. I wasn't doing anything but sleeping," I say, firm but desperate

for him to believe that I had been a very good girl and that this was some bad mistake.

"I know. I know you didn't, sweetie. But let's think harder about your actions next time before placing blame on others, OK?" he says kindly as he takes hold of my arm and ushers me out of the office with a nice pat on the back, quietly shutting the door behind me.

I stand shaking and tear-stained, in the now-empty hallway, alone and hopeless. I climb into the big green chair that sits in the lobby and try to disappear into the sunshine-drenched velvet.

AGE 45 AFTERMATH

CHAPTER FORTY-ONE

"I think Will eventually got that basketball, right?" I finish trying hard to convince my daddy of my honesty, looking for any proof he can cling on to.

My daddy has only cried twice in his life that I have seen, once when his mother died and once on my wedding day. So it's no surprise when I can see the rims of his eyes brimming with sadness, but he doesn't let them escape. He sniffs and quickly swipes his nose and face, refusing to be weak when his little girl needs his strength.

He grabs my hand with his tanned callused one and warms it with a squeeze. "I'm so sorry, baby. I never knew."

"I know. I made sure of it," I say with a weak smile, "I did a really good job." It is one of the proudest accomplishments of my life, and this is the first time I have said it out loud. "I protected you and Dave and Jack—"

A flicker of a phone call, a threat, my little boy clutched in the arms of The Mother screaming on the other end of the line. She has him.

My boys are safe with me. They will never touch us again.

I push the thought away, not important now. My boys are safe; I made sure of it.

"You did, honey. I just wish you didn't feel like you had to," he says with a nervous chuckle. My daddy is always a man of few words so we sit back and listen to the world a bit.

Exhaustion settles into my bones as I slow down, bending my body with weariness. I give my daddy a quick kiss on the cheek and head into my bedroom to lie down. The day too much for anything more than pillows and blankets.

I lie on the bed staring at strips of sunlight on the floor, fatigue settling the fear and anxiety into a buzzy sort of rest. I remember I can try some pink clouds to help soften the edges. RC says that's OK if I don't use too much. So after a few minutes I get up to get my vape pen and see my daddy standing facing me through the door.

The sun is bright today, reflecting his own image back rather than the view of me standing inside. He is alone, smoke curling in delicate tendrils up his hand. Sadness bends his head and shoulders as his left hand sneaks up to wipe away a tear.

I freeze, staring at the intimate moment, feeling like I'm intruding but unable to look away. It's a picture I have wanted my whole life, someone to cry for me, to care that I was hurt. For my daddy to know what I did to protect him. For him to be angry at Them and tell me it's not my fault.

For today, this single tear will do. Because I know with that single drop is an ocean of love that is real. That my daddy really didn't know and he does love me.

I take a hit off my pen and lie back down on my feather pillows, drifting into a warm pink glow of hope.

CHAPTER FORTY-TWO

[Evening]

Me → More memories are coming. It's hard to write them all down!

RC → I am not going to be on top of my phone this evening. Just keep breathing. If you need me, call me.

Me → OK, that works. Thank you!

[Next day]

RC → How are you doing today?

Me → Current situation is melting face emoji.

Me → Kicked it up a notch when I started to remember they used to Jack to control me.

RC → Yeah, we sort of ended there yesterday. But it doesn't sound like it ended there.

Me → It did not.

RC → Holding space for you. Let me know if you need to talk.

RC → You are all OK now. Safe. They don't have any more power. Remember that. Without violently and visibly breaking the law, they cannot do you any more harm.

Sunday 7:00 p.m.

Me → *+Voice recording - The Grandfather*

* * *

[Monday]

Me → Doing a little better today. Still more coming up, some good things in there too.

RC → The fact that you are seeing some good and bad things is a good sign. It makes sense that not every minute was horrible.

Me → Yeah, I hid the good ones like little treasures that I could pull out and look at when things got too bad.

RC → Try to set it down and just be for a while. You need to rest.

Me → I know. I will try. Thanks again.

[Wednesday]

RC → Are you OK to drive to our session tomorrow or would you prefer virtual?

Me → Yes, I am OK to drive. I think I am going to go home with Nanny and Poppy to Oklahoma this weekend. Nanny said she would help me put together a timeline. But I will be at our session in person tomorrow.

Me → I have been painting, I might bring some.

RC → Bring whatever you want. I look forward to seeing it.

* * *

"How are you doing?" It's a simple question 99 percent of the time, but today it's a thinker

"I am exhausted," I don't even try to polish it up. I have no makeup on, hair in a bun, stretchy pants and a t-shirt in the middle of the workweek. I am a wreck, the worst I have ever looked in my life… and I don't even care. "I just need to get it all out of my body. The shaking and episodes are exhausting."

She nods knowingly. Gives me space to breathe since it's so much harder these days.

My body is exhausted. The trauma releasing from my joints and muscles is debilitating. I shake and tremble all over like a scared rabbit.

Trembling at any sound, eyes darting and nose twitching even when I am in my favorite spot on the couch at home. I am terrified to close my eyes, to let my mind wander, the flashes of violence flickering at warp speed with any tug of a thread.

We rehash the stories from the first wave of memory, details turning up the more I talk. Feelings and images swirling like brownie batter— sticky, gooey, lumpy, and oddly velvety. The exit of the arching narrative is traumatic, but the release of no longer being sole owner of the horror is like an elixir. The more I force myself to say out loud, to see in words, the more I feel the black invasion of terror in my center recede.

"It's just so hard to believe myself," I blubber. I don't even pretend I don't cry anymore. I am a fucking fountain of tears. "How could I have kept these secrets for so long? How could I say these things out loud about my family?"

"The truth doesn't go anywhere because you cover it up," she says gently. "It just waits. I'm sorry you had to wait so long carrying this. I'm sorry your family treated you like this. You don't deserve to be treated like this."

I look up, searching. "It's that bad?" I ask again.

A lifetime of one story, one person I trust saying, "Yes. It is absolutely that bad. It's the worst I have ever heard."

We let those words sit between us, sinking like a stone into my subconscious. My session hour fades away. She steers the conversation up out of the past. "Did your dad rally a bit?" she asks as we both glance at the clock.

"Yes, he did. I think he believes me that he wasn't supposed to know. That I did my absolute best to make sure he never knew. But when I told

him what really happened at the nature center, he adamantly refused to believe it," I finish with a sigh. It wasn't even surprising, just another person who didn't believe me because it's just too hard to hear. I know it's not because he thinks I am lying.

"You know he has no right to refuse to believe anything," she says softly, kind but firm.

"Oh, Nanny did," I say with a small smile. "She jumped him real quick and let him know that he had no idea what the heck was going on, and he just needed to sit down and shut up." Nanny is an act of God when she wants to be; even my daddy was lost for words.

"He just ended up leaving for a while. That's on brand for him, just take some space until the fire dies down to a manageable flame. Sure something is lurking there," I finish. Honestly, I was amazed he didn't just leave for Oklahoma that minute. I had already had a few ideas of what to do if we had to be bailing him out of jail for murder in a few days.

* * *

Sunday, 7:24 a.m.

Me → Sleep is hard when you can't let your mind wander.

RC → I heal loudly because I suffered silently my whole life - unknown quote Me → Damn. That hits.

RC → Happy Mother's Day

Me → I don't even know how to process today.

RC → Be kind to yourself.

Tuesday

RC → Done for the day. Checking in. Sending hugs. Take care of yourself in this process.

Me → I am at my daddy's. Trying to put all the pieces together into a timeline of events. My memory is all over the place.

RC → "Enlightenment is when a wave realizes it's the ocean." GG, I'll check in later.

Me → The sheer volume is overwhelming.

Wednesday

Me → [[photo of notecards]]

Me → Need to talk about The White room (this one is a jumble) +
recording

Monday

Me → 2 LDS missionaries just dropped by. Pretty sure The Grandfather sent them.

RC → You OK?

Me → I mean, no. Not melting down, but not feeling safe.

RC → What do you need?

Me → Safety.

RC → And what is within your power to do that would make you feel safe?

Me → ….

CHAPTER FORTY-THREE

The days pass slowly. Long periods with the hum of fear seize my spine and vibrate through my mind. Attempts to watch movies bring unexpected bubbles of memories floating to the surface, bursting with feelings so strong they kidnap my consciousness and drag me down into the pain all over again.

I lie in bed for hours, staring at the light from my bedroom window creeping across the floor. Holding myself together with the strength of a Greek god, straining and stretching to keep my mind from falling into the abyss.

Keeping secrets from myself is the hardest to understand. Knowing I have an entire other life that I endured, all the experiences I spent a lifetime being told didn't exist or "weren't that bad," is surreal. It's like being at a fabulous party, all the flashing lights and confetti and thrumming bass abruptly turning into a big mess when the lights come up at the end of the fun. Knowing there was an entire team of people working their asses off to serve drinks, clean up puke in the bathroom, throw out the drunks, and play the right music. I see all my support team, the scared little girls, the managers, the planners, the executors, all visible and standing in the middle of the mess, proud of the work we have done but knowing so much more must be done before the venue is ready for the next party.

I religiously practice yoga classes on YouTube, glassy-eyed and breathing deep to try and keep my body healthy. I listen to endless uplifting meditations, believing the positive messages will reach some

part of my brain to keep us all above the dark. I watch documentaries about other survivors, but their stories are so sad and so often without retribution that I can only watch a few. I play video games to keep my mind from wandering but still keep it sharp. Then a sad cutscene will creep in and trigger some off-the-wall connection my brain made long ago, and down the rabbit hole I spiral.

I did not know the big memories were causing panic attacks until I got a professional diagnosis. I responsibly make an appointment with my primary care doctor when they get so bad I am collapsing at home alone.

"Yeah, that's what anxiety is. What you are describing is exactly what a panic attack is," he says kindly as he writes me a prescription for a mild anti-anxiety medication. We will work our way up to the *big stuff*—don't want me getting addicted.

And even then, "a panic attack" is a dirty phrase that no one really wants to use because it means you just can't control your emotions—how embarrassing. Looking back, of course I have had them for years at awful points of my life. I just hid or excused myself to the bathroom until I could get enough air to breathe and stop freaking out. Getting control of the racing heart and the labored breathing are only the symptoms compared to the real work of getting my mind out of the vortex of awful.

Unexpectedly, while I am watching a show or listening to a song, I lose myself to memories of the past. Pent-up pain, despair, and fear finally bursting through my carefully crafted defenses and raging all the more violently for it. Emotional reactions to trauma stored in my body for decades, never acknowledged and now roaring to be heard. Emotions that will not be ignored forever, and they grow angry and violent. Panic attacks are the consequences of my control, a chaotic ride through my

worst memories complete with a 5D experience. Every poke, pinch, needle, and jab fresh as new. Every glare, evil twinkle, and locking door as vivid as the day it happened.

I am turning to medicine to stabilize myself. RC or Dave need a rest. They are the only ones to get me to believe I am safe now. Those assholes will never touch me again. The aftermath recovery takes days.

* * *

Each memory is so carefully coded I can't avoid the triggers. To keep my secrets safe, I coded each memory with titles and odd props inside the memory so I could keep the information safe without being triggered and spilling the secret. It's a strategy that serves me well, yet now it's a field of landmines just waiting to go off as I walk drunkenly across the path of revelation.

Me → Worst thing I ever did came up on the way home from our session - Voice recording: Bite

RC → Why were you screaming and yelling?

Me → At The Mother because I didn't want another blue dress.

RC → That wasn't a bad thing. It was self-defense before they beat it out of you.

Me → Oh. I think I am making progress, but then you say something that I can't even comprehend. I don't think I ever tried self-defense, didn't think I was allowed to.

RC → The whole shtick about being a lady is just to keep you under control so you can be abused.

Me → I don't understand.

RC → *If you are ladylike, you don't protest and fight. If they let you be a normal person, of course you're going to protest what's happening to you.*

Me → *"Of course you are going to protest what's happening to you" "This is not happening now—you are just remembering" – I am working on listening to them, but it's like the words get jumbled in my brain, and they don't make sense.*

Me → *That's how crazy I am now.*

RC → *You are not crazy—you are healing.*

Me → *I fucking hope so. I am tired of this shit.*

RC → *In being tired of this shit, there is a seed of anger. Get so pissed that you're having to spend so much time dealing with the shit instead of doing other more fun stuff.*

RC → *Also, I think this might be something good for you to try: Website: Karen - Body Trauma massage therapist*

Me → *I'll try anything.*

* * *

I sit in a small office suite, with a massage table in the middle, a small counter connected to a wall, a bookshelf and a couple of chairs. I sit on the edge of the chair, jiggling my foot as I stare at my busy picking hands. "I'm not even sure what I am doing here, but my therapist said you could help, and I will do anything to get through this," I say in a rush.

I don't have the energy for small talk. I know my eyes are glassy and red, filled to the brim with meds to dull the pain, anything to keep the horrors at bay. I glance up to see her staring at me intently listening, empathy on her face.

I don't even know what a body trauma massage therapist does, but RC said she thinks it could help so I am here. I am willing to try anything to help my body feel better. The constant fear and worry is like an electric wire cut and waving around, spurting electric panic inside me. I shake and wiggle constantly; I am exhausted.

"I'm glad you are here. Let's just go slow and see what feels good. OK?" she says as she stands and gestures for me to do the same.

"Is this like a regular massage? Do I need to take off my clothes and lie down?" I ask, panic rising. I love massages but not sure I am ready for that today.

"Hmmm…" she says with a serene face and a thoughtful look, "how would you feel about being wrapped up in a blanket? Like a baby?" She looks at me straight-faced and totally serious. I stare, confused. Her kind eyes sparkle like she has a surprise in store for me, something that might help. I trust her.

"Uh, OK," I say uncertainly, turning around in a circle, unsure what to do. What kind of therapy is this? How will a massage help when I am wrapped up?

"Let's just try it. We can stop if it doesn't feel right, OK?" She seems confident with the idea so I perch on the side of the table fully dressed, watching her prepare her supplies. She takes a little flat cotton blanket, folded square, out of a humming box, flapping it out to its full length. I can feel the warmth from the flapping. It's been heated and smells of lavender. She then folds it into an intricate pattern I remember from swaddling my son when he was a baby, corners and folds that keep the fabric tight, then picks it up to wrap around my shoulders. She pulls it tight, the warm pressure enveloping me, melting my anxiety down a few

notches instantly. She tucks in the folds tight and lays me gently back on the table, throwing another blanket softly over my feet.

I lie on the table, wrapped and warm, and tears slide down my cheeks. I look at her in alarm, but she just glances and turns away, busying herself readying other supplies I can't see. "You OK?" she asks nonchalantly, checking in without the searching glances of discernment.

"Yeah, just a bit weepy. This feels nice," I say softly, tears just leaking down my chin because my arms are too tight to brush them away. I don't think I have ever been wrapped this way before, even when I was young. It's warm and comforting, a feeling so foreign it makes me cry even more. How fucked up am I that I can't even feel warm and safe without crying?

"OK, I am going to just sit here at your head, and we are going to breathe together," she says closer now, pulling up a stool and sitting behind my messy hair hanging over the edge of the table.

I nod and close my eyes, concentrating on taking deep breaths—in through my nose, out through my mouth. We sit in silence breathing for a few minutes.

"Open your mouth as wide as you can and push that air out," she instructs, demonstrating a large "Ha" sounds behind me. I try. I cannot get any breath out. I try again—I can't. It's like there is a block in my thought, preventing me from breathing that loudly and losing all my air at once.

Like my body is scared to make a noise or move the air with a deep exhale.

"It's OK. It's something to work on. It's harder than you think," she says delicately, just holding my head and breathing with me. The tears flow more freely.

256

"I don't know why I can't do that," I say, frustrated. What a weird thing not to be able to do.

"At some point in your life, you have learned to be invisible. To breathe shallow and not make a sound. Your body has learned to behave this way. We need to relax it into realizing that you are not in danger anymore. It's OK to breathe, to exist and be seen." She speaks softly behind me, gently rubbing the sides of my head and neck, soothing the trembling flesh. I just close my eyes and concentrate on breathing.

"This is not uncommon. I noticed you hold your breath a lot when you came in. Women who have been abused often have a hard time breathing in that way. It's too noisy and unladylike." She speaks softly and surely, holding my head still as I struggle to breathe normally now that I am aware it's not normal.

"I would like to try something else, if you are feeling OK," she says quietly after a while, as she stands and comes to the bottom of the bed by my spasming left leg, "I know this shaking is annoying. Would it feel OK if I put my hands on it? Not massaging or anything, just putting my hands on the shaking limb. Is that OK?" She holds her hands above my legs to show her intent but intentionally doesn't move toward my leg. Very clearly she is waiting for permission.

"Yes, OK, that might be nice," I say carefully, not at all sure what will happen.

"OK, just keep breathing. I am going to rest my hands on your left hip in three, two, one..." She lowers her hands as they finally come to touch my quivering hip. The hip continues to shake and shiver, but calms a bit at her touch.

A few moments pass. Then she instructs me, "Now, close your eyes and tell me what you feel. What does your left hip want to tell you?"

What an odd question, but this is my life now so I close my eyes and ask my hip—*Hey hip, what do you want to say to me? Why are you shaking?*

A flash of memory burns bright and overtakes my mind.

I am in a hospital bed, giving birth to my son. The pain is unbearable, ripping my body in half. Pressure in my pelvis, straining to push and trying to hold in the creature inside. I look up, beyond my trembling knees, to see The Mother's face smiling in the corner. Her eager gaze focused on the small head pushing out between my legs, ravenous hope of another female baby being born into the family naked on her face. My body shakes and shudders violently as my mind fights to keep the baby safe and my body pushes it out to save my life.

"My hips hurt a lot when I carried my son. He sat very far out from my body. I was sick a lot during pregnancy and had a lot of difficulties with my body and the strain." I let the words flow out of me without thinking. "During labor, my hips felt like they were going to pop out of socket. I was holding them so tight, scared of what was coming out. I can see The Mother sitting in the corner of the hospital room, her Cheshire smile greedy to see if another little girl will be on offer to her father soon. I chose not to know the sex of my baby—I couldn't trust myself to carry to term if I found out it was a girl. So this was the moment. She planned it so she would be the first to know. I was so afraid to give birth. My body was fighting itself, and it hurt so bad I just wanted to scream." Words stream out of my mouth like the other memories, her hands holding firmly to my hip to provide stability as my entire body starts to shake.

"I can see her smile collapse as the doctor holds up the squirming baby at last and announces it's a boy. My body turns to water with relief and exhaustion." My hip settles and stops shaking under her hand; she still holds on in case. "I have never been so relieved in my life."

I blurt it out and sob openly. I didn't even know that memory was hiding in there. It rips through my mind like a serrated blade, leaving jagged and bleeding despair dripping in my mind. The pressure of having the baby, of protecting it by not finding out the gender until it was born. The relief when the doctor says it's a boy.

I cry and cry, wrapped in the swaddling with her hand resting gently on my leg. Karen waits. My leg stills at last.

I open my eyes and look at her, surprised. "I've never told anyone that before." She nods with tears rolling down her cheeks and lifts one hand to rest on my shoulder, leaving one hand solid on my hip.

"That's fucked up, but I'm glad you got it out," she says with a sad smile, a little pride shining in her eyes.

"Me too," I say, a little confused but relieved, my hip relaxed as it hasn't been in months. I sit up slowly, still wrapped tight, and sniff up the trauma dripping off my face. All this time I have been shaking, it's just my body screaming at me because I wouldn't listen. So much work to do.

* * *

It's been weeks, and it still seems so surreal. Logically, I know this all happened—to me, to the body I currently live in….yet it seems so extreme, so outrageous. How could it possibly be true? That means this has been going on for more than 60 years to at least three generations of women, and no one said anything? That just can't be right.

But the sessions with Karen have put a new dose of reality into my mind. My body reacting to her touch, bringing up stored memories like a vault long ago locked away. It's wild to recognize that a huge part of my memory is not stored in my brain, no thought or logic or intention behind it, just raw experience stored inside my bones. Finally erupting violently into this trembling exit after too many decades of being ignored.

Me → quote of the day: "If you're wondering why nothing made sense growing up, it's because you didn't have the proper terminology to describe it."

RC → That's good and accurate, and doesn't even begin to scratch the surface of trauma like yours. You had that AND so much more to escape.

Me → Really?

RC → Yeah, she's just talking about the emotional needs of kids that are neglected. She's not even talking about the kind of abuse you endured.

Me → I am still not quite believing mine is that bad.

RC → Think about it this way. Try to imagine Jack in the closet at The Grandmother's for the weekend. Think about leaving him with a friend for the weekend and coming home and finding out some of the things you remember had happened to him.

{dots}

{dots disappear}

{dots}

{dots disappear}

RC → You are not making it up.

Me → I think that's why so many of the memories are third person. I watched it like a movie.

RC → Where would you even have gotten source material to make that kind of stuff up?

Chapter Forty-Three

Me → *I read a lot. I watch social media. And documentaries.*

RC → *Yeah, 'cause you were dissociated because your little body could not process what was happening to it.*

Me → *Oh.*

RC → *The worst kind of child porn erotica doesn't have the stories you're telling. What in the world could you have read that would have planted those ideas?*

Me → *Really?*

RC → *Do you think Jack at his age right now has any concept about some of the stuff you're talking about?*

Me → *It just doesn't seem that bad. There are people who fight in wars and die in the Holocaust.*

RC → *Would he have been able to describe anal rape to you at seven years old?*

Me → *Oh. I guess not.*

RC → *Pain comparison does you no good. Yes, there's always somebody who has been through something worse. But when your bar for comparison is the war and the Holocaust...*

Me → *Oh. Yeah, I guess that's not great.*

RC → *Just keep doing what you are doing. It will sink in at some point.*

Me → *It's just frustrating.*

RC → *You can try doing something destructive to shake something loose. Like break a plate or smash a watermelon. Write all the names of the people who hurt you on it and smash it.*

Me → *Hmmm.*

RC → *You have a powerful defender inside you that is determined to protect you. You can't break things because it's gonna be the death of you, but that was then, not now. You are an adult. You are safe. Maybe start tapping "It's safe to be angry" into your chest in the mirror. You need to believe yourself.*

Me → *That's powerful, but I don't believe it yet.*

RC → *I totally get why those protectors are there, but they are going to have to rest at some point. You need to talk to the little girl inside you who is protecting you and tell her she can rest.*

Me → *Let me work on it.*

Me → *That's powerful, but I don't believe it yet.*

CHAPTER FORTY-FOUR

I count the days that turn into weeks. The time since I broke. The days I have not been producing income. The money leaving our bank account and not being replaced. I count the number of pills, the milligrams of THC. The number of memories I have shared and with whom.

I stare at the walls for hours, trying to do the math. The years and the ages of the stories, how old the adults were, what was going on in the world at that time. What did I say was happening, and what was actually happening? Untangling all the stories from the truth.

I track my schedule so I don't get lazy, attempting to fill my days with mindful and healthy activities to keep my mind from getting lost in the sea of agony. I give myself deadlines and push myself to do productive things like text friends and go for walks and paint. Each day is a marathon, dragging with each tick of the clock, but the weeks fly by, my old life getting further and further away.

I watch TV shows and movies I have already seen, hoping the predictability will protect me for surprise trips down the rabbit hole. But with the new capacity of my full intelligence now accessible, I can see layers deep into the writer's narrative. I can see through the layers upon layers of story to the writer's insight, the thoughts and feelings they can't put into words so they write them into visual imagery and clever dialogue.

My love for prestige drama has always been strong, a love of creators who bring a fresh perspective and unique voice to stories I have not considered before. A way to learn, not directly, about other's lives and lessons learned, to widen my awareness covertly.

Today I am watching *Station Eleven*, one of my favorite shows. I love the books of Charlotte St. John, the intricacy of her clever writing discussing heartbreaking insights. Upon first viewing, I appreciated the artistry of the acting. Seeing a person bring to life a character who has only ever existed in your mind, always interesting to see those emotion and movement choices. Obviously, I adore the character Kirsten, her strength and courage so palpable in Mackenzie Davis's performance.

But as I rewatch her journey, I begin to see a deeper meaning behind her flashbacks in time. I see her reliving her own trauma that has never been dealt with, and (spoiler alert) just before she may die, she has to step through the door of her own mind. Her door, like mine, has a scared little girl behind it, and she cannot heal until she listens to that little girl's story.

My watch pings me that my heart rate is too fast. The TV show fades from my vision as I see the door in my mind and wonder if I have strength like Kristen, to walk through and face what's on the other side. My breath begins to hitch, my eyes darting everywhere and seeing nothing. I open the door, and I am in the White Room….

Me → Voice recording: The White Room

Me → Can you talk???

RC → Briefly, I have an appointment in 15 min. I'll call you.

* * *

The screen flickers as the storm rages outside. It's one of those wild Texas summer storms, sunshine one minute and pouring rain the next. I tap the button to turn up the volume on my phone as I sit huddled on the couch shaking.

"I can hear that storm, wow!" RC exclaims as we exchange panicked hellos. "Are you safe?"

"I remember. I remember the babies. And the food wasn't safe to eat. And The White Room," I trail off as I gasp and heave for breath. Panic like bile rising in my throat, choking off the air from reaching my lungs as my vision sinks into blackness—and then white.

It's like remembering a scene in a movie, but not knowing which movie it is. You know the actors' faces, but can't think of their names. You don't remember this person being there…wait, that can't be how it goes. Images flashing bright as the lightning in the swirling clouds outside, horrible acts and feelings pressing on my conscious mind, searing their truth back onto the dark spots in my memory.

"Slow down, breathe," she says gently and firmly, always a kind coach. "You catch your breath. Let me see if my next appointment can reschedule. Just stay on the phone with me, OK? Keep breathing. Tap your finger into your chest and repeat, *This is not happening. I am just remembering. They can no longer hurt me. I am safe*. Let me hear you," she says distractedly as I focus on the words and repeat over and over.

A moment feels like forever. Fighting a war in my mind, to breathe, to let the searing images burn and sting and rush my system. The only way out is through.

"OK, my next client was able to move. We can talk for a while. Take a deep breath. Are you physically OK? You sound like you are breathing better." Her gentle tone is like a bright light shining on my embarrassment. I never thought I would be the kind of person who has panic attacks in the middle of the day and has to have other people move their appointments because of me. I cringe into the shame.

"I'm OK. I'll be OK," I pant as my airway relaxes a bit with the tapping. Weird how thumping my own chest and repeating those words pulls my brain out of the spiral.

"OK. Now, start at the beginning… you said something about The White Room. We already know about that. Are you remembering something new, or is it just more of the same?" She pauses to let me think. Logical thinking is helpful. Figuring out a timeline like a puzzle is easier than sorting through my childhood memories. It's hard to pick just one frame of the wild images flashing in my mind.

"How about telling me how old you were during this memory? Do you remember what grade you were in school?"

"Yeah, I was seven. First grade was really tough. The Mother pulled me from private school after my sister was born. Putting me in public school was a bold move on her part, but The Grandparents had bigger fish to fry, I guess. Honestly, I was kind of relieved. I didn't have to worry about members of the church working there. No one knew me. It was a totally new set of adults. Which was nice." I manage a small smile at the thought. The first place I remember being safe was at Fulton Public Elementary School.

It wasn't easy making the change. I didn't know that there were different kinds of schools with different rules, so I kept getting in trouble. There were rules about sitting down and going to the bathroom and talking, different rules than the Montessori School philosophy. They had double the class size and half as many teachers. It was hard to adjust to the control of having to ask to go to the bathroom or blow my nose. The structure of learning was difficult too. I was used to doing my work as fast as I wanted to, but learning at a slower pace left me time to daydream.

"Actually, it ended up being a life-saver because I was able to get access to a library for the first time." A small smile whispers across my lips at the thought of the old elementary school library room. The old tattered arm chairs and the smell of aging paper. Ms. Bailey, the sweet librarian who knew me by name the first week of school.

"They would let me check out three books at a time, and I checked out the max every week. I gobbled them up like candy. I love reading stories about different kinds of people, how other people live, are loved by their families, get through the bad times. It was critical access to information I would never get at home…" I trail off as I realize that's not normal. "I think people read books for fun, but I have always read to learn. I guess that's weird," I finish awkwardly, lost in reflection. RC stays quiet, letting the story ebb and flow.

"I was absent from school sometimes, when the inspection days are got really bad. Sometimes The Mother would give me too much special soda, and I couldn't leave the bathroom. Sometimes my insides hurt so bad from The Grandfather's experiments that I just couldn't sit in the desk all day. The Mother was down with what I now suspect is postpartum depression. She laid in bed for days, forgetting to make us food or take care of the baby. I didn't know how to cook so sometimes I didn't know what was bad to eat. My daddy had an important new job, so he was away on business during the week. Sometimes it was all too much, and I couldn't deal. I would just lie in bed with my sister, trying to keep her quiet so I could rest." I sound sad. It was a sad time, I remember. I was trying to manage so much; it was difficult to keep energy in my body.

"It turns out that The Mother was so sick because she was having another baby," I finish glibly, trying forcefully to shake off the sadness of

the little girl's story. "My little brother was born the summer after first grade. Finally a baby to name William. My daddy was so excited. He always wanted a little boy." I smile at the flicker of joy I feel for my daddy finally getting his wish.

"When they told me The Mother was going to have another baby, she was already six months pregnant. It was close to the end of the school year, and Rebecca was just beginning to walk. Anyone with a toddler knows how hard it is. Now I was going to have another baby to look after. I was exhausted just thinking about it." I stop to take a drink of water. RC coughs. The storm grumbles outside.

"I was relieved when they told me he was a boy. Boys, like my cousin Rick, don't have to be prepared for celestial marriage like girls do. They have a different process," I say, almost like an accomplishment. "The relief was almost enough to make it exciting. Then I realized I would have to help take care of two babies now. I could barely handle one, and now I would have two." The urgency rises in my chest, the old familiar buzz of panic.

"I worried all summer as I helped change diapers and clean up spit-up. How would I help take care of two babies and go to school? Taking care of one baby in the first grade was hard. Taking care of two babies in the second grade sounded impossible." The exasperation comes through the sadness. "I would sit in the old rocking chair with the two babies on my lap, rocking and singing little songs I made up to soothe them, worrying about schedules." My voice is soft now, the despair blanketing the burn of panic with its numbing heaviness. "The Mother could breastfeed, thank god, so I knew they would eat, but they would cry a lot and need changing and baths. If The Mother got too upset, she would hit, and

then the babies would cry some more. It seemed endless." I stop, lost to the loneliness. The responsibility like an albatross around my neck.

"I learned life just moves on anyway, whether you are ready or not. No matter how many prayers I sent up to heaven or how many plans I tried to make, I just wasn't ready for the new school year when it arrived…" At last the storm dumps the flood, and I am carried away into the whirlpool of memory.

AGE 7 THE WHITE ROOM

CHAPTER FORTY-FIVE

The first day of the second grade, I watch the sunrise peek over the houses across our sweet suburban neighborhood as I rock a just-settled three-month-old. His teeth are starting to come in so he is drooly and grumpy, loudly waking several times during the night. I decided to just rock him for the rest of the night so we could all get some sleep. But I couldn't go back to sleep, just sitting quietly watching the shadows fade into the pink glow of morning.

I gently lay the sleeping little boy down in his crib, sliding the side back up carefully so he doesn't fall out. There is drool on the shoulder of my nightgown and something sticking in my hair on top of one of the little pink rollers clacking in my ears. I hope it didn't ruin my curls. That's The Mother's most important job since The Grandfather buys my dresses. She will be mad if I mess them up.

I creep over to my dresser and smooth a hand over my dress I laid out the night before. A blue dress to wear today. Always a blue dress for special occasions. I have decided I will be glad about blue dresses. That's what my new favorite movie, *Pollyanna*, says to do, and she smiled when her legs got broken, so maybe it works.

I pull on the dress, carefully buttoning the three tiny buttons behind my neck, connecting the white lace collar in back. I stand in front of the mirror and carefully take my hair down from the rollers, snapping and unraveling each perfect brown curl. When it's done, I look like Shirley Temple, curls bouncing and flopping with a flip of my head. My hair is my best feature; everyone agrees.

I take my shoes with me as I walk into the hall, shutting the door softly behind me. I pad down the hall on bare feet, muffled footsteps in the blood-red carpet. It's quiet—that's nice.

I walk into the dark kitchen, searching for something to eat. My daddy is away on business so no meals are prepared this week, and I have learned my lesson about taking a chance on things in the refrigerator that I don't know are OK to eat. So I grab an apple that doesn't look too bruised. I munch on a bite as I sit at the table to pull on my new jelly shoes, my favorite part of the "first day of school" outfit.

I am doing my best. I am doing my best.

I think it over and over as I walk out the door with my new school supplies in hand. I pull the door shut tight and take a deep breath as I head out to walk to my first day of second grade.

Second grade seems pretty much like first grade. It's a lot of the same stuff repeated AGAIN. So boring, but I really like school. Every day, there is food. Every—single—DAY, I get a lunch tray. I have favorites, like mac-and-cheese day, but I don't mind eating any of it because I know it's safe to eat.

We get time to play with our friends on the playground after lunch. We don't have to work or be productive or even be learning, just play. I love the swings best. It almost feels like I can fly when I swing high, making the railing creak and knock. It's when I feel my body in a good way. All the zings and buzzing feel good, not like when it's hurting. Sometimes I am extra daring, and I jump off the swing right at the top, soaring for just a moment before I land crashing onto the dust.

And we have music class! Art and music are my favorite subjects, but The Mother HATES art, so I don't get to like art anymore. Our teacher,

Mrs. Creekmore, is so nice. She lets us be a little bit silly, which makes the working time so much easier. She teaches art with Ms. Bailey sometimes. We sing and paint and have a good ol' time.

All in all, it is a first day of school. I stuff my art project in the trash outside school on the way home, hoping the teachers don't see. But I can keep my music. She can't take that away from me, so I sing the new songs I learned all the way home, humming the words I can't remember yet.

When I walk in my front door, it's chaos—babies crying and The Mother screaming. I drop my bag by the door and rush over to pick up the toddler reaching around the fireplace corner. I soothe her with a finger in the mouth and stoop to the baby in the carrier to give a quick check to see why he is crying. A fallen binky quickly popped back into his mouth brings instant silence, leaving only the huffing Mother exasperated in the kitchen.

"Where the hell have you been?" she demands viciously. "We are going to be late," she says as she grabs her car keys and heads out the garage door.

I give little piddles of encouragement to Rebecca as I set her down and pick up Will's carrier, using the other hand to usher the wobbling toddler to the door and down the back stairs. Stairs can be tricky on new legs so I tell her to wait until I go set down Will and get him settled. Of course, she doesn't listen.

Tumble, hit, BUMP

I turn to see Rebecca lying at the bottom of the two small stairs leading down to the garage, feet over head, ruffled butt in the air, screaming at the top of her lungs. I just close my eyes and wait.

My sister has been angry from the first moment of her life, but as a toddler she is unbearable. She doesn't know how to turn it off. She will scream and wail for HOURS and HOURS, only stopping when she falls asleep. There is no talking to her, nothing will make her stop, and nothing is as bad as when she gets hurt. Which happens a lot for someone who has only been a human for one year. So I stand there frozen, knowing this means we will be trapped in the car with a wailing little baby. No matter where we are going, it's going to get worse.

* * *

My heart sinks when we pull into the driveway of The Grandparents' house. I never know when The Grandfather plans an inspection day, but this is the worst possible time. With Rebecca still screaming her head off, The Mother is in a real bad mood. She is going to tell The Grandfather that it's my fault Rebecca is crying, and I need to be extra punished—I just know it. Shit.

"You stay in the car," she says, looking daggers at me. "Rebecca, you better stop that crying and get out of the car right now," she commands as she gets out of the car and reaches for the back door to get Will.

Rebecca sniffs and quiets when I silently give her prayer hands and say pretty please with my lips. She knows something bad will happen if she doesn't obey the pretty-please hands. She scoots out of the car, and I turn back around quickly, just as both car doors slam shut. It's hot, but I don't mind. The window is down, and the magnolia tree is giving some shade. I almost doze off when I hear The Mother close the front door and head out down the steps. She gets in and starts the car without a word, heading down the street deeper into the neighborhood.

When I see the familiar white steeple poking above the trees, I begin to steel myself for what's to come. I know I can't stop it. This is coming from a higher power. It's important to shape me into an obedient young bride. That's what The Grandfather says. There are lots of rules and requirements to being a celestial bride. I am lucky I have him to prepare me for a man worthy of me.

But being prepared hurts A LOT. The Grandfather gets very angry if I cry or scream. It hurts his feelings because he is just trying to help me. So I am learning how to send my brain far away from the pain, like I saw in a TV show, so I don't scream or cry. And the inspection goes much quicker if I am silent and do whatever I am told. So I stiffen my back and start to think of some songs and stories I can remember to help my mind go away for the next few hours.

CHAPTER FORTY-SIX

The Grandfather is excited. There is a buzzing in the air; I can hear it. It sounds like bees.

I look around the White Room for the first time today, curiosity bringing my mind back to the room. I lie on my back, bare butt at the end of the bed, knees up and my dress flipped up on my tummy, white lace peeking up at the sky. I can see The Mother in the corner of my eye, sitting behind my right ear where I can hear her panting like a dog. I turn a little to see her eyes are big and black, fixed on The Grandfather. I follow her gaze to look down at the man standing between my open legs.

The Grandfather looks like a scientist standing at the foot of the raised table—feet apart, white clothes, gloves, little round light on his head. I can see a black cord connecting to something in his hands, but I can't see what it is. He reaches with his finger to flip a switch on the object, and the hum gets louder, changing pitch with the turn of a dial. My body begins to worry and suck inside itself. I roll my head back straight and desperately try to send my mind away from this.

FIRE

Fire enters my body through my butthole and races directly to my eyeballs. My body arches on the table, and my teeth clench shut real tight as the fire burns my insides and steals my breath.

The fire goes away, and now there is hot lava everywhere inside me. I can't see anything but white, white light, white, white, white.

SLAP

"Stop it! Stop it! Stop it!" I hear The Mother screaming in my ear as her long nails dig into the soft flesh inside my outstretched arm. I hear an animal dying. Is that what she is upset about, I wonder?

Slowly, I begin to realize that I am the animal that is crying out. The pain racing through my body is like nothing I have ever felt before. It's hard to breathe. I think I would just go ahead and die rather than feel this. I wonder if The Grandfather would let me go then. If I am not sealed to him.

I know I hurt, but it all becomes fuzzy, and parts go missing. The Mother slaps my face a few times, but I can't focus. The fire is raging so hot inside; I can't see or hear anything right.

The Grandfather picks me up. I get so scared I guess I black out because the next thing I know, I am sitting in Dr. Parks's house. Dr. Parks is our next-door neighbor. He is a dentist. I am confused, running my tongue around my mouth to see if I lost any teeth. I don't feel anything missing, just the lava making my whole body scream at my butthole. Dr. Parks says he is going to pinch me, and I start to cry, fat tears rolling down my cheeks. I can't help it. I hurt so bad already. I can't have another Uncle Brad right now. But the pinch feels soft after the hurt, and then a pink cloud comes and takes me away.

CHAPTER FORTY-SEVEN

I drift up from sleep to coals in the fire, still burning and hurting but not the lava level. I feel sticky, wet but cold. There is something cool on my forehead, soft on my cheek. It smells like roses and lemon Pledge, so I must be at The Grandparents' house. I lie still and listen. The house is quiet, and I hear soft breathing near my head.

I lift a corner of the washcloth on my eyes and peek out at the room. It's nighttime, everything outlined in blue and black, little slivers of silver where the moonlight comes through the window. I am lying on a couch in The Grandparents' room. I have a sheet and blanket wrapped around me on top of the couch, with a pillow under my cheek like a guest. I have never slept anywhere but the closet at The Grandparents' house.

I can see The Grandparents sleeping in their big bed across the large room. Fancy oak furniture looms in the night, dolls' eyes and small figurines looking less friendly in the dark. I need to go to the bathroom, but I am too scared, so I carefully roll over and drift back to sleep.

* * *

I stay on the couch at The Grandparents' for three days. The Grandmother brings little tiny sandwiches and soup, helps me to go to the bathroom. The Grandfather sits in his chair next to my head, watching *Matlock* and *Murder She Wrote* reruns and keeping track of my medicine. I sleep a lot. It is better than feeling the pain when I am awake. Even with the medicine, I am afraid to poop. I don't want anything to touch my butthole ever again. I hurt inside and out.

On the fourth morning, I wake up to The Grandmother sitting next to me holding my hand. I don't know what to say, so I just look at her and wait.

"You have to go home today," she says sternly, like maybe it's hard for her to say. "It's time your mother takes care of her own child." She is disappointed at how The Mother turned out; everyone knows that.

"I am sorry they did this to you," she says in a quiet voice, almost a whisper even though we are the only ones in the room. "I didn't know he would go this far. And your mother's an idiot, so she just goes along." She pauses, purses her lips, takes a deep breath, and continues. "Anyway, I wasn't going to let her torture you while you recovered. Lord knows that woman hates when anyone else gets attention. You'll have to look out for yourself now. I think you're strong enough." She gives me a little bag with my bloody dress and my medicine, a little pat on the cheek, and she leaves me alone.

* * *

It's been a week, and I still haven't taken a poop. My butthole is scabby and hurts still. I don't want to push anything out or wipe it at all. So I just hold it in.

But now my tummy hurts; my guts are cramping and full. I wiggle and twist on the couch as The Mother and I watch TV.

"Have you had a BM yet?" she says slyly. She and The Grandmother have been asking a million times a day.

"No, I don't need to yet," I say casually. She knows I am lying, but what can she do? She can't make me poop.

"Hmmm…" she says, picking up the phone and punching in rapid numbers.

"Hey, Frannie, how are you? Good to hear. Yeah, I was just wondering if you wanted to bring DeDe over and have dinner tonight? Maybe stick something in the crockpot?" She pauses to listen to the bubbling acceptance.

I brighten. DeDe is my best friend. It's fun when she gets to come over. But then my tummy gives an angry poke, and I wince at the pain. Slowly, I look up at The Mother, rocking in her chair, still talking on the phone. The Cheshire smile spreads across her lips as she gets up and heads into the kitchen. She pulls the special strawberry soda from the back of the fridge and grabs a glass.

"Uh-huh, yeah," she responds into the speaker as she makes the special treat for my cramping tummy.

She nods and mmmms as she listens to the latest gossip, handing the glass of soda to me with a shove of her chin. Drink it, she mouths.

A few hours later, I sit on the toilet miserably staring at my dangling toes. My butthole is ragged and bloody. It feels like I am pooping fire. I can hear the merriment happening in the other room with The Mother playing games with my best friend while a week's worth of poo explodes out my burned and scabbed butthole. I don't get to play with DeDe very long since I keep having to use the bathroom and then fix my face from crying. I am so embarrassed and upset; I can't even enjoy the little time I do get to play.

DeDe gives me a tight hug goodbye and promises me that we are still best friends. She doesn't mind if I have the poos—it happens to everyone sometimes. She is a nice friend.

I sit on the porch eating an apple and enjoying the cool cement on my burning butt. I think The Mother is using the special soda to make me poo. That's the only thing I can think of since I haven't been eating much, 'cuz my tummy hurts. I sigh and lie over on my side, pressing my cheek to the step as a tear slides down my nose and drips on the concrete.

Chapter Forty-Seven

AGE 45 THE FACILITY

CHAPTER FORTY-EIGHT

"That's awful," she says with a sniff. What else is there to say, really? It's a lot.

"You believe me?" my seven-year-old squeaks out, her little shivering presence still sitting cradled in my mind as she recovers from telling her story.

"Yes. Absolutely. Every word," she says firmly, without hesitation. I know it's her job, but it's a job I pay her to do. It's stupid to pay someone to do a job and then not listen to their expertise. I can't quite believe it yet, but I am going to make myself listen. And that means starting to believe myself.

"You are so lucky I had a flexible client today and had time to talk," she says a bit shakily. "We may need to talk about getting you some more help. This is so much, and I am not set up to support you full-time. I want you to be safe and have resources when you need them."

I know she is scared. This is getting worse and worse, and there is still a little bit down there I can see sulking in the shadows. "Are you thinking I need to go to a facility?" I ask meekly, like a child taking their punishment for being too bad.

"Well, maybe. But it would need to be somewhere that specializes in trauma and NOT addiction. Those two things are often together, and that's not what you need. And you need to be at some place with women only. I don't want you trying to talk about this stuff with men in the room, at least not at first..." She trails off. She is worried I will be mad. I don't want to be sent away.

"I understand," I say meekly. "It's a lot for you to handle alone." I am always a lot to handle. Dave is struggling with the stress of my life—my work schedule, my grand parties, my insane family—and me being out of commission has been more than he bargained for.

"You are not being sent away. You just need more time than I can give you right now," she says quickly. "There is a place I know of that is women-only and doesn't treat drug addition. It's in the Keys. Do you like dolphins?"

Making the decision to commit yourself to a mental health facility is a humbling process. It requires extreme patience and dedication to navigate our healthcare system to get the care you need all while being at the absolute lowest point of your life.

There are two mental health facilities that are women-only, do not treat addiction, and accept out-of-network insurance (there are none in-network) in the US. I have been out of work for months, but am lucky enough to have a husband who works at a job with good benefits. Paying thousands of dollars out of our quickly emptying pocket to go to a nuthouse is tough to justify, let alone advocate for.

But that's what I am going to do. I make dozens of calls to facilities, coordinate maximum use of benefits, connect the right people in behavior health coverage and physical health coverage because those are different companies and they don't work together without patient request. I gather confirmation numbers and case numbers and fees and phone numbers. Submit to telling and retelling the grand arcs of my story to advocates and admins, proving I need the care I am asking for. Finally, spending hours on an application to be accepted into the healthcare center of my choice. Sharing the most intimate details of my life with a stranger I will

never meet to get care that only 30 years ago would just be electroshock treatment or a lobotomy. I shake and shiver and float in silence as the interview goes on and on. The hardest process of my life during the hardest moment of my life. It's easy to see how easy it would be to give up.

But I have too much to live for. I have my son, my husband, my daddy. My best friend KB checks in on me and sends me funny memes about being crazy old ladies together. My husband books a flight to come with me so I am not alone on the plane. My daddy and Nanny come to visit, sharing support and kindness even though they are dubious about sending me away. We can all agree—this is too much for any of us to deal with on our own. We need help. This is what's available. So I will go and fight.

* * *

I cling to Dave as he hugs me goodbye in front of The Facility van at the Miami airport. I sob openly, and so does he, wrapped in an embrace that needs to last a lifetime. Airport traffic honks and whips around us, the driver from The Facility patiently waiting to get me in the van as we say our last goodbyes.

"Get better. You can do this," Dave whispers in my ear through choked sobs. "I love you. You are always my favorite."

"I love you," I whisper and turn away to step up into the van. I climb into the back seat and slide across the vinyl to the window, not looking back. I pop in my earbuds as she slides the door shut. Stereosonic guitar drifts through my head as I settle in for the 1.5 hour drive from the airport.

I have never been away from my boys this long. A 30-day commitment is the minimum they require for admittance, with an expectation that I can extend to 60 or 90 days if I need it. I can't imagine why I would need to be in 30 days, let alone 90, so it's all open-ended for now. One step at a time.

Today is day one. Today, I just had to get on the plane and get in this van. If I can't take it, I can quit and go home. It is a voluntary facility; I am not captive there. Dave, Nanny, my daddy, KB, and RC all send me messages reminding me I am loved and I can come home any time. I hug my phone to my chest, their numbers resting safely inside, a lifeline when before I had none.

I lay my head against the glass, watching the palm trees and ocean waves slide across my reflection like a girl in a movie. The salty tang of the air like a dream remembered. I like to pretend that little girl is in a movie, the music a thoughtfully chosen score to set up the scene of trial and triumph to come. Or at least, that's what I hope happens.

CHAPTER FORTY-NINE

It's nighttime, and I am hiding in the tiki hut in the backyard of The Facility. I am drawing in my scribble notebook, long palm leaves with sharp points and wild jagged circles. I have an official journal I am supposed to keep while I am here, but I brought another to write the stuff I don't want the staff to read. I switch from drawing and slash in my messiest handwriting a scathing entry:

Journal Entry - Day 1

This place is hard. Today was a goddamn shit show. The five-plus-hour intake process is excruciating. Seeing my entire life dumped on the floor exploded and messy. People I don't know or trust sorting through my things, looking for the tiny crumbs of personal dignity that aren't allowed.

No razors to shave my legs. No outside food or drinks. No phones (at least for the first week). No soft pink clouds of comfort.

I sit for hours, answering questions about the rot and ruin that brought me so low. Intimate questions. Challenging questions. Endless details of medical conditions and symptoms experienced. Detailed descriptions of physical abuse and reckless behavior. They grill me over details, but I can't do anything but squirm in the hardback chair and try to take my mind anywhere other than that open suitcase on the floor with my life hanging out the side like intestines hanging from a disemboweled corpse while this evil crone pokes even further into my life. I have been traveling all day. I am irritated, scared, and exhausted, but there is no comfort here. This is a facility to work, they say.

I tell them I need my medication. With the time change and the early travel, I am off schedule. I expected them to trust me that I know when I need my meds, but I am an unassessed crazy person now. I am not to be trusted. So they tell me to wait until I am fully processed and my meds can be verified. So I wait.

As the light fades outside, I start to get really shaky. I am hours past due for my meds, and the staff doesn't seemed concerned about it at all. "I need to take my medication, or I am going to have a panic attack," I tell them over and over.

"OK, when are you going to have a panic attack?" one of the staff asks straight-faced and hard-eyed. I stare at her aghast.

"Uh, any minute now since I am HOURS past due for my anti-anxiety AND antidepressants," I snap. I am shaking so hard my teeth are chattering; my spine is stiff and sore.

"OK, we are here to help you through that." She dismisses me like a child and sends me to sit and wait as they continue making arrangements to move me to a new location to finish intake and get my room set up.

I sit in hopeless fury. I am a fucking adult, I am not an addict. I should be able to make a health decision about myself. Meds I took in the wee hours of the morning before I got on the plane are long gone by this point. I feel the fear take over my mind as the dark threatens to creep in and swallow me whole.

They take me out to the van to move locations, the driver running back inside to get something forgotten. Sitting in a soupy hot van alone and unmedicated brings a wave of uncertainty—*Why did I do this to myself? Can I do this? Why am I doing this? What am I doing here? What am I doing!*

Seeing words like *mental illness* and *abuse* so many times on those forms, the probing questions bringing up thoughts I haven't yet been ready to face bring the heat of panic rising in my face.

The hot van sweltering in the Florida sunset fills my lungs with the swampy humidity as I fight to breathe through the building panic. *What did I do to myself? What if they keep me? What if they say I am too crazy and send me away, and I never get to go home?*

I melt. I gasp. I shake. The shaking, the vise grip on my spine is ever vigilant. Nowhere is safe, or never has been before.

I drip and run and crumble. *And they don't know me. They don't know me, and they think I am crazy. They are afraid. My radioactive damage too hot for anyone to look at. I am the only one who can carry all of this. All of it.*

Through the haze of the oncoming attack, I hear my logical self whisper, *I will have to fight myself. Fight for myself again. Fight for the control that comforts and crushes me. The only weapon strong enough to withstand the heat and calm the scared child within.*

The driver comes back to find me collapsing in my seat and runs to get a therapist inside. The unkind lady who poked and prodded me all afternoon tries to soothe me enough to get out of the van, her tough-love approach grating on my every nerve. "If you don't calm down, we are going to send you to the hospital and send you home. You have to want to be here and fight this. Come on. Get out of the van and fight it," she commands, barely audible over my gasping and sobbing. "Sit down right here in the shade and take some deep breaths."

"I can't. I can't breathe," I gasp and heave. Visions of being lost in the woods, running and sweating, flash in my mind.

"Yes you can. If you don't want to be sent away, you have to try," she barks through the trauma erupting through my body. So I try.

I focus, I breathe, I try and try and try. Until I finally get my mind out of the memories and focused on my own hands in front of me. Her stern face willing me to calm down. The van driver and interns staring at me like a circus act. I am mortified.

The rest of the evening is a long drawn-out blur. Arriving at the lodging house. Lonely though there are kind faces around. It's hard to look at the kindness when you were so bad at judging what was behind the mask for so long…or at least out of practice. And I am so embarrassed of the meltdown some just witnessed. Shame and despair claim my voice so I silently follow whatever orders are given until I am FINALLY able to sit alone for a few minutes. I am going to get my meds and go to sleep and leave this day behind.

But I made it through. Because that's what I do. And I will do what it takes, and do it well, because that's what I do. But this is awful. More horrible than I could have imagined and I know this is a good place generally. My heart breaks for all those women who did this alone in places not surrounded by palm trees and a pool. guess it's just awful no matter where you are.

* * *

I close my little scribble book when one of the ladies comes out on to the patio. "Time for lights out."

Ever dutiful, I immediately grab my water mug and leave the soft couches. I walk carefully around the pool deck beaded with condensation in the cooling night air, up the steep winding staircase to the second-

story patio. The stairs are slippery. Everything in the Keys is wet outside, so I take them cautiously one by one, water slapping on my bare feet.

Shoes line the patio outside of the sliding glass doors, mine still in a box downstairs. I step over them and into the deserted common room. It's large and spacious, lined with a large sectional and several fluffy chairs. It's where this house has group every day, so I am told. So much of the information is a blur at this point.

I head through the common room and into the long hallway, padding down the worn carpet to my room at the end. I hear Pink's "Hey Now" blasting from our room, and my body slumps. I don't want to be the person who has to tell her new roommate to turn down the music at lights out on my first day. Rather than face her, I turn and head back down the hall. At the entry to the common room, I turn right and head down the stairs instead. It's FINALLY 9:01 p.m., time for my night meds. I can get those and just go to sleep. (I hope.)

In the Keys, the houses are mostly built on stilts or with the ground floor more of a patio area in case of a hurricane. Though the weather is hot and the view is beautiful, being this close to the ocean on both sides brings its challenges. Most houses are prepared for flooding, with main living areas usually being on the top floor.

I creep down the stairs across the entryway to the office door. The top half of the door is open, where the therapist on duty is preparing for meds distribution before lights out.

"I'm here for my meds," I say softly with my head bowed. Setting myself up as a good girl now will help me when dealing with my troublesome roommate later. I met my roommate for just a short time earlier; it wasn't pleasant. If I think with compassion, we are all not at our best here, so

I am postponing making judgements and will avoid her until I get on meds and get some rest. I would think in a house of damaged girls it would be pretty acceptable to just be quiet until I am ready to talk. I think everyone can respect that.

"Sure." She smiles and turns to get the little pills.

"Are you settling in OK?" she asks casually as she watches me take the pills and records it in her notebook.

"Yes," I respond quickly before gulping the water, "although my roommate is playing some music kind of loud. I know I should be able to talk to her about it, but I am not at my best today and don't want to make it an issue and risk a bad reaction. Do you think you could help me out?" I say pleadingly, leaving the solution open-ended for her input.

"She shouldn't be playing that. I'll let her know," she says smartly, like a school proctor attending to a possible distraction. She has a peculiar way of speaking, like each word has been measured and assured of its importance. Fitting with her short cropped hair and tiny pink bow barrette.

"Thanks, I appreciate the help," I say gratefully and step back for her to lead the journey back up the stairs. I decide to make a quick trip to get some water before bed, giving the little bow lady time to chat with my roommate. I loiter at the fridge until I hear her clipped walk downstairs and then I creep quietly down the hall. I tiptoe until I reach the half shut door, listening through the now-deafening silence for a hint of what's going on inside… but it's quiet.

I push open the door carefully, but the room is empty. Maybe she is downstairs getting meds?

I quickly dash into the bathroom we share and brush my teeth, pee, and pull on my PJs. I turn off the lights and jump into bed, my reading lamp and book snuggled up under the covers to take me away from this awful place.

CHAPTER FIFTY

I wake up to an empty room. I close my eyes in relief, a new day with a quiet start. 6:30 a.m. yoga class is not my first choice of activities today, but I put myself into this place so I am gonna do everything the best I can.

It's already above 80 degrees. The humidity is beading on the screened-in porch as the sun peeks over the horizon. The other girls roll out in their active wear, wiping sleepy eyes and nursing cups of coffee. We line up in a row and spread out mats, the kind yogi talking softly about breathing and setting intentions.

The movement is familiar; the heat is oppressive. As I move through the poses, sweat drips down every part of my body, straining in the soupy air. My mind struggles to stay focused. Morning meds aren't available for another two hours. I shake and quiver, but I participate to the best of my ability.

Some girls do the advanced moves, most just participating because they have to. One girl lies on her side and never moves, tears sliding down her cheeks silently. I try to focus on the yogi, breathe into a space that is calm, but my eyes are drawn to the variety of ladies around me. Most especially my roommate, who has appeared at the other end of the line radiating hate like a shield. I avert my eyes to avoid meeting her black stare. I can feel her gaze burning a hole in my head.

When we finally blissfully rest in corpse pose, I struggle to keep calm lying on my back in the open air. I grip the mat with my fingertips, eyes open, straining to keep my mind here on the patio—not on my back in

the White Room. I don't want to make another scene for everyone to discuss. The panic attack I survived yesterday making a show for all the girls in the house to see was a grand enough entrance that I intend not to repeat.

We namaste and file back into the blasting icy air of the common room, most girls padding directly into their rooms. I avoid my roommate and slip back to my room carefully, her heavy trudge audible behind me. My spine tenses, and my mind flashes on potential solutions to be safe in the coming confrontation.

She wastes no time bursting into the room with a purpose. "You didn't have to tell the staff on me," she spits, her jowls quivering and her hands flexing. "You could have just asked me to turn the music off. You don't have to tell on me. I don't know what kind of person you are, but that's not how we do things where I am from. You need to talk to me directly, not go to tell Mommy."

I imagine steam coming out of her ears like in the cartoons, her red face and messy hair adding to the wildly over-the-top frenzy that is coming from her mouth. Her body radiates hate and anger. Mine responds with fawn and flight.

"Oh. I'm sorry. I just mentioned it while I was getting my meds. Won't happen again," I say without making eye contact as I grab my robe and head into the bathroom and shut the door. I stand quietly, listening to her bang around and grumble about "this place" and "put up with this shit" and then stomp out the door.

A sigh of relief escapes as I slouch over the sink and drop my head. I can survive this—I must. I have worked too long and built too much to

just let it all fall now. I give myself a hard stare in the mirror and turn on the shower. One more step.

* * *

Journal Entry - Day 2

I have never been to a group therapy session, but it's pretty much the same thing you see in movies. Everyone sits in a circle, shares stories, the group nods and listens, and the facilitator provides insight.

Today is another girl's last group. She is going home tomorrow. As a final project, she had to compose an artistic timeline of her life. This is an important project for all the girls that "graduate" to go home, to make a timeline with all the important events in your life and talk about them. For some, it's a line with a few hash marks; for others, it's an elaborate painting with dates all over the place. Creative expression is extremely important, as long as it helps you tell your story.

Her story is a sad one, filled with a mother similar to mine—always controlling and belittling, the building blocks of a woman's life who was built to serve others. The constant criticism of her weight and face and her demeanor being a necessary tool to capture the ultimate prize—a husband. Living with those expectations and then being confused when her marriage turned out to be a house of lies. I capture some of her words to help remind me that I am not the only one with a mother who is awful:

My mom laughed when I fell down but got mad when I laughed at her falling down.

I didn't want to wipe the blood off; I wanted someone to see it. They kept going until I screamed. Then they just kept going.

I realized she fucked with me on purpose. I would never be enough.

My husband didn't know what to do with me when I was crying so much, so he ignored me, and it made me feel worse.

I realized it wasn't me, it wasn't personal, it could have been any kid, I was just born her daughter. *(This one hit hard.)*

She was an adult; I was a kid.

What would it mean if I stopped looking for validation from her?

Explore what it would be like to sit with it, to work it yourself, trusting yourself to figure it out rather than reaching for a friend/partner.

I've learned I need to love myself before I love other people. <3

It's fascinating, hearing another person's story from start to finish with everything laid bare. No cover-ups or editing. No "we don't talk about that," skipping over the triggers, or family members correcting you. Seeing the strengths gained from the work, of saying it out loud knowing it is the truth. Your truth. That's what I want, to say it all out loud and believe it.

That feels like a lofty goal sitting among these girls, shaking and twitchy, listening to more stories of parents who cared so little, partners that build worlds of lies for people they are supposed to love. So many men who are angry and hurting, reaping devastation into so many lives just so they don't have to live their own. Adults who hurt little girls, tear apart families, cheat on spouses, hit and rape and ignore the women who try to fix it. Building structures to protect their bad behavior, rules and laws that keep their kind in power to ensure their safety.

It's heartbreaking because I am so lucky. My daddy loves me. He has always loved me. He has his flaws, has struggled and toiled, and he is still a kind and loving man. My husband is a giver, always helping others.

He loved me when he didn't know why I needed what I did, went along with capers that were ridiculous because he loves and trusts his wild wife. He has helped me create a young man who is a joy. Jack is kind and thoughtful, never hurting or raging, learning from the incredible men I am lucky to have in my life.

The Grandfather and The Uncle are also men in my life, the bad kind that the girls in this room can relate to, but I do feel so grateful that I have examples of both. I know the truth of the full spectrum of what kind of men are in the world, and knowledge is power.

I am a bit weirded out by the lack of comfort in this setting. It's weird to see girls openly bawl, cry, rage, and have outbursts with no gentle hugs or dramatic exits. Some girls cry while others stare vacantly. A girl is silently bawling into a pillow next to the therapist who sits silently ignoring her, all focus on the speaker. It's nice in a weird way, but so lonely. To know I will be the one suffering alone soon, with no gentleness of a friend or family to comfort me. It's not a pleasant thought.

But I listened and took notes like a good student. I learned a lot from this one session, from the speaker and reading the room. I plan to learn more no matter what it takes. I am going to get better, damn it, even if it kills me.

I am continuing to scribble because I need to have something to focus on so my eyes don't wander to my furnace of a roommate staring daggers at me across the room. That's going to be a problem.

* * *

After group, Jessica the lead therapist asks my roommate to speak with her privately. I watch them whisper a minute and then walk quietly,

heads still bent together as they walk away. I sit frozen, doodling absently in the margins of my journal, listening to the chatter of the girls as they awkwardly pat the girls who are crying. No one else seems to notice their exit so I relax a bit, accepting this may be taken care of without my input.

A few moments later, Jessica pops her head back around the corner. "Can I talk to you a minute?" she asks me with a pointed stare.

I look up and smile a big bright smile and stand up immediately, "Of course." I walk around the side of the divider wall and into the hallway where she stands in her flowing broomstick skirt and jangling jewelry. Very Professor Trelawney in a Pacific Northwest kind of way.

She smiles her soft, kind smile and looks at me directly. "I know there was an issue with the radio last night. I'd like to help you and Shelly work things out. Are you open to that?"

"Oh, sure, of course," I say at once, eager to please and get this person on my side. I like Jessica. Being in her presence is like stepping into the art room or the library at an elementary school, all bright colors and kind, softspoken words of encouragement.

"I appreciate your willingness to participate." She smiles as we walk down the hall to the room I share with Shelly. There is loud banging and swearing coming from the partially closed door, but Jessica confidently pushes it open and steps right into the light, my shadow slipping behind her onto my bed, grabbing a pillow and hugging it to my lap. I can do this.

"Shelly, can you stop that activity for a moment and come sit with us?" she says so sugary and sweet. It floats like cotton candy into that wild whipping machine that is my roommate.

"Sure." She throws down a hanger she has been preparing and stomps over to sit on the floor like a cross child. Fuming and puffing, crossing her arms and looking at the sky. It looks like she has been packing to leave. I feel a little guilty at the relief that sweeps through me at that thought.

"OK, Shelly, there was an incident last night with the music. You wanted it on. She wanted it off. Are those facts right?" she asks logically. Her voice is high and girlish, almost like she is speaking to toddlers to soften the blow of the intelligence behind them. It's an interesting technique, hiding behind the rainbows.

"No!" she screams, building to a rage ready to burst. "I ASKED her if she liked music, and she said YES!" Exasperated and huffing again like an angry elephant. "I told her how much I liked Pink, and SHE said she did too so I put some on. You know, upbeat music! Since we all feel so awful here! You know, because I still don't have my meds. And this is NOT what I thought I was getting into here. This place is awful! I thought you were going to take care of me! And instead, I can't get my meds and you make me do yoga at 6 a.m. after I didn't get ANY sleep at all because I can't take a shower in there because there is no lock on the door and I don't want to talk about why I can't take a shower without a lock on the door because my father molested me and he used to come into the shower and she doesn't even understand that I am having a hard time and I just wanted to listen to music and if she had just TOLD ME that she wanted it off I would have turned it off but NOOOOOOO!" I cower reflexively, jerking with each syllable as she gets louder. I can see her anger ignite as she watches me sink back from her, rage exploding as she sees my overreaction to her as the same she suffered so many times. "We don't treat people like that where I am from! You have a problem

with me, you come talk to ME about it!" she screams as she throws down the notebook in her hand and stands up. "I'm leaving. This place is crazy! Or you have to move me to another room or something because I am NOT spending one more minute with this girl," she spits and snarls as she throws clothing into a suitcase.

"Shelly, I understand you are upset, but throwing things is not acceptable. Do you understand?" Jessica does have a big girl voice. It is the same one I use when the dog is in the road and he better do what I say so he doesn't get in trouble.

"I just don't want to be here!" she screams, but she's losing steam and drops to the bed in sobs. I sit frozen in a ball, knees hugged tight to my chest, hands gripping my shins. Jessica and I have made eye contact a few times. I like that she checks on me. I give her the look that says I will trust her to handle this if she keeps me safe, but we are on thin ice here. She nods.

Jessica guides Shelly gently back to her seat facing my bed, the bunks side by side but not far enough away for either of us.

"OK, what is your response to Shelly's concern of coming to her to discuss issues directly?" she says as she turns to me. It's a soft little bubble she bats over to me for my chance to participate.

I take a deep breath before I respond, "I understand why you are upset. I recognize I could have handled it better. It was a hard day, and I was not at my best. We are all struggling here. I understand that. I hope you can too." My voice is steady and calm, practiced and poised. I think it's the composure that breaks her.

"Oh, I don't give a shit. What you did was WRONG," she roars. "I have been having a hard day for my whole life! My dad and my uncle hurt me, and my husband hurt my kids and—"

"Lady, I was still being abused two years ago. FORTY FUCKING YEARS of abuse. We are ALL FUCKING ABUSED HERE. You are not special. There is plenty of abuse to go around," I burst out, a flame of defiance I haven't seen in so long I forgot it was there.

Her eyes bulge, and her steam turns to a raging inferno as she surges to her feet and I dart out the door. I give a shrug to Jessica as I pin her with my eyes. I tried.

* * *

"Can I speak with you a moment?" Jessica asks some time later. I am sitting in the common room with the other girls, discussing our assignment for the day as if nothing happened. Ta-da!

"Thank you for not discussing this matter with the other girls." She speaks low in the hallway so the other girls can't hear. "I'm really sorry that situation happened that way," she says quietly. "I appreciate you trying to communicate and participate." She looks at me with her big Bambi eyes, and there aren't any clouds of deceit, just sadness.

"Me too. I tried—I really did. I mean, we are all having a rough time right now. I just couldn't take it anymore," I plead with Jessica to believe I am not a bitch who would treat someone like that. "I just couldn't stay in there anymore," I finish lamely, panic rising in my throat again.

I am so embarrassed, cowering and fleeing like a scared child. I am 45 years old, and that lady is a bitch. I should have turned the other cheek and ignored her. I just didn't have it in me today.

"I understand. I watched your reactions to her throwing things. You stayed much longer than you wanted to, I think," she says with a smile, surprising me. She looks at me imploringly, seeing how much I am willing to share, how much I am holding back.

My head snaps up to search her face. "Yes, when she threw things, it scared me. It reminded me of The Mother when she was angry." My face is burning, eyes bright and brimming. "I feel sorry for her kids. I bet it's worse at her house," I say, lip trembling. "I don't want to go back in there. Can we maybe change rooms?" I ask meekly, but I don't know what I will do if she says no. I can't be alone with that woman again.

"I understand. Let me see what I can do. Today, we are going on a field trip so maybe that will cool things down. We are going on a glass-bottomed boat with all the girls. Should be easy to give each other some space," she says breezily. I nod, advice I intend to heed immediately.

"Take a deep breath. Try and find your calm. Trust the process," she advises as she steps around the banister to the stairs. "I am going to check to see if the van is here. Go get ready to leave, OK?"

* * *

The glass-bottomed boat ride did help. Spending an afternoon on a boat in the ocean is the best thing that's happened since I got here. Not too hard to avoid Shelly—she seems to want to avoid everyone.

I stick to myself and don't say much to anyone. The other girls are all chatting around me like a cloud of birds as we move from the boat to the coffee shop and back to The Facility. It's easy to stare out the window and pretend you don't exist; there are lots of girls here who do that.

I'm relieved when we finally get back to the boarding house. I hurry upstairs to my room and tuck myself up with a book and my journal on the bed before Shelly is out of the van. I turn away from the door, hoping to establish my willingness to coexist but not to congregate.

But Shelly never comes back. I eventually join the other girls at dinner, small talk over bland chicken. I am fascinated at the stories behind these girls' eyes, written on their skin and in their bones. It's written in the tension that a new girl brings up old guards so I stay quiet and only speak when spoken to, retreating to my room until lights out.

And still no roommate.

Journal Entry - Day 2 (cont)

We went on the water today. I spent the entire boat ride on the top deck soaking up the salty breeze and the waves. Didn't speak to any of the other girls. I met two young people, twentysomethings starting out in life. They had tattoos and blue hair, went to fancy art school, and studied abroad. They love literature and sculpture, and have opinions on movie directors. One had decided to change their name and discard gender norms. Their parents loved them openly and proudly, hugging and laughing with them both equally. I eavesdropped on their beautiful family and missed my own. My beautiful boys whom I love just like that.

Jessica and I talked briefly on the ride home, checking in on the Shelly drama. Jessica was proud of my handling of the situation. She thinks I did well managing my own fear until I had to leave. We will discuss it in more detail at our next 1:1 session when we have some privacy, she promises. She did remind me that I did not do anything TO Shelly; she was only impacted by my choices. She is an adult who chooses her own actions, and that is not my responsibility.

It is OK to ask for what I need in a way that enables me to feel safe. I didn't do anything wrong. I just need to grow into the person who is better equipped to manage asking for what I need.

Always more work to do here. Hopefully, I can rest before I start another day.

CHAPTER FIFTY-ONE

Shelly appears in the lobby the next morning as we are preparing to leave for another building for orientation. She shuffles around hugging her blanket and looking sheepish. She pouts like a baby, puffing cheeks and blowing little tufts of air, drooping her bottom lip and exaggerated puppy-dog eyes. Her delight at the caregivers' attention is her only flaw in the performance. We avoid eye contact as we board the van and head to the other building.

Shelly and I are attending orientation today. Two other new girls join us, a spicy Latina and a demure Southern blonde. Rules and restrictions, warnings and advice—I am here of my own accord, I am an adult, and I will leave if I want to. Safety rules I absolutely understand, keeping razors and meds locked up under supervision, but no junk food? Seriously? Feels like a dumb idea to isolate traumatized women and limit their access to chocolate and wine.

We four head up the stairs to share lunch with the girls arriving from the other building. The chef waves us in. "Lunch is ready. Come fix you a plate." We file in, carefully stepping over the girls draped around the small coffee tables and sitting on the floor picking at their plates. I fix a small salad and sit on the floor next to the blonde from orientation.

"Hiii," she drawls with the most lovely Southern accent, "you doing OK?" She gives me a little rub of a circle on my back. "The first few days can be pretty rough, I know." Her eyes darken for a moment, then refocus with a smile. She is a lady; she knows how to keep that smile in place.

"Yeah, I'm alright, I guess. It's been rough at the other house," I say, desperate to talk to someone. I don't want to spread rumors at our house, but I am worried sick about my roommate who is currently picking at the salad and complaining about some ingredient.

"Oh really? Yeah, I hear there was some ruckus over there last night." She doesn't pry; her manners are too good. "Well, I'm Cardinal, but everyone just calls me Cards. I'm from the great state of Mississippi. Where you from?" She says it with the weary smile of a beauty queen at the end of a meet-and-greet. She is a beauty, with bright blue eyes and bright pink cheeks. We all look a mess in this place, except for the young ones who still insist on the black eyeliner and mascara, and her warm glow is a light in the gloom.

"Dallas. Dallas, Texas… I'm a lucky girl to be all this way from home." I smile back, the first genuine smile in days.

"I'm Catalina! You can call me Lina, Cat, Catalina, or Hot Bitch. I like them all," says the other girl as she plops down next to us, swinging her gorgeous long brown hair and laughing, dark eyes sparkling. Her energy is so different than the other girls here, sparks flying to the point that everyone else seems a black hole.

"Hi, lovely to meet you, Lina. And where did you say you are from?" I ask politely as she settles back into the couch, snuggling up close to Cards like a little child.

"Cards is my momma in here. We got here on the same day and hit it off, and we ended up roommates! It's amazing. I don't know what I would do without her." She snuggles in tighter as Cards laughs and gives her motherly pat.

"Oh, well now," Cards twangs like lemonade on a summer night, "you just needed a little extra love, right?" She smiles at Catalina; Catalina smiles back. Two peas in a pod. I couldn't be more jealous.

Journal entry - Day 3

Friday is when we have group all together. All the girls from all three buildings come do activities and discuss a topic together. After lunch, we all sat together in the upstairs living room and discussed today's topic: existential questions. For example:

As a human, I see myself as _

My views on freedom and responsibility for myself include

It's an odd thing, trying to describe who I am as a human being. I scribble some answers on the worksheet quickly so I can get a peek at the other girls. One girl is only 18, dark eyes, blue hair and parallel scars running the length of the arm she uses to write. A lady well into her 60s sits sour-faced and silent on the end of the couch, hugging a pillow and staring at the floor. There are old ladies and young women, beauty and courage. And pain. So much pain tugs at the faces and pulls the eyes down, shame and loneliness heavy in the room.

As the more-tenured girls share their thoughts, I find I begin to get wiggly quick. It's uncomfortable being with this many women who are so hurt. Wounded beasts who slash and cut with their input, eager to spew the venom to make it go away. It's scary, seeing the way some women use their abuse to justify their behavior. I try to pipe in with a cheerier perspective, but we are not here for sunshine.

My abuse is not a weapon that I use to control others or guilt them into softer treatment. Kindness is more genuine and feels more real

when it is earned from an invested relationship. Unfortunately, so many people wear shiny, happy faces to hide their malcontent. Then they get very uncomfortable when they see that I have more pain than they can imagine and still I am not an asshole. It's an awful mirror I carry without knowing it.

I am at a facility that caters *only* to females with trauma. It used to be, when I said that, I thought only of those who chose an abusive relationship or suffered a horrible accident. Now I realize how many men and women like to hurt little girls. Moms and dads. Friends and husbands. They walk around like everyone else, pretending that no one can see so it isn't wrong. There are enough for us all, and they find us like a dog sniffing through the trash. They look for the abuse cower, the flinch and the inability to say no, or stop. They feed on it like caffeine or cocaine, craving that next jolt of power when they learn they can do anything and never get in trouble.

Because the truth is that they have been ruthless enough to create power structures to protect each other and to facilitate narratives to destroy any fool who dares have tits and speak out. I see this as plain as day on the faces around me. I know I came here to work, but I was not prepared for the lack of empathy. Everyone is on their own here. You can't save someone from drowning when you are at the bottom of the sea, I guess.

After the session, a counselor pulls me aside and quietly lets me know I will be moving. They have arranged for my things to be moved into a room in this building with Cards and Lina. I breathe a sight of relief. Anything away from Shelly is a step in the right direction.

I sit in the new building, my new roomies in the kitchen, chatting and cleaning and putting things away. It's soft and timeless, the fabric of the bonds that are weaved over olive oil and salt. These women are thoughtful and work with each other rather than yelling and ordering people around. No snide comments or honey-dipped bee stings of insecurity and criticism. There is laughter.

People take turns. A gentle rise and fall of the conversation that shifts like the breeze. I want more of this with people I love. And never again with those I left behind.

(Update)

It's god knows what time in the morning and I can't sleep. It's been a long night of tummy aches, bathroom rushes, and a racing brain. All I want in this moment is rest. My body to calm. My mind to drift.

I cannot keep food in my body. It's like my stomach doesn't trust me to make good choices. Like my body is screaming at me to take care of it, but I don't know how.

I cannot take a Tylenol PM. I cannot have any medicine or Gatorade. I can't take a walk outside. I can't have a little snack. I can't pet my dogs. There is no comfort here, only the bald face of reality. The reality is I am sad. I am scared. I am exhausted. I want soothing and comfort. I always want what I can't have. Story of my life.

* * *

"Day four is the worst," says my roommate kindly as I collapse on my bed, exhausted. "My fourth night here, I said I wanted to leave too. It's guess maybe that's when it really starts to sink in where you are and why."

My new roommate, Anne, is a sweet woman, with a dark cloud of black hair and slightly olive skin. An absolute delight compared to my first roommate. I don't know why she is here, curious but not rude enough to ask. This house has three rooms, two girls each to a room. I can hear Lina and Cards singing softly in the room next door. The third room is empty. All of these girls have been here a week or more so it's nice to have roommates to show me the way.

"Thanks," I say softly, not trusting myself to say much else. The meds mix-ups have been awful, the staff ill-trained and the tools used for distribution a mess. I assumed food and medicine would be the simple part of coming here, so much worrying about the therapy and the stories of other girls. Yet here I am, day four with fucked-up meds and an empty belly.

I am still struggling to keep food in my body. It's in one hole and out another. I can't help but look at the bright side that if I keep this up I will be thinner in my swimsuit. Then I feel awful because that's not what I am here to worry about. Then I get sad because my body is such a weapon no matter the size and start to get upset and cry.

I lay on the bed trying to read my book, relax my mind, escape to my stories. But it's been a long time since I have given autonomy of my body over to anyone else. To give up my freedom to make decisions about myself, stupid in hindsight.

But I have made a commitment to be here so I am going to work. I can be uncomfortable and live. I know what I am capable of, so I will endure and stick it out. I have a lot to live for.

* * *

Chapter Fifty-One

Journal Entry - Day 4 - A Letter To My Dearest Dave

The past few days have been so challenging, yet they pale in comparison to the last 40 years.

When I think of it like that, it helps a little, but I continue to miss the one thing that saved me so many times before—my loving partner.

For decades, I was too scared to even whisper my true love for fear of losing you. Everything I treasure was used against me so I learned to treasure my mind, but then they took that too.

You came into my life, and I couldn't let you go. You are so gentle and kind. I didn't feel like a conquest but instead a dazzling jewel you were happy just to be with. You forgive my weirdness, my distance, and nature to hide. You made me feel safe and cared for the first time in my life.

You are the love of my life. Your heart, hands, and wonderful mind are the perfect counter to my wild life. I loved you the moment we met, and I have protected that treasure with all that I have in me.

Thank you for supporting my time to heal. Having something to go home to gives me the strength to put myself through this pain and endure.

My love, soon we will be living the life we deserve,

No fear

No trauma

No threats

No more of

Them

Love you always.

CHAPTER FIFTY-TWO

There is a schedule hanging on the billboard in my room with times listed for each day's activities. Always yoga at 6:30 a.m.—seven days a week. Some girls lie in blankets and sleep, some do the motions blank-eyed like robots, and some go all out doing advanced moves on their head. I do what I can. Every time I lie on my back, my breath quickens, and my mind wanders to other horrors that happen while on my back. I leave class frequently to throw up in the garden just outside the door.

"It's more of a guide than a hard schedule," says Anne as she enters our little room after her shower. "It depends on what staff is working that day. There have been some changes lately. They usually try to plan the activities around some 'theme' of the week they choose based on the residents' needs. This week we are focusing on anxiety," she says with a playful wink, "fun." Deadpan delivery with a friendly smile. I give her a genuine smile, the first in days, and politely leave her to get dressed.

Per the schedule, group therapy will consume the rest of our day. Multiple formats are used, varying the approach to accessing different emotions, but it's going to be hours a day working on myself and my problems. Traditional group discussion sessions happen every day, moderated group sharing about an assigned topic (grief, anxiety, depression, anger), followed by activities to help process those emotions. Sometimes we will do an activity (meditation or nature walks) or alternative therapy (music or art assignments), different ways of expressing how we feel and healthy ways to process and connect with those feelings. Once a week, we go on

field trips, using boat rides and aviary tours and seaside yoga to lift our spirits.

Fridays, I meet with my assigned therapist one-on-one. For one hour. I have already met her; she moderated the first group session I attended. She is the kind one who helped me with Shelly. So far, she is my favorite counselor so I am relieved she will be my person.

I putter around making a cup of herbal tea as our small group sits down for our group discussion. Cards and Lina snuggle on the couch, my roommate and the girls from the other room draped around chairs and on poufs. I choose a lounge chair by myself in the corner and settle in for the work.

* * *

"Morning everyone," Jamie says with a big ironic smile, "how's everyone feeling today?" She is an interesting lady, this counselor I haven't met yet. Middle age, dark brown hair and razor-sharp stare. She smiles and laughs with a few girls, though she actively banters with them about their negative attitudes.

"I'm handing out a worksheet. I want you to take a look at these quotes and tell me which ones resonate with you and why," she says commandingly, as she efficiently hands out worksheets and small critiques around the room. (Ex: "Here you go, Lina. Please put away the blanket.")

We settle in to read, and the room goes quiet as the discomfort grows. Girls wiggling and adjusting as they read the statements on the paper:

Anxiety is not who you are; it's a part of who you are. It's a symptom of your experience.

Gut punch on the first one. I stare at the words as they swirl on the paper.

I can learn to accept it's a part of me without it consuming me.

Uh… how do I do that? It's not like I WANT to have panic attacks.

I put the paper down in my lap, look around at the other girls. My roommate Anne looks quietly thoughtful. Progress almost complete at The Facility, she is further along in her journey and doesn't appear too distressed. She drifts though her interpretation, starting us off but not dominating. "I have to accept who I am, flaws and all."

Jamie smiles kindly but hardens a bit as a challenge. "What flaws are your favorite, Anne?"

Anne's sunny light dims a bit. "I like that I do the right thing, even when my family doesn't like it." The words drop like stones, but she throws them out for everyone to see without too much trouble.

Now Jamie smiles the real smile. "Me too. I like that about you too." Lightning fast, she looks over to Lina. "What do you think? How do those phrases resonate with you?"

Catalina and Cardinal are a darling duo, the spicy Cuban and the motherly Southern momma. Lina keeps everyone in line with her unfiltered feedback, a force of nature, and I like her immediately. "I accept that anxiety is a part of me, but I think I am going to get rid of it. I don't have no time for nothing like that in MY life," she says with conviction and a Miami Cuban beat. "I mean, come on, Jamie. No one wants to live with that shit. It's exhausting!" she appeals to the room and catches my eye. I smile back in encouragement.

She has the confidence and intelligence of the kind of girl who will let nothing stand in the way of her goals, yet she melts as the discussion

moves forward with Jamie's insightful prodding. Her heartbreaking tale of anxiously waiting to hear about her ex-boyfriend's trial. The anxiety of waiting to hear if they will believe her, if she wants them to. The challenge of loving a man who beats that fire out of her, not understating what she did wrong.

Cards holds her tight as we dismiss from the session, Jamie focused on getting her to process rather than push away the emotions pouring into the room. The rest of us scurry to our rooms to avoid the mess. We have our own trauma. Like I said, there is plenty to go around.

* * *

Journal Entry - Day 5 - Housemates

Living in a house with five other women who are admittedly at their worst is no picnic. There are petty little jabs of lingering anger from comments thrown in session. Short-fuse tempers and silent tears sprinkled among those who just want to escape. With Anne's departure coming up tomorrow, new girls move around the houses.

Cards mothers us all, prepping meals and rounding up the chores list. She gives the warmest hugs, always the first to wrap a crying girl in a comforting embrace. She smiles and listens, reads her Bible every morning and talks to her abusive husband every night. She wails like only a mother who has lost her child can, my heart breaking every time she collapses from grief into a puddle on the floor. We all do our best to give her comfort. She does so much for us, but what can you say to a mother grieving a son taken too soon?

Lina continues to fascinate me. She is so beautiful and confident and intelligent, and yet she cannot see her destructive patterns well enough

to avoid danger. She is so bright. I want to show her all the ways she can get away, but she is just not ready for that yet, as evidenced by her challenging session today. My heart breaks for these young girls.

Lolly is a new girl who joined us in the empty room today. A young colt of a girl, just barely 22. Her trauma written all over her face, with piercings and makeup and whip-smart sarcasm, always followed with a hollow chuckle. She boasts that this is her fourth facility. She knows all the tricks and doesn't know how they will fix her. She calls her abusive parents every night, has a panic attack sometimes after she hangs up. So many secrets in that girl's little body that she is physically ill constantly, collapsing and wobbly like a broken doll, starving for someone to cradle her so she can be safe to recover. I know the feeling.

Harriet rounds out the group, a stoic woman, with watchful eyes and a soft voice. She tends to stay silent unless spoken to, choosing to share only what is asked. Her trauma is drawn out over decades of a complicated family which she minimizes and refuses to discuss. She sits on the couch all day, listening but not doing anything else. She is baffled by her depression, glued to her safe little seat in the corner, yet has no inclination to confront the demons she came here to discover.

Today's session veered to Lina quickly, and we stayed there for the rest of the time. It was a big moment for her, which was fine because I needed time to process.

Anxiety is not who you are; it's a part of who you are. It's a symptom of your experience.

Logically, the panic attacks are real. Therefore, the experience is real. But some of the stories that come out of my mouth are so awful—surely someone would have seen. How could a kid even survive what I say

happened to me? These girls are a mess, and they haven't been through anything close… I should be dead, right? Is this real, or am I just making it all up?

This is the loop in my mind that goes round and round. I can see the little girls in my mind peeking out with big hopeful eyes—am I finally ready to listen? Will I survive it if I do?

* * *

Journal Entry - Day 6 - Food

I am sitting on the deck watching the palm trees dance in the storm. The sound of the delicate rain is getting heavy as the thunder rolls overhead. I have always found calm in a storm. A way to turn an unexpected challenge into my own moment of respite.

Today is my sweet little boy's birthday. He is 14. First day of high school is just a week away. He is strong and tall; he is kind and smart. He is the best thing I have ever made, and he is everything I ever dreamed he would be. I am so proud of his mental quickness and gentle heart. I love him more than I imagined I could.

It's the first time we haven't been together on this day. No morning kisses, silly songs, fun adventures, or cookie cake.

I feel shaky and new, like after the birth of my son. Exhausted and aching from the exertion of the last couple of days, the sadness at missing him. But the soft glow of hope sits delicately in my heart because I know I am doing the work to get better. If I can improve just 1 percent each day, that will be enough to heal. To get better for him, to be the mom he deserves.

So, this morning I am worried about food. The little girls in my body are scared it's not safe. We are starting to talk, the Littles and I. I am just going to accept that I have little bits of myself, memories of who I was when I was a little girl, who live in my body and need to be heard. I need to listen to my body, so this is how I am going to do it. If that makes me nuts, well, call me crazy. All the coolest creative people are.

The Littles remind me of when food was a weapon. It could be withheld, and my tummy would hurt. I could be presented with choices, careful not to choose the wrong one or my tummy would hurt. Strawberry soda always meant trouble. And pizza. The Mother's homemade pizza when I was too old to be tricked by the soda.

Last night, we heard the chef talk about me not being a good girl and eating all of my dinner. The Littles are scared she will be mad and poison us. I really do love food, the tastes and textures and smells! Logically, I know this chef is making delicious food. I need to somehow convince The Littles that the food is safe and won't make me sick. I am learning how to do that, but not successful yet, hence the exhaustion.

The courage to change even for the better is always difficult. But this journey to see change within myself is one that so few brave to endeavor. I am grateful I have the people of my life to help me. Sending birthday hugs out to you, my sweet Jack. I love you enough to suffer this sadness as an investment in a beautiful future for our family.

AGE 7/8 BAPTISM

CHAPTER FIFTY-THREE

The LDS church is like most churches, believing they are right and everyone else is wrong. In the summer, I go to lots of different vacation bible schools (VBS) at local churches because it's basically free summer camp. Each camp, a pastor or bishop or priest or whatever tells us stories about how Jesus is the best person ever and he is going to save us all for heaven.

When I was little, I used to pray to Jesus to save me when The Mother was hitting me or The Grandfather was inspecting me. I would close my eyes real tight and say all the words I could remember to say to get him to come save me. But no one ever saved me. So I figure he is just like all the other make-believe people grownups use to trick little kids into being good—like Santa and the Easter Bunny.

So when my eighth birthday is getting closer, I start to worry. In the LDS church, people can't get baptized until they are eight years old. Catholics baptize babies, but they don't know what they are doing because they are babies so they can't really make a commitment to God. The Mormon church believes that children should learn about the church and then can make their commitment to God by being baptized when they are old enough.

Turning eight is a big deal because then I will be old enough to make the decision to be a full member of the church for time and all eternity. But I don't really believe in God and Jesus so it feels like lying to make a commitment like that. I don't like to lie.

I know I say the prayers and sing the songs at church. I have to for The Family, but it's not lying because they are somebody else's words I just read. I memorized lots of kids' prayers in Sunday school so I could use those if someone makes me say a prayer without a book or paper. But I am worried because in preparing for baptism, the seven-year-old primary class has to write our testimony. I am supposed to write a speech I will say in front of the whole church after I am baptized that tells everyone why I love God and why I love the church. But I don't love those things, so I am not sure I should be baptized.

Ever since The Big Ouchie on my butthole, I haven't been a good girl. Every time The Grandfather tries to have an Inspection Day, I start screaming and crying and lifting my butt off the white bed, scared of letting The Grandfather hurt me again. He says he understands my limits now and won't do that again, but I don't believe him. The Grandfather lies better than anyone.

The Grandfather gives his testimony all the time. He is in the Bishopric so he sits at the front of the church on the stage. On the first Sunday of the month, our church has a special meeting where members can stand and bear their testimony. The Grandfather stands at the microphone and welcomes everyone to the meeting and gives his testimony every time. He talks about how he knows Joseph Smith founded the only true church and how he is so grateful for our Heavenly Father. Everyone in the crowd smiles and nods except my family, who stares woodenly ahead trying to be good.

The Mother is always busy with my brother and sister, scribbling and wiggling; she never listens. My daddy doesn't go to church much. He is too smart for this silliness. The Grandmother always looks beautiful

sitting in her Sunday best, accepting hellos and invitations like a queen at her court. Aunt Ivy sometimes comes to church with Uncle Anton, sometimes not. Uncle Anton doesn't like the church much either.

The Grandfather is disappointed that his own children didn't marry in the temple like he planned, so he is going to make sure that I am worthy of a good celestial marriage. He has done a lot of work on me to make sure I am ready, testing my body and preparing me for my sacred duties.

This preparation is all part of a plan that leads up to the big event, my baptism. When I turn eight, I will be ready to become a full member of the church through baptism. Once I am a member of the church, I will be ready to begin my training to be a celestial bride and be sealed in the temple. It's a very important step and The Grandfather is eager to ensure I am ready.

So as my eighth birthday approaches, my bishop calls me into his office to begin planning the event.

"So, you are approaching your eighth birthday, and your mom tells me you are worried about getting baptized. Is that right?" he asks with a grownup smile, the one that says you are a dumb kid causing problems.

"I'm not worried. I just don't know if I am ready yet," I say meekly. It's important to look down and speak softly when talking to the priesthood leadership. Always be a sweet and obedient girl. This is the story I have come up with, that I am not ready. That way I am not lying (because I don't want to get baptized) and I am not hurting The Grandfather's feelings by quitting. I just need some more time.

"Hmmm," he says as he folds his hands into a steeple under his chin. "Why do you think you are not ready? Do you believe that Joseph Smith is the true prophet of our Lord and Savior Jesus Christ and our Heavenly

Father?" He tilts his head just a little and looks at me inquisitively. I can't tell if it's a period or a question mark.

Careful.

"Yeees," I say delicately, like blowing on a candle without putting it out, "but I don't know if I am ready to make a commitment for the rest of my life. I am only almost eight. I don't know what I want for the rest of my life." I finish a little rushed, eager to see if the words work. I have worked on them all week, knowing this appointment was coming up. I want to tell the truth and I don't want to lie *and* I want to wait to get baptized. This is the best way to say I don't want to get baptized, by saying I just want to wait. I think.

"I can understand that sounds like a long time," he says with a relieved sigh. He is glad I am not a heretic. "But this is your salvation and soul. It's important that you protect it now, while you are growing, so that you can grow strong and straight as the rod." He gives a little nod, very pleased with his input. I slump a little. Defeat is better accepted quickly so I can move on to the next thing faster.

"I understand," I say, looking up with my big blue eyes and blinking my lashes. "Would it be OK if I waited just a little longer? My friend Joey turns eight in a few months—can I wait and do it with him?"

I resist the temptation to say more. The priesthood doesn't like lots of words. Short and sweet, they say.

He stares at me a long time, silence getting heavier with each tick of the clock on the wall. I drop my eyes back to my lap and wait. I would pray, but I don't think that would help in this situation even if there was a God.

"Yes, I think that would be OK." He breaks the silence, and my spine unlocks. "I'll let your family know to work with Sister K on the arrangements. I am glad you are giving this such careful thought. It's a big decision. I know you will make the right choice."

He puts his hands on the desk and pushes his chair back, smiling. I peek at him up through my lashes and venture a small smile. "Thank you, Bishop," I say politely as we both stand and shake hands, my little hand devoured by his big one. I quietly walk out the door. It is not the outcome I wanted, but it at least gives me more time to think of what to do.

CHAPTER FIFTY-FOUR

After church, we go to The Grandparents' house for a late lunch. Family dinner on Sundays is always a busy affair, with all the daddies and sometimes family friends who join us. While the dishes are being washed and put away, The Grandfather grabs my arm and pulls me into the foyer. "Did you ask the Bishop to change the date of your baptism?" Quiet rage, The Grandfather is scarier the softer his whisper. Ice water floods into my blood, and I begin to shake.

"Yes," I say meekly. No point in lying, he already knows.

He doesn't respond, just stands there breathing. He licks his lips with a snake-like flicker and releases my arm, standing up tall to tower over me. I keep my head down and my hands clasped tight in front of me, trying to look as small as possible. I am hoping he is only a little mad. I didn't say no; I only asked for a little time. But The Grandfather is no dummy. He knows that my going behind his back was a risky move. He's not sure if I am trying to get out of it altogether or if I am just stalling for time. Getting the date moved is pretty smart—I can see he respects the play—but it messes with his plans so now he must adjust.

Without a word, he turns and walks back a few steps. Popping in his head to the kitchen, he says, "Pam, can you come with me on an errand please?" It's not a request; it's an order.

I hear The Mother quietly whisper to the others. She sets down something with a clang and jangles her purse as she picks it up. She appears, looking confused, adjusting her bag on her arm and looking at me like "what did you do this time?"

"I need to run to the church. I'll drive," he says to The Mother as he sticks his hand out to me to follow. Reluctantly, I take his wrinkly withered hand and follow him without comment down the dark steps to the garage. The Mother snaps the door shut behind us, walking importantly like she does when we go for inspections.

* * *

I stare at the blue dress lying in a heap on the floor, my little black patent shoes tossed aside. I lay on my back on the white bed under the white ceiling and try to send my brain away. It's cold in the church today, so I wrap my arms around my chest to try and keep warm. My knees are bent so my little white-socked heels are just sitting on the edge, my privates exposed for The Grandfather to do his inspection. I am worried I might start screaming again. I am so scared he is going to use the electric wand on my butthole again. I am squeezed tight, almost lifting my booty off the ground, shaking with fear. I hold my breath and take shallow sips of air, hoping to keep as quiet and still as possible. The Mother sits in her chair behind me, nails at the ready.

The Grandfather stands between my knees, staring down at my body. His eyes take their time, feasting on every inch of my naked flesh. My tiny boobies that I can't quite cover completely with my little hands. My tummy that pokes out just a little. The Mother says I am getting fat. The white creamy skin that slides down from my tummy to cover my private parts pimpling with goose bumps from cold and fear. My little legs trembling with the effort of being propped up, ready to brace themselves for his experiments.

stop, but then I remember there's no poop in there—The Mother gave me strawberry soda this morning. I thought it was because I was being naughty and wanting to miss church, but now I look at her in dismay, her black doll eyes and smile painted on her stone face staring at the wall.

The Grandfather pushes in too far, and I scream. I can't stop it; it escapes my lips with a cry from something old inside me. And then the pressure is gone. My body collapses with the release of the intrusion, panting as the fire from the pain crashes over me in waves. I feel like I couldn't stop any poop if it came out, a hole open onto my insides for anyone to reach in. I barely catch my breath before I feel him push in and rip open my vagina hole, filling me up deep inside and hitting my middle. I open my mouth to scream but am silenced with The Mother's hand clamping over my open lips. "Be quiet." she whispers violently in my ear as her nails dig into my cheek. "Women have done this for centuries. You are not the first," she says as she stares fixated on the wall, not looking at The Grandfather pumping below.

The Grandfather is now holding my hips and shoving his pee-pee into me hard. I feel like I might break into pieces. I try to breathe through The Mother's fingers so I don't have to smell her horrible, rotten breath, but her hand is so tight on my face it's hard to even move. I struggle to breathe through the tearing and pounding and suffocation, nothing to do but close my eyes and wait for it to be over.

Finally, The Grandfather gives a big moan and collapses on my legs. His pee-pee slithers out like a snake. I feel wet and empty and embarrassed. I need to go to the bathroom real bad, but I don't dare move. The Mother just sits with the greedy expression on her face, waiting for orders. I

alternate between closing my eyes tight and wildly looking around to see what is going to happen next.

The Grandfather stoops as he takes a deep breath, stands wiping his pee-pee off with my blue dress. He bends down calmly again and pulls up his pants, tucking in his shirt and fastening his brown leather belt.

He scratches his head and gives me a skinny eye. "You ruined everything." He says it softly, like something he told me not to do and I did it anyway. He wipes his hand over his face, his lips tightening, getting meaner by the second. I struggle to stay still as I lie on the bed, dripping and shivering, eyes fixed on his face for a clue as to what happens next.

"You were my little golden girl." He is angry and disappointed. I bet I am in trouble because I screamed. "I got you from the start, put all this effort into preparing you for a celestial marriage, and you ruined everything before you are even eight years old." He tsk-tsks at me, like I made a big mistake that breaks his heart.

I stare up at him, confused. I can still be baptized; it's not too late. I can still fix this so I am not ruined. Fresh tears start to leak down my cheeks, I don't know if it's safe to say something.

"You just had to be such a perfect little vixen, with your sparkling eyes and shiny hair." He sounds like he is a villain in a movie about to kill the hero. But I am not the hero; I am just a little girl. I don't know what the right thing to do is, so I just stay still.

"I taught you the dangers of vanity, of tempting men." He is gaining volume now, towering over me as he circles around the bed to put his face close to mine. "But you just had to tempt me. You had to have such a soft fragile body that isn't able to take the rigorous testing I created to ensure you would be the perfect celestial bride. But noooo, you had to go

be a weak little girl, not my special heavenly bride." He says the last bit as he pushes away from me, disappointment clearly fueling his disgust. "I don't even want to look at you anymore. Pam, take her out of here."

That's it? That wasn't as bad as the electric wand. I sit up slowly and slide off the edge over the sticky goo and blood (where did the blood come from), reaching down to put on my soiled dress since I don't have anything else. I sit on the floor to put on my shoes and grab my panties, putting them on carefully over my shoes. I really need to go to the bathroom—I feel like my potty is about to fall out of my holes—but I don't know if it's time to ask.

The Mother grabs her purse and skirts around The Grandfather's back as he stands facing the wall, thinking. She grabs my arm and hurries me out of the secret door. I am still sticky, and my privates hurt, but I can walk so I hurry along without complaint. I can go to the bathroom upstairs and clean up when we get to The Grandparents' house.

"Quit crying," she orders as she drags me down the hall to the back door of the church. I sniff and wipe, trying desperately to do anything right.

* * *

I didn't get to choose when to lose my virginity so it is a real shock to me when we get in the car and The Mother shouts, "You slut! How could you tempt him to take your virginity like that?!"

She pounds on the leather-wrapped steering wheel with her hands and shakes her curly hair in fury. "You always have to look so pretty. Always have to be sooooo perfect that no one can resist you." She sneers. The evil queen is going to eat the beautiful princess.

I slump in shame, sliding down in the seat of the car. My bare legs stick on the seat where the sticky goo is smeared.

"Sorry, I didn't mean to," I say in a tiny mouse voice. I know it won't make any difference, but I really didn't mean to be extra pretty today. I didn't even get to choose my dress. And The Mother did my hair herself.

"Ugh! You are such a little tease, always egging him on like that." She sounds almost jealous, like when my daddy gives me loves after a long business trip and forgets to love her. "Now you are ruined. Who will ever want you now?" She seems to cheer up a little at this thought, building control to start the car. I stay quiet, usually the safest response at moments like this. I am not sure what virginity is, so I don't know how I lost it. I wonder, if I find it, will I still be ruined?

My mind races—does The Grandfather have my virginity? Where was I hiding it? Can I get it back? Is this about sticking the pee-pee in the private hole? If I am ruined, will The Grandfather stop hurting me?

My head swims with questions that will go unanswered until I can get to the library. Teachers ask too many questions, and people at church tell The Mother when I ask these kinds of things so I find what I can at the school library. I wonder if I am a vixen like the reindeer? That makes me smile just a little as I press my forehead to the glass window of the passenger's door and close my eyes to think.

CHAPTER FIFTY-FIVE

I open my eyes, and the room comes back into focus. I am breathing hard, but I am able to slow it down with concentration. Lolly sits stunned in the seat across from me, uncomfortable but here. I can see in her eyes that it's nothing too shocking for her. I feel a flicker of guilt for making her listen to it.

"I was baptized on a warm spring evening with my church friend, Joey. The Mother planned a fancy reception in the social hall. We said our little speeches, and everyone gave us hugs and welcomed us to the church as members. I remember sitting next to Joey on the green carpet of the social hall at the end of the evening, legs crossed, laying my head on his shoulder. The adults walking around with their little plates and drinks, smiling and talking.

"I was so grateful that he still wanted to be friends with me even through I was ruined. It took me a while to figure it out, asking my friends' older siblings and covertly watching MTV, but that was how I learned about sex. It was the '80s, purity culture at its height. The message that I was ruined for not being a virgin was everywhere. I just accepted that I was ruined and tried to do my best from then on," I finish lamely. So embarrassing to say it out loud. My face burns in shame as tears continue to stream down my cheeks.

"After that, Inspection Days were mostly just that. The Grandfather usually just wanted to stick it in, call me bad names, shoot the goo, and then I went home. It wasn't that bad, really, much better than the agony of the purity tests." The air gets sucked out of the room, and everyone

freezes. It's one of those moments when I say something so weird that people get upset.

"My friend said, 'I don't think you are ruined. I think you are wonderful,'" I say with a little laugh, an attempt to lift the mood.

"I think you are wonderful too," Jamie responds softly. Her glibness gone with our pain scattered on the floor like glass. "Let's take a break from this and have something to eat."

I slink into my room and shut the door. Lie on the bed and cry. How will I ever survive this?

AGE 45 DO THE WORK

CHAPTER FIFTY-SIX

I wake up shaking and shivering, the night heavy with rain rustling in the palm trees. Sleep has always been an escape. Precious moments of blissful oblivion where I don't have to plan or analyze or remember anything. So I chase it and cherish resting hours, looking forward to that moment when I can lie down and not be on. But since I have arrived here 10 days ago, I haven't slept a peaceful night through.

Sleep was a weapon like any other The Mother used, hard to show blame but brutal to endure. I look back at the years I was going to elementary school and raising two babies and wonder at my focus. In high school, I was at scripture study at 5:30 a.m., returning home late into the night after school, activities, and my job were done, and somehow I endured it all. Now here I am, forced to get up at sunrise again to participate in more work at the cost of rest.

These past few days have been a grind of group worksheets, art projects, meditations, and talking. So much talking, listening, and processing. I feel hollow and exhausted. The therapists have been wary of me since I have been sharing more, uncertain of the wildness of the accounts. I can't muster the energy to care what they think anymore. I am here to be messy so I am a fucking mess.

It takes so much energy to manage The Littles now that I know they are there. Little pieces of me holding all the horrible stories we endured, eager to tell their story next. They crowd around my mind as soon as I close my eyes, flashing images with white curtains and blue dresses and cashmere. Tea towels and sticky icing. Images of stories I am telling for the first time. Stories of those yet to come.

Accepting that I have little parts of myself keeping secrets is tough. Listening to them and believing them is tougher. I've been up every night, fighting the images bubbling to the surface. Now that the floodgates are open, the only way is through. I boldly face the onslaught as much as I can endure, but it's so hard to practice compassion for yourself when you have never *felt* it. No one has ever heard them before and believed, comforted instead of punished. I can see the disconnect, but I don't know how to fix it.

I feel at war with my body. I see all the broken, battered, and beaten little girls cloaked in the manipulation I use as a weapon and protection in my own mind. My denial and disbelief is like an assault on their already-ignored wounds. Logically, I know I should treat myself better. I would absolutely believe my child if they were telling me these stories, would rage at anyone who hurt him. But when it's myself, I keep thinking that I am strong enough to hold it all. That these can't all possibly be true. Surely my family loves me a little bit.

I roll over and look at the clock, 4:32 blinking bright green back at me. I lie on my back and try to focus on my breathing until suddenly a light flashes and an alarm starts blaring. I freeze, hold my breath, count the sirens. The seconds tick by, punctuated by blaring WAH WAH WAH.

Lina knocks softly and opens my door. "Hey, what the heck…" She trails off when she sees my corpse-like pose with tears streaming down my cheeks. "Oh my gosh, girl, it's OK. We are gonna find out what is going on together, OK?" she cajoles as she crosses the room to help me up into a hug. "I got you, girl. Those assholes aren't gonna get you here."

I hug her fiercely and take the comfort as I stand and join the other girls in the hallway. Sleepy eyed and PJs flapping, we all huddle together

as Lina marches in front. She rants in half Spanish, half English as she stomps downstairs brandishing a rolling pin. "I don't know what's going on, but you better get out of here, Punta!"

She disappears down the stairs as Lolly, Harriet, Cards, and I wait frozen with fear. The siren continues to blare as flashing red-and-blue lights blink through the window. I'm vaguely impressed the police got here so quickly, not my usual experience.

The panic shakes and shivers in my tummy. Miss Stick-up-her-ass (my least favorite staffer, Karen) stalks up the stairs and asks if we are all OK. Karen is the one who seems real intent on shaming me for being immodest and unladylike. I also found out she is from Oklahoma. She may be reporting on my progress to The Church, and they are getting scared, I worry. What if she told them to come get me, that I am telling the secrets? I duck behind Lolly to avoid eye contact as she searches the rooms and veranda.

As the girls notice my trembling, instinctively, they move a little closer, Lina back with the group demanding to know what happened, Cards and Lolly sharing a kind touch or gentle reassurance quietly as we wait. The police check around. Karen does a sweep inside. Nothing seems out of place, and no intruder is found.

Miss Stick-up-her-ass takes charge roughly of the men and shoos them outside to finish up the report. Us girls creep into the stairwell to peek at the empty entry just to be sure. She finishes with the men and shoos us up the stairs to make coffee and cuddle for comfort. She calls me back to have a chat. I droop down the stairs to the office.

I don't want to have a chat. I want to hide under the covers and shake. Let my Littles take over and plan my next move. But that's not what I

am here for. I am here to learn a new way, and that requires accepting opportunities as they arise, even with people I don't like.

So I sit with Miss Stick-up-her-ass and spill out my concerns. Not wild and rushing like the first day, but heavy and slow like molasses in winter. But I do it. I tell her how I found out she is from Oklahoma, that she is the one who picks at me for being immodest in a sports bra and that she is the one here when intruders come (real or not). I tell her I don't trust her. She seemed amused, but then surprises me by denying any connections to the church. I have to make a choice to believe her.

I am tired of being afraid all the time. It's exhausting always trying to do everything myself. That asshole is 100 years old. He can't see, hear, read, or walk very well anymore. The church is a cult that will protect its own. I know that The Church will discredit me. They will lie about me and try to intimidate me. But at some point I have to believe that not everyone will believe them. Some will believe me too.

So I will step bravely into this fight, because the fear of speaking up is no longer a burden I am willing to carry… come what may. I let my crazy thoughts out to this person I don't like and just let it be messy. She seems pleased that I told her what's bothering me and that I accept her denial of her connection. It's just a bad incident; it's not part of a bigger conspiracy. I am out of that world now. I am safe.

Even with the commotion, our yoga instructor starts on time. I remind myself I don't have to be the best in class. No one is watching me. I am giving myself permission to be gentle and listen to my body so maybe it won't keep screaming at me. My body has served us, me and the Littles, so well, looked out for us, protected us, even when my mind didn't know what was happening or was minimizing the damage.

So from now on, I am going to listen to myself and just be messy. To be gentle on myself because I have been through a lot, because I *deserve* it. No matter what that damn yoga instructor says.

* * *

Me → This is hard. I miss home. Damn I have so much fucking shit to work through.

RC → I get it. Muck out the stalls and get rid of the shit. Did you get your gut under control?

Me → Sort of. I did OK yesterday but then I ate an apple today and immediately got sick. The Mother used to love playing the queen in Snow White. Had to swing in the tree swing to calm the Littles down. But at least now I can understand how to calm the Littles down so one step.

RC → Are you being messy? Are you talking about it? All of it?

Me → Yes. A lot. I cry a lot. And pick at my food. And make snide comments. I am a hot mess.

RC → Good.

Me → I'm blabbing all of the secrets when I can. I don't like it, though.

RC → You don't have to like it. It will get easier the more you do it.

Me → I know. I don't like any of it, but I am busting my ass to get through it. They keep saying I am angry and I need to let it out. I laugh and tell them that's what you said.

RC → Your Littles are angry. They deserve to be angry. You need to get angry. It's safe to be mad there.

Me → I don't feel angry, just tired and sad. But I am here for a reason, to get it all out. I am working on a timeline of everything, trying to get it all down. It's still bits and pieces all over the place.

RC → *It's OK to be messy. It's safe to be mad. You are there to say it all out loud. However it comes out is OK. Keep up the good work. I am proud of you for leaning in.*

Me → *You told me I can't say I can't or I don't know so this is what I am doing. It's your fault.*

RC → *I suggested. You had to agree. Nobody can make you do anything ever again.*

* * *

There's a buzz in the air as we walk into the midafternoon sunshine streaming into the main meeting area. All the girls are here today, huddling in small groups of roommates and housemates. New girls shuffling near the door, uncertain what to do. Angry girls crossed up tight sitting away from the group with stone faces. All the furniture has been pushed against the walls, opening up the main area for movement. Huge bins filled with baseball bats, foam pool noodles, and large solid sticks are placed around the room next to menacing slack pillow men. It's anger class today.

Jamie steps to the font of the room. "OK, everyone, settle down," she announces as we all take seats on the floor around the room. "So good to see you all looking ready to take this big day. I know everyone talks about the anger exercises, and some of you are more than eager to jump right in," a sly eye at some of the angry girls who are eyeing the buckets of weapons with determination, "but we are going to take a moment to prepare."

She and the other counselors walk around the room helping get girls spaced out among the pillow men, helping each of us select a weapon

of our choice. I sit in a group with two girls from the other house, not wanting my anger to be close up with anyone of my sweet housemates. A beautiful Indian girl with sparks flying snatches a baseball bat and kneads it with her hands, preparing for violence. A new girl, older and trembling with shock, politely accepts a stick and lays it in front of her.

I haven't ever hit anything in anger. Not a mad swipe of a hand at a stack of papers. Not a boyfriend or a best friend. Never thrown a vase across the room in a heat of passion with a lover. Never slapped a petulant child. The idea of hitting anything feels so scary I tremble as I choose a pool noodle from the weapons. Jamie gives me a frown but lets it slide. I sit with my soft noodle in my arms like a baby, waiting for instructions like a good girl.

"Anger is a human emotion, like love and sadness. It is good to express your anger. It's vital to your health, but doing so in a healthy way." Jamie doesn't even try to hide the pointed glances at the stony girls seething by the wall. There must have been some drama in the other house. "So before we work that anger out, let's talk about it." She walks around the room, looking at each group of girls, stopping and turning quickly around to point to a new girl on the floor. "You. What is your anger like?"

The lady looks retirement age, flyaway grey hair and sagging face. "Well…when I get angry…" She trails off as she tries to stop the tears already leaking down her face. "I yell and scream and hit. I know I shouldn't. I know I have hurt people. Sometimes I just can't control it…" she says through escalating sobs. "I have hurt my kids. I don't know why I get so angry sometimes." She collapses in sobs as Shelly scoots away from her like she has a contagious disease.

"Yes, bottling up the anger doesn't make it go away. It just makes it squish out in different ways. Ways we may not choose. Ways we may regret," she says gently but stands her ground. Comfort is not the goal here. "When you do this exercise today, I want you to think about how you can move that anger to this dummy on the ground rather than at your kids… and yourself." The lady is still crying but gives a slight nod.

"So, what is your anger like?" I look up, startled to find Jamie looking directly at me. My mind races.

I'm not an angry person.

Pushing. Pushing. Pushing.

I don't hit things or throw things.

It's safe to be angry. It's safe to be messy.

"I am an evil genius." It flies out of my mouth like a firework bursting into the sky. "When I am angry, I am calculated. I create a barrier of silence around me to protect the white-hot fire of my temper until it fades, so I can think clearly."

She smiles and lifts her eyebrows. "That's a first. But what happens when the white flame is first lit? How do you express that anger?"

I stare at her, confused. It's a feeling that I have spent so much time managing, but never shown to anyone in its full force. "I don't know."

I said I wouldn't say that. I promised myself. Of course I know; it's my brain. I know what my anger looks like, from that one time when I was four. That's the last time I remember being so angry I couldn't control it. "I bite," I reply belatedly.

"Well, that's a bit outside of this activity, but good to know." She continues whipping her words across our tempers, forcing us to wake up the sparks of fury within us. After everyone is sufficiently fidgeting, she

asks us to rise and prepare for violence. No hitting anyone else, only the pillow men on the floor.

"We are going to play music. You may begin hurting the pillow man however you like. Take out your anger. Picture your aggressors and antagonists. Yell, scream, do whatever you need to do to get this out. Once the music stops, we will lie down and rest, processing and deconstructing your experience."

The fiery girl next to me stands and gets ready to do some damage. The weepy girls stand like they are going to the gallows. Determined, I stand and breathe deep, forcing myself to impose the face of The Grandfather on the dummy doll. I do not want to do this. I don't want to hit anyone. I am afraid to be violent.

Wailing guitars and banging drumbeats fill the room as the angry girls begin beating down on the dolls. Huge thwacks starting over their head and squishing the soft filling with sharp thuds. Girls scream and yell, cuss and accuse. Some girls kick. One girl picks up the dummy and throws it down with a Viking-like yell of war.

The spicy girl next to me is beating the dummy mercilessly, pelting the torso and head with hammering blows as a stream of violence pours out her mouth. I stare. I can do this. I can try. It's what I am here to do.

I kick the dummy in the crotch. The soft cotton inside gives, and I watch my bare feet sink into the seam with delicious satisfaction. I lean down and pinch the legs, first softly, then really hard. The canvas of the doll twisting and causing the leg to twitch. I whap the pool noodle right in the middle with a big yell, making myself kick and hit more. I whip myself into a frenzy, kicking and stepping on the man. I knock him

across the head, I shove the noodle under his butt, I kick and hit and yell mean things.

The music stops, and I freeze, limbs limp, breath heaving. "Good job, now take a few minutes to slow down and lie down on your stomach to relax." Girls pace and shake; the sound of deep breaths and last-ditch insults float around the room. I roll my shoulders and try to relax, let the venom leak out.

Jamie and the other counselors walk around the room, softly rubbing small circles on girls' backs and murmuring soft words. Delicate piano music wafts like a cooling breeze across the gutting fires as everyone begins to settle on the floor.

"Give yourself compassion," Jamie suggests as we lie there exhausted. "It is OK to be angry. It's human. It is OK to be angry here. It is safe." She helps each girl calm and relax. Small discussions of topics raised and comments yelled. Nothing too challenging after that expulsion, but enough to start questions stirring in an active mind.

"Ask yourself—who am I when I am angry? Do I act on rage? Am I ashamed of my anger?" She asks these questions to the room as she continues to soothe the fading black tempers melting into tears.

I lie numb on a pillow. Abating anger leaving a void that fills with sadness as the memories rush in. Memories of fighting to not wear another blue dress. Of fighting myself to stay still while my body screams in protest. Anger at The Mother for holding me down, digging her claws into my arms to keep me on the dais. Rising frustration and temper at being a kid raising two kids as The Mother lies in bed and goes shopping. Anger at The Grandfather and his power to always keep me silent.

Chapter Fifty-Six

AGE 9 THE QUEENS & THE LIGHTNING

CHAPTER FIFTY-SEVEN

Being a big sister is a lot of responsibility. Being a big sister of two babies is overwhelming.

The Mother likes little babies. She likes the little ones that can't talk back. She likes to sit and hold them while they eat from her boobies, soft and quiet. She sits in her rocking chair and smiles down at their tiny faces and is quiet. It's nice.

But babies grow up. Now my brother and sister are walking and talking. Their crying and demands make Mother angry, a lot.

Rebecca is the worst; she cries about everything. She often wails for hours over the smallest slight—a dropped sucker or a torn coloring page—so it's difficult to manage her temper enough that The Mother doesn't get upset and give her something to really cry about. I use every song and story I can think of to help keep her from crying so The Mother doesn't get angry, but I can't save her every time. The summer is almost over, and I will go back to school. I have to teach her how to control her emotions, or The Mother will do it "the hard way."

Little Will is as good as they come. He never cries, is always smiling, a beautiful happy little boy. He is a sweet little brother, patient and kind. He is three now, walking and talking a little, following his beloved sister everywhere. He and Rebecca are only 13 months apart so they often get mistaken for twins. They go everywhere together and scream when they are separated. I do my best to keep them together and out from under The Mother's watchful eye, but they have to learn to do it on their own.

I am the oldest so it's my job to take care of them. I clean and cajole, rock and feed, whatever helps them stay calm and out of The Mother's hair. I work very hard to keep things picked up, but I can't do everything. I can't drive or spend money yet which makes things difficult. It's frustrating to know what needs to be done but gently having to maneuver The Mother into doing it. It takes so much time and energy when I could just do it myself so much easier.

I finish writing the list of things we need from the grocery store and carefully fold it in half to tuck into The Mother's purse. She and my daddy are going to run errands this afternoon, and I need to make sure she remembers Rebecca's ear medicine, milk, and cereal. It's been a while without fresh groceries since my daddy was away on business, but now that he is back, he will get the things on the list even if The Mother says we are spoiled brats. If I am lucky, they will stay away while the little ones are napping, and I can read my book in the apple tree.

* * *

I stand on the top stair of the step stool over the kitchen sink, a twig in one hand, a knife in the other. Afternoon sunshine spills through the window across the faucet as I scrape the knife down the wooden shaft.

She must learn. I don't want to, but she must learn. I tell myself this over and over as I desperately try to cut the little knots off of the twig. Those hurt when they hit you, so I am trying to remove them before I use it on Rebecca. I don't really want to hurt her, but she has to learn to be a good little girl. She makes me so angry when she won't listen. Maybe I can teach her a lesson so The Mother won't have to.

She has started biting and screaming at The Grandfather when he tries to prepare her for celestial marriage. I understand it's awful. I want to bite and scream too, but The Grandfather will hurt our daddy if we aren't good little girls. I can't live without my daddy.

She is too little; she doesn't understand how important having my daddy protected is yet. He is the only one who gives snuggles and real kisses. He is the only one who calls me sweet names and means it. He never hurts or hits, only tickles and tight squeezes. And safety. My daddy is always safe. I am working out how to be more careful at family dinner, learning how to avoid The Grandfather more by staying close to my daddy. It doesn't always work, but it's less than before my baptism.

So I bend over the sink further, shaking as I try desperately to scrape away the last little knots on the switch so when I hit her little legs it won't break the skin and make her bleed. But I have to do it. She has to learn.

I look up through the window as the wind picks up, watching the late summer apples fall like gravity in a picture book. I love my apple tree. I shift my gaze to the two little children playing in the sunshine, running and laughing like best friends. I'm jealous a little. I never had a friend to laugh with like that.

Pinch

I startle as I look down and see red. Blood everywhere. The knife sits lodged in my pointer finger. Blood so red it's almost black wells out of the wound and makes crimson splatters in the white porcelain sink below. It doesn't hurt; I'm surprised by all the blood. *Is that coming from me?*

I drop the knife but don't move my gaze from the deep red now flowing over my hand. I grip the side of the sink and lean over the wound, panting to catch my breath. I look up at the window again, seeing the

little girl run and play, and a wave of sadness sweeps away the anger and settles like a heavy rain on me, I lose my breath under the weight of it. I stare at the blood now running down the drain.

What if I just let it bleed?

I could just let it bleed. Let all the blood flow out of my body and I can rest. Go to sleep and never wake up. Never worry about my purity or celestial preparation. No dishes or groceries or temper tantrums. No school work or homework. Just rest. Sleep. I am just so tired of being afraid.

I look up at the little kids now rolling in the grass, making a proper mess of their hair.

Who would protect them?

It comes to my mind like a bolt of lightning, jerking me awake and making me grab for a paper towel. I act on instinct, quick like it is somebody else who is hurt. I wrap the towel tight, like we learned in first aid, and call the first number on the emergency list taped up next to the phone.

"Patten residence," says The Grandmother in her proper matron voice. The Grandmother is always polite and proper.

"Uh, I cut myself," I blurt out before thinking. I am shocked at myself for calling this number of all the numbers. I just did it without thinking. Stupid me.

"We'll be right over," she says and hangs up the phone.

I stand there listening to the dial tone, the phone frozen to my ear. Why did I do that? Why did I call them?

I hear Rebecca squeal outside, startling me so I drop the phone, the zzz-zzz-zzz sound softening in volume but still audible through the

speaker. My eyes snap to the window and the little kids still playing in the grass, and my heart skips a beat—what have I done?

If The Grandfather comes over… if they take me somewhere or something happens to me, who will protect them? Who would give hug Will hugs after he falls down or give Rebecca snuggles when it storms? Who will help Rebecca after inspection days, give her little snacks when she is in trouble? Who will take care of them if I am gone?

It is an unbearable weight on my shoulders, heavier even than the dark cloud of sadness as my responsibility. To protect them forever, as they grow, it is too much. I can barely make it myself. I am just a little girl with no help. I can't do it; I can't take care of them both all the time. It's too much.

I feel like I am breaking into a million pieces, my insides crumbling under the pressure shoving me down. I stand in the middle of the kitchen, clutching my seeping, red-toweled hand, and throw my head back and howl. The pain comes out like a wolf crying for a lost cub. It's wild and vicious, and then it is gone.

I breathe deep, demanding breaths to recover from the pain. No use crying over spilt milk. This isn't helping anyone. What are my options? I can keep silent and keep doing what I am doing… or I can tell.

I stand real still, listening to the wind blow through the apple tree as I think. I have told before; it didn't work out well. But keeping silent means protecting all three of us. I am strong, but I am only nine. I will need allies. That means I will need to trust an adult enough to tell them a little.

Then they can get more help.

That makes sense, maybe help instead of telling. Who would be able to help without getting The Grandfather in trouble… My best friend Adriana lives three blocks away, in a big house by the neighborhood pool. She and her twin brother Adam live with their eight brothers and sisters in Brother and Sister Queen's house. They are members of the church so they should know all about celestial preparation. Maybe she can help me teach Rebecca better so she doesn't get into trouble and I don't have to worry about it.

It is not a great plan, but it's all I can think of. It's better than doing nothing. Even if they kill me, maybe I can save my brother and sister.

I turn and run to the back door, throwing it open so hard it lifts up and bumps in the tracks. "Hey, you two, I gotta ride my bike somewhere. You stay here and come in if it starts raining. Looks like a storm's coming. I'll be right back," I yell and turn to shut the door on their startled faces.

They will be OK for a few minutes. I can ride my bike really fast.

CHAPTER FIFTY-EIGHT

I pedal on my bike as fast as I can, riding one-handed, cradling my bleeding finger to my chest. A cherry stain is blooming across my t-shirt, but I don't care. I am flying on the wind to my friend's house, hoping she is home. I want Adriana to hold my hand when I tell her mom. Maybe Adam too for luck.

I dump my pink Huffy on the lawn and race up to the door, slowing down a little to knock politely three times. It is always a little rowdy at The Queens' so I bang on the door a little harder than usual. Adam throws open the door with a huge grin under his wide blue eyes. "Hey!" he says as he sees it's me, turning to leave me standing in the doorway. I am a friend, but I am not a boyfriend, and boys are more fun so I am a disappointment.

I roll my eyes and step into the hall. "Don't be a butthole. I am on urgent business," I say importantly, a little out of breath. It is a fast ride over on my bike, and I am winded. "Is your mom home?"

"Yeah, she's in the kitchen," he says as he wheels around on his heel lazily and heads off toward his room. Guess I am not interesting enough today to get an escort. I turn to walk through the living room into the kitchen and run into Adriana in the hallway.

I reach out and snag her hand as she smiles to say hi. "Walk with me." I cut her off and drag her into the kitchen where Sister Queen is cooking. Adriana stutters a bit but comes along willingly as we walk into the warm baking cloud of the kitchen.

Sister Queen is bustling around the counter, stirring something that lifts little tufts of flour into the air, sprinkling her nose and apron. She is a large, cheery woman with curly cropped hair and round jolly cheeks. She looks like The Mother if The Mother was nice. She is like Mrs. Claus and Jesus all rolled into one, with cookies and hugs always at the ready. Adriana and Adam are so lucky she is their mom. I tell them all the time. I spend as much time at their house as I can. It's heaven.

I walk around the counter and into the warmth of the oven and her hip and tug on her apron. "Sister Queen, can I talk to you?" I say it soft and with big watery eyes, then dip my head to focus on my finger. It's still bloody, but not dripping or anything. I don't want Sister Queen thinking that is my problem when I have more important things to discuss.

"Sure, darlin', what is it?" she says with concern, putting down her bowl and dipping to look me in the eye. She takes my hands and looks real hard, seeing my fear and worry all swimming around in the corners of my eyeballs. "Goodness, what happened here?!" She instantly begins to pull me over to the tiny kitchen first aid kit she keeps in the cupboard, but I pull back and stare her in the eyes real hard. "Let's take a seat," she relents.

She gently guides me as I walk woodenly to the big kitchen table. The urgency and confidence I felt on the way over about this plan is starting to fade into doubt and fear. I don't know if I have made the right choice, if she can help. If anyone can help.

"Now, what's on your mind?" she asks, giving me her full attention, glancing nervously at Adriana's face above mine, looking for clues. I begin to shake. A lot. The words won't come out; they are stuck in my throat. I haven't told anyone anything since The Bishop. I know The Grandfather

will not be kind if he finds out I told again. But I need some help. This is an emergency.

"The Grandfather hurts me. Sometimes he sticks things in my private places." I pause to gulp some air. It's so hard to breathe through the snot and the choke, but I don't dare look up. I keep going. "I can be prepared for celestial marriage. I am a good little Mormon girl, but my sister…" I pause again, taking a big swallow before I continue. "She is having trouble and it's too hard to take care of her and teach her what to do and I don't know how and I am really worried and wondered if you could help me help her get better." I blubber and cry so that last words are slippery and wet. But I got it out. I took the risk. Now was it worth it? Did I choose the right person to help me?

She is quiet for a long time. I sniff and snivel, shake and fidget, breaking to pieces under the pressure. I want to beg her to believe me, but I don't have the voice. I used it all up.

"Honey, I think you might be confused. Let me call your mom and let's see if we can't talk this thing out," she says kindly. "Now let me take a look at that finger."

My heart stops. I have failed. I chose wrong.

My body slumps a little lower, and I drop my head to my chest, letting her look at my finger. Adriana squeezes the hand I forgot she was holding, leaning her head on my shoulder in comfort. Her life is too perfect. She doesn't understand these things yet, but she understands I am hurting and that she is my friend so she sits with me in silence as we listen to Sister Queen mumble softly into the phone as she puts a bandage on my finger.

Adam wanders into the room and sees Adriana and me snuggled together and changes his path to join us. "What's the matter?" he says with concern. He is a boy but a kind one.

"She told mom about The Grandfather hurting her, and Mom didn't believe her," says Adriana softly. I look up in surprise. I guess I knew she was listening, but I didn't realize she believes me. The first person ever to believe me. She is truly a lovely friend.

Adam's eyes narrow as he peers over our heads to where his mother's back is now turned, hunched over the phone talking so softly it's almost a whisper.

Adam looks at my red, ruined face, and his blue eyes light with fire. "Run," he says. "You need to run and get home before your mom gets here. Just pretend it never happened. We will back you up. Now GO!"

So I run.

CHAPTER FIFTY-NINE

I feel like Peter Rabbit running from Mr. McGregor, leaping over toys and furniture, bounding through doorways, out through the front door. I grab my bike with both hands, gripping tight to get my leg over the top, and I am already moving before my feet find the pedals.

The band-aid on my finger flies away as I start to pedal, blood seeping down my hand and scattering drops behind me. The clouds overhead are swirling and black, with blue sky still peeking through less and less. There's crackling electricity in the air, thunder rumbling above. My legs gain momentum as they pump furiously, my tires flying across the slick pavement. A car turns onto the road as I turn the corner. I swerve around to miss getting hit. The Mother stares out from the passenger seat of our minivan as she passes me going the opposite direction.

I give her a defiant glare, put my head down and pedal faster, hoping somehow we can just forget this whole thing ever happened. As the raindrops start falling around me, I feel the road turn to water under my bike. I slip as I come around the next corner and have to slow down a little to get balanced when

CRACK

A ball of lightning gathers overhead, and a single bolt sizzles down, lighting up the sky as it reaches down to scorch the earth. The crack of electricity is louder than the scream of the metal it strikes, causing me to jump off my bike and land wobbly to gain my balance. My legs start pumping a million miles an hour, and I fly down the hill through the creek overflowing with the sudden downpour.

The air stinks of burned rubber, the sound of sirens and car alarms and house alarms all blaring. I have seen a house fire before; I know what that smells like. But I don't stop. I just keep pedaling to get home. I have to. The Grandfather is coming.

* * *

I throw my bike in a heap on the lawn and run inside out of the storm. I know I will pay for the trail of raindrops I leave across the floor, but I have to see if they are safe.

My little brother and sister sit on the green turf of the patio under the awning, holding sticks out to the rain. They look up together as I slide open the glass door to greet them, relief like a drink of cold water on a hot summer day rushing through me. It's only been about 30 minutes since I left. They didn't even notice I was gone.

I smile back through my huffing to get my breath, wave hi. They are happy and quiet, so I step out on the patio and sit on the steps to rest. It's been a difficult day. I know The Grandfather is on his way, but I have a plan. I will convince him that it was a big misunderstanding and that The Mother is the one who messed up telling Sister Queen. If no one gets in trouble, I might be able to pull it off. We all know The Mother is crazy and does stupid things all the time. Might as well put that to good use.

But it gets later and later, and no one comes home. Not The Grandfather or The Mother. I sit on the steps for a while, then head inside to get a book. The phone rings just as I am on my way back out.

"Hello," I say politely, trying not to sound out of breath.

"This is your grandmother. I am at the hospital. Your mother has been struck by lightning."

Turns out that everyone wanted to pretend that day never happened. The Mother forgot everything because she was struck by lightning. Actually, the car was struck by lightning, and she was holding onto the car so she got shocked, but it's more fun for her to be dramatic. The Grandfather didn't know about me telling Sister Queen. He did come help me with my finger eventually, but nothing else.

Sister Queen tries to ask me if everything is OK once or twice more at the hospital, but I just give her my sunny smile and say of course, I was just confused. Adults like it when you are shiny. And now I know that no adult is ever going to believe me. This is just the way it is, no use getting angry about it.

CHAPTER SIXTY

Journal Entry - Anger

This week's topic is anger. In group this afternoon, we beat man pillows and howled and raged. It feels so wasteful of the precious energy I have left. I learned a long time ago that getting angry doesn't do anything but lead to poor decision-making. Rather than let it pass, I let it sit and cook me from the inside. I process and dig to the root of the anger until I can define what I am angry about and create a plan to fix the problem.

But I am here to change. So I am going to do everything they tell me, no matter how hard or dumb it feels. I hit and yelled; I stomped and kicked that stupid pillow guy. I howled in rage and collapsed in exhaustion. I don't really feel much better, but I do feel different. I feel heard.

After the violence, when we all lie down and have little private sessions of what memories came up, I felt the overwhelming need to talk about the consequences of my anger. How when I chose to express my anger, at a blue dress or an obtuse adult, I was punished. I was punished so severely that I never acted out of anger again.

Learning and growing requires I change my behavior, even if I think it's silly. So I am angry no one listened. I am angry that my family made me stay silent so they didn't have to talk about what was going on. I am angry at The Grandfather for deciding to groom me for his twisted path to being a god. I am angry at The Mother for never being a mother. I am angry I am losing an entire life that never really existed.

I feel tired, sad, messy, and weak. I feel sad when I think about the Littles never having known comfort. I miss the tiny slivers of attention I got when I was a really good girl. I miss the kindness and comfort of my sweet family I made for myself. I miss the ability to trust my own mind and body.

I am halfway through this journey at The Facility. The pain and suffering required to heal has been beyond anything I could have ever expected. I knew coming in that getting messy would be necessary, to allow myself to feel and react without control. To let others see me be at my worst. All while real life is moving forward around me.

My body's continued fear of this path is not unreasonable. This body has served me well, protecting me from facing the worst of unimaginable horrors. My mind's strategy and logic crafting incredible narratives to buffer those impossible situations I had to survive. The Little girls inside of me who worked so hard, waited so patiently for the moment when I was ready to listen.

I am working on thanking those defenses and encouraging them to evolve into something that is better suited to my life now—soft and fun, a beautiful life I built. I worked hard to create a life I want, with kindness and comfort and love. Now I have to learn how to live that life with new tools. I don't need this constant hypervigilance; I don't need to be afraid of my emotions anymore. Those assholes will never touch me again. I can express my emotions and be safe.

Jessica and I are working on thoughts to help me navigate this transition. To learn how to listen to the body's whisper so it doesn't have to roar. The sooner I respond to my body, the easier it will be to calm myself before it escalates. To validate instead of dismiss my emotions.

Acknowledge how I feel to help my mind create healthy pathways of communication with my body, replacing those damaged by frequent dissociation.

I am learning to love my emotions. Ride the waves instead of fighting them, appreciating the range and intensity as a part of my own self-worth. Everything is not all or nothing. A small success is not a total failure. Little steps are still steps forward. I am using evidence from credible sources to validate how I am feeling and believing them. Deciphering if the response in my head is that of The Mother or what I really think of myself.

Self-respect is not apologizing for things that are not wrong but may be uncomfortable for the other person. Feels like the hardest lesson to learn. I apologize a lot. Yet I never really do anything that wrong. Learning to respect myself more than my abusers sounds absurd, but it's going to take time. I spent a lot of years programming myself to believe them instead of myself. I am committed to this, learning how to live a better life. I won't fail myself.

AGE 45 TIMELINE

CHAPTER SIXTY-ONE

Journal Entry - Atone

I just booked my flight home. I waited until I was able to get my phone this evening and quickly booked it for next Thursday. I committed to 30 days, and I won't do a single day more in this place.

They kicked me out of the program this morning. Said I broke protocol for taking two ibuprofen when I only had clearance to have one. I yelled at the nurse and took the meds without her permission, so they were going to kick me out immediately. Just take me to a hotel and drop me off and leave me mid-mess.

It was tempting, to leave. To go home to my warm bed and kind boys and leave this awfulness behind. I sat and looked at her blankly when The Administrator told me, clearly expecting me to scream or protest. I quickly ran scenarios in my head, what going home would mean. It meant junk food and sleeping in and my dogs. It also meant going home in the middle of my learning. I am not well, yet. I still need to learn more. Going home means I would have to start all over at a new place, with new staff. I've been through worse than this. I have endured so much over my life. What's a little contrition?

So I bowed my head and put on the show, said I was sorry and asked if I could atone. She was shocked. I don't think her harsh delivery ever gets responses of calm. She looked confused and asked what the heck that means. Meekly, I told her that I realized I made a mistake but that I was willing to apologize if that was an option. I am really sick, and I need to be here. She sat stunned.

"How old are you right now?" she asked, out of the blue.

"Eleven," I replied softly.

I forced the words out of my mouth. We are not too far away from a time when women deemed crazy got sent to shock treatment and a lobotomy. This woman has just threatened to throw me out of the program for being too crazy, and here I am, laying the biggest crazy at her feet. But this is the work. Laying it out there when it's the hardest, scariest thing in the world to do. Because when I get in trouble for asking for what I need to take care of myself, I feel like I am 11 years old. That part of me that I built to protect myself from caretakers who want to control my access to care. I am proud of those skills I began to carefully craft at nine and build until I was a crafty cat able to get what I needed without help. Those little girls are warriors, survivors… and used to putting on the show to get what I need.

She didn't respond, just stepped quickly out of the room to talk to the other counselors. She arranged a face-to-face with offended staff where I provided an Oscar-winner performance of humility and penitence. I am allowed to stay but no more outbursts like that.

So I booked my flight home the moment I could. I won't stay here a day longer than I have to, but I am going to endure the next 10 days to get everything out of it I can. I have suffered through worse than these idiots. I made a commitment to myself, and I am going to keep it.

* * *

Me → I had to beat on a man-shaped pillow with a pool noodle. Then I cried real hard. You would be proud.

Me → *They were going to discharge me for breaking protocol and taking two ibuprofen instead of the approved one. I did what I do and talked them out of it. Because you said I need to be here. I trust you so I am doing this.*

RC → *Uh. Yes, I am proud of you for beating the man. Don't trust me beyond your own safety. I'm not there. I don't know what it's like.*

Me → *I am just gonna suffer and stop fighting. I have lived through worse, and it's only 10 more days. I trust that you know me and know what I need to heal. The rest is just noise.*

RC → *You just need to beat the pillow man and cry.*

Me → *I did! I even yelled real loud.*

RC → *That's awesome!*

Me → *I am also eating, but managing what I eat and what activities I do and don't tell anyone what I am doing. The Little warriors and protectors are trying to adjust.*

RC → *OK. Be kind to them. They are there to help.*

Me → *Whatever it takes.*

RC → *And you got mad and loud and the world didn't end.*

Me → *I mean, it's almost like you know what you are doing.*

CHAPTER SIXTY-TWO

"It's been a rough week for you, hasn't it?" asks Jessica as we walk across the street to the other building with the private space. It's Friday again, our week of anger mercifully over and time to process our feelings in private therapy time.

This is the third time Jessica and I have met one-on-one. I was surprised at first to learn we only have one one-hour private session a week. I thought I would be having intense two-hour sessions a day to work on my shit. Instead we do the bulk of the work in group therapy, writing and reflecting after group discussions. It's unique, telling strangers the most intimate secrets of your mind with no preexisting connection. There is definitely enough therapy time; the one-on-one feels like a special treat of getting to process in quiet.

I appreciate Jessica's knowledge above all else. She has experience with religious childhood trauma from around the world, giving context to my experiences in a new way.

"Do you think I have multiple personalities?" I blurt out once we are inside. The question waved like a white flag, signaling me finally giving up trying to be a "normal" person and just trying to figure out what the heck is going on with me.

"That's an interesting question. Do you think you have dissociative identity disorder, DID?" She smiles but gives me a pensive look. "Is that something you are concerned about?"

"Yes. After saying that I felt 11." I stutter, lost for words, "I mean, what else could that possibly mean?"

She gives me a long look, settles in for a chat. I grab a pillow to hug, a huge sigh of frustration, and steel myself to find out if I am totally crazy.

"Let's forget about labels for a second. Instead, let's talk about why you might have felt 11 in that situation..."

"I felt like I couldn't get what I needed because an adult was holding it back. I could see it—it was right there. I am 45 years old. I should be able to have a couple ibuprofen if I want without permission." I feel the heat rising in my cheeks, the climbing pitch of my voice as it turns from a story to a whine. "I came here to get help, not suffer more."

"Agreed. So let's talk about what happens when your adult brain and your Littles give you conflicting information." She nods and encourages me to continue to work it out.

I don't have dissociative identity disorder (DID) or multiple personalities. I do have little versions of myself living life alongside my adult version. Each lucky little girl holds some horrific memories. I am carefully tending to them so I can escape my abusive family and live the life I want. I don't lose time, black out, or switch personalities. It's always me. I somehow managed an extreme form of compartmentalization that functions similar to amnesia. When I felt threatened or like I was not being cared for by a caretaker, the Littles used to rise up with wild emotions, overwhelming my adult mind. It's a defense against decades spent trying to hide what I need from those who want to withhold it for power.

I learned quickly how different I was from other children. I knew things they didn't. I couldn't behave the way they did. Once my trust in adults crumbled completely, my psyche fractured. Not all the way, but enough for me to get some space between my non-family life and my

abuse to learn to live. These sweet little girls who kept me safe for so long don't trust my adult self to make good decisions. I spent years shutting them up as I went to holiday celebrations and summer vacations with the monsters whom I called family. I ignored them so fully I could pretend to love my family publicly to protect myself, using distance and silence to cover my escape.

But my Littles are still living in my body and will not be silent anymore. If I don't listen to their stories, they scream at me through jabs and twists of my muscles, expelling my food or stealing my sleep. I cannot ignore them any longer. I have to listen to their stories and say them out loud. Speak them into existence, acknowledging that they happened to me. That those assholes will never touch me again. That I am strong enough to break the cycle of abuse.

My job for the rest of the stay in The Facility is to learn about each one and tell their story out loud. And believe it.

"Have you started on your timeline?" Jessica casually asks at the end of the session. My exhausted brain swims in this new insight. "This might be a good place to start. Just identify each part of yourself. What do you remember about them, what stories do they tell, what role do they play to help the system? Think about it." Rainbow smiles and gentle hugs, only a small respite when there is so much work to do.

* * *

Journal Entry - Timeline Notes

I am working on a trauma timeline. It is the big assignment I came here to accomplish, though I didn't know exactly what it would be. But this

is what I am working for, to get it all down, all out there for the first time. The goal is to obtain a better understanding of the events in my life that have led to trauma over the years. But I have so many. I still can't remember so much. But I have to start somewhere, so I am going to organize this like a book. First, the characters.

Understanding that my psyche is fractured is unnerving. It's the kind of realization that scares me to the core. Less than 30 years ago, women were committed or shocked to placidity in my condition. Realizing that my brain is hiding things from me is tough, and there is comfort in the knowledge that I am brave enough to accept it. Let go of the perception of what this condition means to others; focus on what it could mean for me.

Rather than fight and try to dominate them, Jessica and I are working to embrace my parts. To listen to their stories, give them attention. Each part brings something unique and valuable to my life. I choose to embrace those skills that have enabled my survival. Maybe acknowledgment will give them the attention they need to rest, no longer on red alert but quietly on standby until their skills are needed.

Three-year-old me is quiet, carries a doll named Victoria (which she was not allowed to touch). She sings church songs. She is creative and optimistic.

Four-year-old me is more cautious and serious. Toys were not allowed, only books and puzzles, which were a bit too advanced, so it led to creative play. She enjoys picnics in the sunshine. She wears a blue velvet dress with white petticoats.

Five-year-old me is a sad, lonely little girl. Because of the Worst Week Ever, with the dress shopping and the picnic, the inspection days and the other grandma. It was a really hard year. She just survives.

Six-year-old me is a quiet, watchful girl with big eyes and zipped lips. She and Five sit together and hold hands sometimes, quiet companionship in their matching blue dresses and black patent shoes.

Seven-year-old me is more defiant, blazing with knowledge and determination. She was the first to get access to advanced education in my gifted and talented class, which changed the way I was able to survive. She reads a lot, scribbles on worksheets and climbs trees to stay fit. Always working to figure out a new way to make things better. She is strong and not afraid to get dirty. She carries the pain of the electric wand like a blazing sword; she survived.

Eight-year-old me is in full armor. She is strong and fierce, willing to try to fight back. She is the one who stalled the baptism. She is the reason we tried to tell Sister Queen. She wears a white lace dress with a pink rose at the neck. She is a problem-solver and a fighter.

Nine, 10, and 11-year-old me's are a team, each more fractured than the last. They are ninjas, decades of protecting the entire system from the truth making them almost impossible to communicate with. I hear their whispers once in a while, how to get food, or avoid detection. They are ruthlessly selfish, sole carriers of the knowledge that we couldn't take anyone with us in our escape. They are the crafters and curators of the fractured collective consciousness, created to enable escape. And they are who I must get to rest. I must listen to their stories.

* * *

Me → I am working with Jessica to identify each of my Littles to help with my timeline. I met one of the more protective ones last night. She is 11. She got me up at 4 a.m. to sneak food, packaged to ensure it's safe, and hid in the closet to eat it... like when I shared with my sister. She is a sad girl.

RC → Aww. I'm glad you got in touch with her. That will be important. You can tell her she did such a good job. That what happened wasn't her fault and that she gets to be protected now.

Me → I'm trying. She is really concerned about the stupid people here. She doesn't trust them. I am trying to listen.

RC → Maybe work on stupid people doesn't mean they are evil and want to hurt you

Me → She likes you. She is the one who has the issues with food.

RC → Tell her she can eat whatever she wants. It's safe. Even if it's not perfect, it's not dangerous.

Me → She is just excited for French fries when we go home next week!

RC → OK, make good use of this last week. Turn her loose on them. Let her get mad!

Me → I present my Timeline on Saturday. That's a big one, but I am ready. Can't wait to show you. It's awesome.

RC → I have zero doubt.

* * *

Another group session, another topic for learning. Today, it's Inner Child work. Jessica and Jamie are co-leading today, I guess to give extra support to the two of us veterans left in the house.

Cards advanced in the program, moved away last week. I hope to see her one more time before she goes back home to Missouri. Lina is

leaving to go home tomorrow so she is downstairs doing paperwork, leaving Lolly and I alone with Harriet. Always the quiet lump passively observing.

I feel their absence, but who am I kidding? None of us want to be here. I can't help but be happy for them and let them go. Leave this place and move on with their lives. I see that fixing the problem isn't really the goal. It's just a place to come learn how to get better. How to weather the storms of life that turn into hurricanes at the hands of men.

"So, todaaaaaay…" Jamie says with a sly smile, "we are working on our Inner Child. Fun, huh!" We are close enough now for me to know that beneath her sarcasm and edgy barbs is intelligent kindness. Jamie is a talented picker, always knowing just what to say to push your buttons.

Lolly and I glance at each other and roll our eyes. She and I have discussed several family picadilloes over the past few weeks, mainly how our fucked-up families abuse us and then punish us for being spoiled, ungrateful brats. Two families separated by thousands of miles yet using the same family tricks to keep their unruly little girls in line.

A big rainbow smile beams from Jessica in her vividly floral dress. "Let's start with some interesting research on this topic. Have any of you ever heard of Erikson's Stages of Development?" she asks as she passes around a worksheet with the same name at the top. I shake my head. Lolly nods and rolls her eyes. "I think it's going to be a great resource to use as you are creating your timelines," she continues, ignoring Lolly's eye rolling. She sits across from Jamie on the floor, leaving space for discussion in the middle.

I quickly scan the page, my mind blooming like a flower. I scribble in examples under each section, lost to the puzzle of it all. Ideas about why

I have a hard time trusting myself. Insight to why, as a child, I believed I was bad and could only rely on myself. Nothing revolutionary, but questions I had never allowed myself to ask until I was willing to listen to the answers.

When I flip back to my list of each little girl's role—it makes a lot of sense. When I was asking myself if I was good or bad, I was going through a mess of conflicting events that both devalued and highly valued my worth. It is humbling to sit in a room of strangers and realize you were neglected. That you have to say you were abused to get accurate medical care. That you never ask for what you want because you were punished for it growing up. No one wants to believe it is *that bad*, least of all me. But here it is. When I listen to The Littles like I committed to doing, this is what they say. That we don't know how to trust or love or believe anyone because we never have. Including ourselves. I have been making myself go back and be abused for years just to avoid listening to those little voices.

I look up to the ceiling, take a deep breath. It stings. It's a piercing moment when the logic and the crazy all make sense. I am trying not to cry. It's all just so sad. I am so sad for those little girls, for myself. Because it's me. I am the Littles. I lived through all of that. The tears leak down my face.

I know I am weird. I don't need to look around to see other girls to know they aren't interested in this topic at all. Lolly's heard it all before, Harriet stoic as ever. I mean, seriously, who wants to pick apart their own mind?! Learning how to deconstruct my personality and understand why I am the way I am helps me feel more at peace, but I see I am the only one.

"You wanna talk about it?" Jessica says softly, peering at me sideways in a friendly way.

"Not yet. Let me put it in my timeline for tomorrow. We can talk about it then," I say quietly and don't say anything more.

So maybe I am built a bit different. There are obvious reasons why. Now I know. My insane experiences have shaped the person I am today. And I like me. I like my life. I have so much to go home to, I have built a beautiful existence. I subconsciously built an oasis of love and peace with my hard work and perseverance—I'll be damned if I give up on it now. So I just have to accept that I am weird. Maybe a little crazy. But I am kind and smart and a fighter. And I have one thing left to do before I can return to that life. It's the job I came here to do, no matter how difficult. I will tell my story, from beginning to end, not hiding anything. Be honest and believe.

CHAPTER SIXTY-THREE

Saturday morning dawns wet and sticky. It's the Florida Keys—everything is always wet and sticky. I take it easy in yoga, just stretching softly. It's just me and Lolly now in this house, empty rooms being cleaned before the new girls arrive Monday. Our bodies and minds exhausted from the week, the yogi takes pity on us and lets us focus on meditation through slow gentle movement. Attempts to calm our minds.

We head up the stairs quietly to get ready for group, or semi-private session since it's just the two of us today. It's my turn to share my timeline, and I am ready. Jessica arranged for this smaller session because she knows it will be a lot. Best to protect the other girls from this much horror… and protect me from their reactions.

I take my time showering and preparing for the presentation. Not like I did in the old days of high heels and power dresses, I choose things to wear that are comforting. Stretchy pants, a tank top, a sweater wrap to use like a blanket. No makeup, hair wrapped up in a bun. Stripped down and bare, I stare at the face in the mirror. I've never been out in public like this, would never even consider doing it for work. Yet here I am, giving the most important presentation of my life, and I look just like me. The real me. For the first time, people will see all of me laid bare… and I am ready.

I walk in like a ballerina taking the stage behind the curtain, soft steps with confident grace. I settle in my favorite chair, arranging my hot tea and water on the table. I carefully lay out my artful timeline like priceless treasures before me—two small rectangles of watercolor paper, carefully

arranged in timeline order. Each paper has three small watercolor icons surrounded by words in shapes. They are beautiful in their misery.

I sit quietly as Jessica and Lolly head into the room and take their seats. Not much small talk today, the anticipation is too heavy.

I take a deep breath and begin. I show the drawings to them, but mostly, I use them as notes to ensure I remember to say each story out loud.

A blue dress, a biting mouth, a strawberry in vivid childlike color— *soldier of God, Oxley Nature Center, don't hurt my daddy* in my swirly handwriting making menacing shapes of the men behind me. *Black pepper, the other grandma, inspection days, and bubble bath* written in the shapes of women who wouldn't protect me. I tell each story with efficiency, telling the bald truth as only a Little girl can. Each Little taking a turn to get it all out.

I flip the first page over and begin talking about the next, a simple white table and curtains next to a cloud with lightning-bright yellow— *the White Room* and *the Queens* scribbled across the paper. Stories fresh and already heard by this crowd, but details about the electric wand and the medical care exposing colors I didn't know were there. Information I never let myself dwell on before, like *why didn't my dentist help me* and *how did I not die?*

I pause, staring down at *The Big Awful* scrawled across a horrible black-and-red stain on the bottom right corner of the page. I was barely able to get it on there. I have never ever spoken of it, not even once. But this is the moment; this is the time to say it out loud. To tell the big awful secret that has brought me to this point of destruction or resurrection.

I steel my resolve and tighten my jaw, open my mouth, and let the words rush out, unafraid.

AGE 9 THE BIG AWFUL

"Get up. Put on your coat." The Mother's harsh whisper stabs into my dreams and startles me awake. I look around sleepily, my brain still foggy from dreaming.

"Wha…" I start but am silenced by a cold hand across my face.

"Shut up and get your coat," says The Crone with her claws in my face and her foul breath creeping up my nose. I nod silently and scramble out of the warm covers down from the top bunk bed.

It's still dark outside. I can hear the crows and crickets. The moonlight helps a little, but it's dark. I'm trying to navigate the baby toys and books on the floor. I can see Rebecca's little cherub cheek puffing on her pillow, and I lean to pull up her blanket to her chin.

"Come on," demands The Crone before sweeping down the hallway. I pad after her on bare feet, silent as a ghost.

I feel the old familiar black goo begin to slither inside me, thick, as we pull into The Grandparents' driveway. It's heavy and sharp, laying eggs and creeping down my insides.

We get out into the darkness heavy with silence. Even the bugs seem to be afraid to be noisy at this house. We walk around the back of the house, using the large wooden gate to enter the backyard from the side. Carefully picking the safe steps in the mud and rocks with my bare feet, we make our way into the back yard where I stop abruptly.

There is a beautiful strawberry patch in The Grandmother's backyard. It's my favorite thing here, providing little sweet surprises when I am sad. But my beautiful strawberry patch is all dug up, fresh black earth in little mounds of roots sticking out. It looks bare and ugly in the dark, not the sunny green-and-red garden that I love so much. I stare at it numbly.

I thought I had gotten away with it, thought everyone had forgotten because of the lightning. I kick myself inside. The Grandfather never forgets.

The Crone reaches back to grab me and makes me walk around to the front of the little patch of earth, sectioned off from the large rose garden that surrounds the rest of the yard. The Grandmother loves her roses, thick with thorns and beauty. Just like her.

I stare at the small little pieces of roots and don't even have the heart to cry. Just another thing to be taken away.

The Grandfather stands tall next to The Grandmother, on the patio so The Grandmother's house shoes don't get wet in the dew. She has on her blue housecoat with the peacocks on it, tucked tightly around her middle as she looks disapprovingly down at me. The Grandfather's face is excited, as it usually is before he is about to punish someone.

"So what's this I hear that you were not happy with being prepared for celestial marriage, hmm?" He is a cat playing with the mouse before he eats it. "And that your sister might not be either?"

I stand silent. I am worried because we don't usually do anything outside where people can see. The fence's high wooden points are over my head, but I can still see the second-story windows of the two neighbors behind us. The dark, black windows… because it's the middle of the night. I just look at the ground at my feet and wait for it to be over.

I hear people moving around and other people joining, my heart rate jumping as I feel more eyes on me. The conversations are too low for me to hear so I finally risk a quick look up before fixing my gaze back on the ground. But I am shocked and freeze when I see a man I do not know kneeling in the dirt.

He is a black man, old but not as old as The Grandfather, with curly black hair that poofs out from his head in a circle. He has big black eyes with yellow around the outside that almost glows in the dark as he frantically looks in every direction for help. He struggles a little, his hands tied behind his back, a rag tied across his mouth. The Grandfather knocks him on the head with something hard. The man goes glassy-eyed for a second and then falls over to the ground.

The Grandfather sighs and bends to grab his shirt, pulling him up by his collar as the man's head lolls to the side. I stare like I am hypnotized. I can't take my eyes off the black man's wide black eyes. He looks like a deer in the woods.

The Grandfather leans down, and with a swift smooth motion, he slices a red line right into the man's neck. Blood arches into the cool night air and covers me as I turn away. The warm liquid coats my left side, warm like bathwater. I don't understand why I am in a bath—I was outside just a second ago.

I stay crouched and warm, wishing I could be away. Away from the warm blanket, away from the strawberry patch, away from the sickly-sweet smell of roses and metal.

The Crone reaches out and grabs my arm, the not-sticky one, and uses her hand on my shoulder blade to twist my arm behind me. I cry out as I stand reflexively to ease the tension, and she shoves my face down to the cut meat of the man's gushing neck.

"This is what will happen to your precious daddy if you ever tell anyone ever again," she spits into my ear, poison from the apple. "Do you understand me?"

I squeeze my eyes shut to try and block out the pink tissue poking out like in a dissection in science class. I nod my head vigorously, anything to get away from the freshly cut meat, the smell of blood and the sound of little bubbles in liquid.

The Mother seems satisfied with my humble silence and lets me stand up as I back up from the corpse. The blood is draining into the soil, disappearing into the dark rich earth. The man lies quietly leaking, forgotten now that the sacrifice has served its purpose.

I stand up straight and look up slowly, directing my eyes at the one person who I think may not be totally crazy right now. I find The Grandmother's steady gaze blazing laser beams into my head, willing me to understand this moment.

This is not a game—this is for life. If I don't protect myself, I will not survive. I can not take anyone with me. It will have to be only me. The Grandmother can only try one more time. It has to be me.

I feel myself crack and shift, like plates in the earth during an earthquake. I can feel the black gaping chasm open in my chest, fracturing my mind into small little pieces to carry the burden of this journey away. Little girls with their secrets floating away on islands, away from my conscious mind so I can breathe. I watch them float away into the dark, their sad eyes shining as they sink deep in the blackness.

I know at this moment that I will never be able to be my whole self with anyone ever again. I am the only one who can carry this and live. So I will. I won't let The Grandmother down. I will keep my daddy safe. I will survive. And one day, I will get out of this family. I will live without them. I will save part of myself away from them, do whatever they want, whatever it takes to get out and be free.

The next morning, I get up. I go to school, I do my chores, I take care of my siblings. Repeat. Over and over again. Past Thanksgiving and Christmas, I don't even remember what I got. It's all kind of been a blur. I feel like a robot just going through my programming. Spring break is over and we only have a month left until summer. Then I can rest.

School has been weird. My teachers are happy I am quiet, getting "usually does" checked on my report card next to "Refrains from unnecessary talking." That's a first for me. I still have inspection days, bathroom checks, and punishments. They just don't seem as bad anymore. I can send my mind away, and the little girls in the dark will hold all the bad stories and secrets for me.

There is one more set of shining eyes in the dark now. She is nine, crying because she couldn't hold on to her sister. She broke off on her island the night The Evil Queen came and found Rebecca hiding with me in the closet. I wasn't strong enough to hang on as The Evil Queen dragged her from my arms. "It's her turn to wear the special dresses now. Stop being a jealous brat."

I try to ignore the crying girls in the dark as I sit in my desk quietly staring at my teacher, Ms. Miller. She is about to announce the big event, the one we all have been waiting for…

"Good morning, class. Today, as you know," she says with a sly glance around the room, "we will be doing class a little differently. We are going to separate into groups, the boys going next door to Ms. Henderson's, the girls staying here."

She says this primly, like a lady speaking about delicate things. Like it's a big secret we mustn't discuss in front of the boys. Everyone perks up as the boys rise to go to the other room. The chatter grows louder as we all

bubble over with excitement at the prospect of our first real introduction to sex—Human Health Class.

I sit on the stairs in the back hallway, crying hysterically in huge gasping breaths. I can hear the health film continuing through the classroom door above my head as I listen for Ms. Miller's footsteps. I hope she saw me leave.

I gasp and pant as I hear her softly approaching on my left, crouched and concerned.

"Are you alright?" she asks carefully, like she is approaching a scared horse. I nod, embarrassed that I can't seem to stop crying.

"Was it something on the video?" She sits down next to me, cocking her head to the side to see my downturned face a little better. She puts a soft hand on my back and rubs a little circle. It's the nicest anyone has touched me in months. My daddy has been away on business a lot, and when he is home, there is fighting. I do my best to stay out of sight.

"All the girls in class talk about the 'red wave.' That at some point you will get your period and it will come gushing out like the crimson tsunami covering you and everyone else like those two little girls in *The Shining*," I say candidly. I can't stop the words from tumbling out of my mouth through the panic. "I thought Health Education would teach me what to do to be prepared."

I pause to get my breath, finally slowing a little with the relief of getting it out. I didn't know anything about periods or sex, but I was getting more worried by the day. Apparently, it's something to do with your private parts and a boy putting things in there. I wasn't sure how that could be right, since I had never had sex with a boy, but I had lots of stuff in my private parts from inspections. I am worried that when the

blood comes, it is going to be extra flowy because I already had stuff in there. So I had hoped that Health Class was going to show me what to do. Instead, the film was a lot about sex and how babies are made and I started to get scared because I don't want to have a baby and if The Grandfather was doing this and it was sex but he is doing special things to prepared me for the kingdom of heaven… it gets all jumbled in my head.

Ms. Miller gives me a tired smile and looks down in embarrassment. "Yes, that would be helpful for girls your age. But the video is standardized by the school board, and they felt it more important to focus on the creation of life. Not as much practical anatomy, I'm afraid," she says with a sigh. "Why are you crying? Do you not have someone to help you with your period?" she asks with concern. I make a mental note to talk to her when the time comes.

"Oh, I am sure The Mother will help me out with that stuff," I say obediently. I am never to speak ill of The Mother.

"Then why are you upset?" Ms. Miller is a kind lady. I think she would help if I asked.

But I will never ask for help again because there is no help for me. I have to do it myself. I can't survive without my daddy. He is all I have left. And I am strong enough to take him with me because he is an adult. I only have to be silent to protect him.

"Just being silly, I guess," I say with a weak smile. The storm has passed, and I can pretend again.

A week left before school ends, I am called into the principal's office during class. I sit in the main office, jiggling my legs and looking around anxiously, scared to death that I am in trouble. I've never had to go down

to the principal's office, so my jiggling almost flies off my leg when The Mother steps through the school front doors. Sunlight streaming behind her, making her outline loom like a black demon coming to get me again.

She is in her nice dress with her hair extra poofy, swinging her purse and dragging my little brother and sister behind. Her shoes don't make a sound so my sister's complaints bounce around the entryway and down the halls. The Mother shushes her harshly but no slaps today—people are watching.

She drags them into the office and gives me a sugary-sweet smile. "Oh, there you are! Are you ready for the big surprise?" she says with her ghoulish smile. It's yellow and silver, reminding me of the wolf who is gonna eat little pigs for dinner.

I paste on my sparkle smile and exclaim, "A surprise!" I am an excellent actress, knowing exactly what response or expression will make the grownup the nicest. I can tell instantly that today will be an I'm-such-a-good-girl day.

"Well, let's get down to it," say Mr. Hale, the principal, his bald head and wire rimmed glasses reflecting the harsh overhead lights and making him wink. "Your academic record…" blah, blah, blah, "very lucky girl, your mother," blah blah blah, "transfer to Byrd has been approved. You will start there next year as a sixth grader. How about that!" He smiles big, proud of me and himself since he is the principal of me.

I make a big smile and squint my nose. "I'm going to a different school next year? Not the one all my friends are going to?" I struggle to keep my voice from quivering. My school friends are the only ones I have; they are the best part of my day. I don't want to go to another school and try to make new friends. I'm already exhausted with these.

"Yes, you are going to Byrd Middle School. You know, the one Ms. Matters teaches at? You and Stacia will both go there next year. We will carpool," The Mother says primly. Her satisfaction at having been grouped with my best friend's mom is a big deal to her. She doesn't have a lot of friends like me.

"Oh good, Stacia is going too," I sigh with relief. At least I will not be alone.

Maria from *The Sound of Music* says, *When God closes a door, somewhere he opens a window.* I don't want to leave my friends, but I know it's not my choice. God doesn't open windows for me, but "what doesn't kill you makes you stronger" is something I read in a book. That makes more sense. So I decide I will look at this as an opportunity to reinvent myself as a different girl.

Chapter Sixty-Three

AGE 45 HOME

CHAPTER SIXTY-FOUR

"As a 11-year-old reinventing myself, there were no self-help books or YouTube tutorials (no internet at all in the '80s!) so I used what I had. I used the resources I had to solve the puzzle of who I would be—logically." I stop to sip some water, but not letting anyone ask a question just yet.

"Obviously, I didn't want to be the broken kid I was in elementary school. I could be somebody different, anyone I wanted to be when I was at school. My friend from dance class, Stacia, was kind and funny, and she didn't care that I was a little weird and outspoken. And she knew sometimes I cried, and sometimes I was really happy, but we were becoming teenage girls so those things didn't seem so weird as we all transitioned into different people." I desperately try to convince Jessica that I did the work. I figured out the puzzle. I survived.

"As with most middle-school kids in the early '90s, I was captivated by the science program *The Voyage of the Mimi*. In it, we studied sea animals and ocean conservation as we virtually traveled along with our captain and kid guide. Turns out an octopus has eight brains and can use them independently or all together at once. That seemed like a pretty smart idea.

"So I decided I could work with the little islands of my brain like the tentacles of an octopus, one main brain to be the happy shiny popular princess, little sad girls sitting out on their islands helping when I needed them to be a sweet obedient LDS girl.

"I am lucky I saw another life for myself outside of the Mormon church and The Grandfather's influence." I finish with a glance at Lolly. "Religious family trauma is enough to fuck anyone up for life. And damned if every single one of the True Faith doesn't have so many procedures in place to deny they ever happen," I finish feebly. The emotions start to creep past the resistance.

The room is quiet, Lolly and Jessica silently crying as they stare at me, sitting straight-backed and sipping from my straw like it's an afternoon tea. I wiggled and squirmed through some of those harder bits, but I didn't have a panic attack or have to stop so I feel a surge of relief. I have never told anyone what happened that night. It's weird to hear it out loud.

"So they murdered him. That's what you are saying," Jessica confirms, staring at me with wonder and confusion. "They killed a man to keep you quiet."

I gulp and look in her blue eyes, red and dripping, but steady and cool. "Yes. They said my daddy would be next if I ever told anyone." As the words sit cooling on the floor, we stare at them lying between us. It's a large accusation that I couldn't possibly prove. Unless the body is still there, I guess, under the roses they planted over the body.

"Do you believe me?" I hate asking, but I need the confirmation. Maybe I just said a whole lot of craziness, and she is about to commit me to the state sanitarium. Wouldn't be the first woman in history to go down that way.

"Yes. I absolutely believe every word of your truth." It's the kind of statement she is trying to imprint on my brain. I can hear the intention behind the words, not making it about what actually happened but

affirming that this is an honest retelling of my perspective. "Do you know who he was?" she asks gently, afraid of more awfulness falling out of my mind.

I look up sheepishly, a quick glance at Lolly, still huddled and shaking but still here for me, the sweet thing.

"I asked The Grandfather if he was going to get in trouble for killing a man. 'It's against the law. The police might come,' I had said in a weak moment soon after. I accepted he wouldn't get caught, but it was important information to have for my further survival, you know." I trail off a little as the memory wraps around my vision and I blink it fiercely away.

"*Nobody cares about a black man disappearing in Oklahoma,*" he scoffed, and that was the last I ever heard of it.

"There are roses growing over that plot of land to this day, last I saw." I am finished with this topic. I have been talking a long time.

"Let's take a break, OK?" Jessica says with a sigh and a deep breath. "Stand up, stretch your legs, and move around a bit."

* * *

Journal Entry - Strategy

I did it. I said it all out loud. I told every secret story, and they believed me. I even told about The Big Awful. It helped. I am honestly impressed that I survived all that.

I knew I had to get out. I knew from that moment in the strawberry patch. It's a puzzle I had to figure out to save my life. I had to learn be clever in leveraging resources. I had to pretend that I was obedient and

content with this Celestial expectation and preparation. I had to fool them all into thinking I was a good girl who wanted what God wanted for me.

Secretly, I scoured the library, TV shows, movies, anything I could get my hands on to learn about different perspectives. I didn't want to be like any of the adults I knew, so I needed to find something else that looked safe to try and be. Away from these people who were liars.

Before the internet and social media, people's lives were behind high walls and closed doors, impenetrable beyond the curated content they carefully crafted for adoration. To gain access to any of that information, I had to learn to speak the secret language of privilege. The privilege of being safe, loved, and cared for equips those who have it with small gestures and little nuances of understanding that they don't even know they use.

It's is why representation in media matters. Providing insight into the kinds of conversations that happen in the hero's mind and behind the hero's back is only unique with diverse heroes. All the stories agree the hero must know how to navigate the dozens of small social cues that are passed around like invisible currency in any story where they want to overcome an obstacle.

The way people carry themselves in social settings tends to be more important than the conversation. The way money is spent. How your family is perceived. I watched and read and listened and learned about the challenges people navigate and share, absorbing the tiny actor movements or descriptions of expressions.

I needed to be successful enough to have a career that could support me such that I would avoid any dependance or reliance on their resources—

money, love, support of any kind couldn't be relied upon, or it would always be a weapon at my throat.

So, my Littles would quietly acquiesce to requests. They helped take extra care of my appearance, made little shows of saying prayers and going to church. I never took unnecessary risks, like drinking alcohol or smoking, was always home by curfew. I was the perfect child. I was an excellent student, participated in a lot of different activities, captain of the dance team, performed in school plays. I nurtured an incredible group of diverse friends who are kind and intelligent. I created a dating strategy, and it worked. I found the love of my life, and he is incredible.

Con artists and predators are my kryptonite—they do the same things I do, but they do it because they are greedy, not to survive. They see me, but I don't see them until it's too late, mistaking them for a fellow survivor. The fatal mistake is asking them to share knowledge or refuse a request. Con artists see an uncomfortable request as a breach of friendship, predators as the moment to strike—and it's usually a pretty hostile event. Hosts cannot feed on prey that requires nourishment to replenish. That ruins the meal.

But I still kept going. I met as many different kinds of people as I could, people who had skill sets that I enjoyed or admired or saw others admire. I learned from them and in exchange I would mirror their own confidence, values, and knowledge back at them. In hindsight, I see how that attracts narcissists, but I didn't know what that was until I was 40—what's a girl to do?

Nurturing a relationship to reach that level of trust is challenging. There is some vulnerability involved. Not everyone is interested in that. But the ones who are willing to try, who recognize the value I bring,

they're incredible people. Truly. The people who have stuck by my side are crafted from the best pieces of humanity. The family I created with kindness and friendship. The girls from high school who rallied to send me slews of cards while I have been here, raising my spirits every time I look at them. Daily texts and voice messages from my bestie, encouraging me to fight through it and come home.

It took me 45 years to find the people who helped me feel safe enough to begin allowing the puzzle pieces to fall into place, to bring me to this moment where I could finally accept my myself as I am. This is the life that I have fought for. I break the cycle as long as I survive this. I have built this life—a family of my own making who loves me, friends who accept me, and a son who is beautiful inside and out. I have spent a lifetime defending it. Now I will blow it all up to finally rid myself of the burden of 40 years of secrets, torture, and abuse and know the people who really love me will still be here.

I got it all out today, but I know there will be more. I just have to make sure I keep the tools in my toolbox sharp, prioritize taking care of myself. Trusting myself, my truth, and my strength. I am worth fighting for.

* * *

Journal Entry - Happy

Yesterday was hard. But I did it. I did it with poise, grace, and honesty and then stepped away. I stepped away from it all to allow myself time to rest. Today, I am protecting my hard-earned peace.

Your roots are so shallow, but you are so vibrant. Jessica said that to me with tears in her eyes at the end of my long tale. She pointed out that it's

amazing what can happen when children are forced to seek the nutrients they need to survive.

The nutrients I had were hurt, cruelty, manipulation, control, and gaslighting. I used them to build the skills to survive, not one world but many. She compared me to a tree in India that grows in the middle of a bridge, roots exposed and concrete-scraped yet vibrant and beautiful. I want to see myself as that tree, even I struggle to keep pampered houseplants alive.

I woke up feeling happy. I slept just a little bit longer than I have in weeks. My tummy was hungry but not painful. The little versions of me were content to be heard at last, proud to let me rest.

It's almost more scary than the screams, the contented softness. After a life of always having to be prepared for the next trauma or challenge, it's even more precious to have a moment of calm. To be able to trust that it will last a little bit, not be yanked away. So I am going to be more thoughtful with this respite from the storm. I am enjoying some gentle music, listening to the chatter of the other girls. Savoring a simple breakfast and calm.

I used to give my peace away as quick as I gathered it, trying to lift others because I know how bad it hurts to be alone. But today, I am trying to create and conserve peace for myself first. A new tactic to be sure, but change will only happen when I try something new. I have fought for this, and now I need to learn to live it.

CHAPTER SIXTY-FIVE

"So how was it?" RC asks nervously during my hour of phone time on Sunday. "Did you get it all out? Even the hard parts?" She knows me better than these counselors; she knows how much I try to edit to make it pretty.

"It was good. It was hard, but it was good." I pace the recreation yard with my phone pressed to my ear. I need her to know I did it right. "There was so much. I had to truncate some of the details, but I said the big stuff. Even The Big Awful, which we can discuss later."

"That's great. I am so glad to hear that you did it. That's what you are there for, right?" The relief in her voice calms my fears. She believes me. She believes me and my ability to do the hard thing even when I don't want to.

"Well, you told me not to say *I can't*, so I did. I just worked and worked on it, trying out using little-kid words and blurting out the scarier parts. It wasn't pretty, but I did it." I allow myself a small smile, acknowledge the warm glow of the campfire in my heart where my Littles are snuggled in close to me, warming up to the new friendships we kindled. "I still have a lot of work to do, but this was a big step, and I did what I came to do. Now I just have to heal."

"Right. Now you have to heal," she breathes out with a sigh, the urgency of my survival ebbing away to the future of stability. "I'm really proud of you. You are doing the work. It's not easy, but I am so proud of you for doing this for yourself."

I sniff as my pride slips a small drip down my cheek. I feel proud but also a little embarrassed. How did I let myself become this big of a mess? How could I put my family through this? But I stop that line of thinking. I am here now, and that is no longer a helpful thought.

"I thought the hardest part was going to be living through the telling, and for sure it is wildly painful, but trusting the peace proves its own challenge," I confide as we wrap up the call so I have time to connect with my sweet boys.

"The hardest part is behind you. Focus on that. You did it. Healing will get easier. And now you have a whole host of tools to help you through the difficult times ahead. You got this, girl. I am proud of you."

Over the next few days, it's a shift in focus from expulsion to conservation. Protecting my peace from the other girls. Being present for their stories but not carrying them. Being polite and kind without depleting my own energy. I feel like a child learning to tie a shoe, complex and thoughtful, but the goal is clear—I deserve the peace I have won, and I don't have to let anyone have it. I can do this; it's worth the effort.

I create a personal dashboard to keep myself focused on areas I am unused to monitoring. I use a 1-5 scale to rate my daily accomplishments in things like Being Kind to my Body and Energy Management—taking time to review my activities during the day and noting progress in listening to my body.

I reflect on the way I talk to myself. Am I talking to myself the way I would talk to my own child or the way my family talked to me? It's an odd thing to self-analyze my own behavior, but one of the biggest revelations of this place has been how hard I am on myself and my own body.

I note my eating habits changing, but it's difficult to separate the trauma in the right buckets. Some food feels unsafe because I am afraid it's spoiled. I have to carefully discuss with myself that I can eat packaged foods for comfort and eat a little prepared food to learn to trust my own judgement. This proves to be challenging because as a child of the '90s, food and my ideal body type are so tangled with my trauma it's hard to get anything in my mouth some days. I want to eat healthy, I want to eat good food, I don't want to be fat, I don't want to gain weight. I have to maintain my figure. But if my body looks TOO good, then I have more problems. Foolish idiots telling me it's my responsibility to ensure men are not enticed to look at me. They can't be trusted to resist. I am just too tempting. Same story since I was four.

I reflect a lot on my attention to relationships. Am I spending my time and giving myself to people who give me energy back? Who love and care about me as much as I do them? I focus on pulling back my attention from The horrible Family, the other girls just starting their healing journey, the friends and coworkers who rail at my absence, and focus on my incredible son who thinks I'm a good mom, my adoring husband who loves me no matter how crappy I look, my dear friends to accept and love me no matter my past. This is what I am working for, to live this life. Now I have to practice learning to live it.

* * *

Journal Entry - Letter to my Littles

Hey, sweet girls, my little me's—we did it! We made it all 28 days, and now we get to go home! I know it was scary, reliving scenes we have

not acknowledged for decades. Never validated that they were even real. Living a double life, no one ever knowing who we really are.

I know how long we held it in. We had to for all of our safety. But I am an adult now so I can handle it. I will carry this from now on. You, Little sweet girls, get to rest now.

Don't apologize for having feelings or crying when it hurts. No one will punish us for it ever again. Humans have emotions. It's safe to show them now. Everyone gets a turn to cry and be comforted.

I am so impressed with our strength to endure such horror in silence. To wake up and go to school or work and pretend like nothing happened. We didn't turn into a serial killer or a drug addict. We didn't shy away from any obstacle in our way, always staying focused on the prize— escape. And now we won. We are free, healthy, and have a beautiful family of our own to go home to.

We are OK living together, all of us. I will drive, and you can rest, but always these stories will be a part of us. A part of me.

Because we are me.

CHAPTER SIXTY-SIX

No tearful goodbyes. No fond farewells. Girls stand in a circle around me as I say goodbye, awkward and silent. Someone leaving is just more hurt to endure, another person walking away. New girls have already arrived to move into my room. This isn't really a place anyone wants to remember or keep in touch, so a few give me a hug and walk away.

Lolly is the only one left that even knows my name. She is young and lives on the other side of the country, yet she knows things about me my dearest friends don't know yet. It's a unique bond that will live without nourishment, just knowing it's always there. Lolly gives me a silent squeeze and turns away softly to join the other girls.

Jessica ushers me down the staircase for the last time, the group session beginning above me allowing me a moment of relief for not having to participate. I need a break. I am exhausted.

She reviews final paperwork and gives me an encouraging smile. "We were not ready for someone like you," she says with a sly smile. "I'm not sure anyone is."

"Thanks," I say, looking her in the eyes real hard, "I couldn't have done it without you." I am not choked up or sad to be leaving, but I will miss her advice and knowledge. Having a teacher as excellent as her is a rare gift.

"I am just another tool in your toolbox. You did the work. You did an amazing job here. I hope you continue on your journey of healing." She gives me a hug, the kind that wraps around your whole body and is soft

in the middle. I try to store her squeeze of encouragement in my mind for comfort later… then remember I have a lifetime of hugs coming my way.

After two glasses of wine, a large order of fries, a full-fat burger, an extra bump of my anti-anxiety meds, and a 12-hour weather delay, I finally sit watching the city lights fade from my window seat as we lift higher into the sky.

I have come so far from that fateful trip to Cali so long ago, yet that Little part of me still enjoys watching as we ascend into clouds. I sit quietly, enjoying the freedom to order another Diet Coke, to stare out the window for a long time, to plug in my headphones and ignore everyone.

I did what I set out to do. I said it all, out loud and without hiding anything. It is still difficult to fully see the magnitude of everything in first person. Much of the pain is still held with my Littles. That's OK because they really just wanted to be seen. To be heard. To be cared for. And that's exactly what I am going to do.

I married a man who supported me every day of this journey. I knew I would need someone who loved me enough, who was strong enough, to brave this level of horror and still be along for the ride. I have only ever loved him within the boundaries of how much I could afford to lose him. I have only ever been able to give him what I could survive if my family ever took him away to punish me. He is about to get a gigantic love bomb. The kind that Lavender Brown would have been green with envy to give Ron Weasley. I suspect he won't mind at all.

I am going home to a Home. One that is safe and soft, with my huge comfy bed and my deep bathtub. My sweet boys. My family. My true friends. Where I can leave my shoes in the middle of the floor or make a

mess in the kitchen and no one wants to punish me. People who love me and don't want to hurt me.

I know what love feels like, even though I had to learn from licking the knife.

ACKNOWLEDGEMENTS

Creating this book as it was happening was a whirlwind experience that (hopefully) happens only once in a lifetime. I began writing this book three months after The Family came to my house, determined to have a record of my story in case they silenced me once again. I am so grateful for the kind humans who supported me through this journey and made this dream a reality.

To the team at Paper Raven, you guys are awesome. You guided me every step of the way to making this dream come to life. Thank you for providing expertise and encouragement to a wild first-time self-published author.

To my writing group, thank you for being kind and supportive from the start. It's tough finding people who speak your passions. You have all been so wonderful in your support of my ambition.

To the City of McKinney, I am grateful for our town providing such wonderful community services. I wrote this book in public parks, on nature trails, in our small downtown coffee shops, and in the John and Judy Gay Library. These safe spaces are so important to provide as a community, to encourage self-enrichment and creativity for everyone. I am lucky to live and contribute to a city that understands the value of community resources.

I am grateful to the millions who viewed, liked, and commented when I first posted that terrifying video with my shaking voice. You helped me find the courage to continue. I am lucky to have friends who gave their overwhelming support, even when things were unreal. My dear friends

who sent cards to the mental hospital, came to my house, and held my hand while I cried, and continue to check in to say I love you. I am so lucky to have some of the most incredible people connect with me through this, believing in me every moment. My elementary, high school, and college friends, my pom pom girls and moms, my business mentors and my best friend for life, Kelley. People who love me no matter how messy I am. This is what friendship is for.

My loving parents, Bill and Patti, who withstood the toxic waste of The Family's influence and hung on to me like a parent should. Hearing these stories for the first time, knowing finally why The Family wouldn't leave me alone, they believed me instantly. I will never forget my nanny, the mother of my heart, holding my hands and helping me carry this burden for the first time. The best parent believes you, even when what you say is unimaginable, because they love you. I decide who is my family is now, who I trust and love, and they are forever bonded to my heart.

My sweet husband, Dave, who has stood by my side every step of the way. He showed my son what it means to truly love someone through good times and bad, all in the same year. He is my most loving partner, my truest friend, and I am lucky to have him in my life.

My beautiful son, Jack, who watched his mother descend into madness and loved me fiercely through it all. He saw the pain and trauma of our family and trusted me to find another way. He gives me hope that cycles can be broken. Seeing him grow up safe and happy absolutely makes trudging through this hell worth it.

And last but not least, I am so eternally grateful to the expert therapist who guided me through it all. RC invested almost a decade into gaining my full trust, the most critical thing that enabled us to get to this point

safely. I would not be here today without her knowledge, intuition, and incredible skill at navigating the mind of trauma. Thank you to all the amazing practitioners who helped me learn the tools to live a life with trauma, and thank you to my rock RC for providing the lifeline when I needed it. Your work matters.

Q&A WITH THE AUTHOR

Why did you write this book? What's your goal?

I needed to get it all out and believe myself. I was abused into believing that nothing bad happened, to not trust my own experience, and that I didn't tell the truth. This book is a huge scream that I saw and heard and smelled and hurt, and it was bad.

The biggest frustration of this journey was my family insisting "it wasn't that bad" or that I was "making things up." Many of these stories were shared at family gatherings, watered down and thrown out at parties to embarrass me. To this day, my family doesn't deny they happened but say I am exaggerating because I want attention.

I want people to read this book and have the courage to question the weird things kids say about the adults in their family. To have tough conversations and believe each other. Our law enforcement systems are not set up to protect our children, but the internet has provided a way to share stories without powerful men deciding what's appropriate. My generation has the wisdom and experience to talk about these taboo topics with followers who want to listen and discuss. Giving young people the respect they deserve to engage them in discussion rather than always protecting through avoidance is what I hope people take into their own lives from stories like mine.

This book is really hard to read. Did you consider watering it down?

If you follow my videos online (@oldladylit, @sabrinacapper), you will know I really struggled with this. My initial feedback from my editors

was that the child perspective of such awful events was too harsh. That people would not be able to invest in the story because it was too off-putting to be inside the mind of a five-year-old being sexually abused. But this is my life. How do I decide what is "too much?"

RC and I had long discussions about how much is too much—my frank narrative, the childlike perspective, the sheer volume of tragedy. My personal views on morality, honesty, religion, and abuse are so skewed by life experience that I sometimes have a hard time understanding where the line of normal human capacity lies. What if the book flops because it's just too difficult to believe?

So I posted a video and asked my followers—what do they want? Encouraged by the incredible online community of TikTok, I was encouraged to publish my childlike horror show in its raw delivery. Hundreds of voices chimed in to declare that they are strong enough to make their own decisions and want to hear my truth my way.

What is the significance of the artwork on the front and section heads?
All the artwork is original work by me. I picked up a paintbrush for the first time in 2020. I began painting things I didn't understand. As my life began to fall apart, I found the process of creating art to be an outlet for things I didn't have the words to say.

The front cover is a piece I created over the two years leading up to the The Break. It's one I kept coming back to to add more as I understood more. It's an abstract representation of how my mind feels inside—a small pink path of my ambition to survive among the chaos of the black-and-white rules of my world. It's wild and messy and beautiful, just like me.

The drawings at the section heads are a mix of some of the pieces I created on the healing journey and some I created as I close this chapter of my story. I see the watercolor drawings as a representation of childlike icons holding those memories in prettier packages. Soft little drawings to focus the little girl trying to keep the dark away.

The digital art signals a switch to the adult mindset, more polished and smooth. I created them as a representation of how I carefully created a more polished story to prepare to share with the world.

What main message do you have for parents who are concerned about protecting their children from stuff like this?

Believe. If a child confides in you, mentions something in passing, or displays signs of abuse, believe. Children do not have the language to make up abuse. They don't understand sexual desire or power dynamics. If a child (or a teen or adult talking about their childhood) says something about weird stuff that happens but isn't "that bad," believe them. Ask questions. Listen. Victims have a hard time admitting they are victims. If someone tells you something that makes you uncomfortable, there is a reason. Listen in good faith and believe what they are saying is they want to be safe, not get other people in trouble.

Do you believe therapy helped?

Absolutely. I have no doubt that I would be dead without it. I wanted to face it head-on. I didn't want my life to be lived in fear. There are so many ways to treat trauma, but you can't treat it until you acknowledge it's there.

First, I got over my fear of medications. Accepting that my mind needed chemical balance gave me the capacity to talk. Finding a

therapist like RC was a stroke of luck, but committing to the work was my responsibility. Talk therapy works best when you talk, a lot, about the worst and best stuff with no holding back. I needed someone who I trusted enough to lose my mind with and guide me to survival. I'm a Lucky girl to have RC as my guide.

Talking is only one way to get it out. Finding out about healing my body was a totally new concept for me. Exploring somatic body trauma massage, Reiki, art, music, group therapy, and meditation was different and weird and really helped me heal in ways I didn't know I needed.

I learned how to vary my approach to mental health to flow more easily with my new life of living fully as myself. I encourage people to listen to their bodies. It stores trauma as much as the mind, and it needs care.

What does The Family say about this story? Are you still in contact?

It's sad to say, but the most sobering challenge has been letting go of those who are not interested in me without keeping secrets. So many people heard my story and rejected it because of the accountability or culpability they would have to admit. My family has raged at me for disrupting their carefully manicured lives. They call me names, shame me, and ultimately all have shunned me. I have no contact with any of The Mother's family anymore.

I have also lost friends who didn't want to talk about it. Part of being honest about this is accepting that this is a huge part of my life and not everyone will like this version of me. Changing my perspective to letting those people go, realizing they didn't love me but the person I was for them is hard… but it makes my real family relationships—my daddy

and Nanny, my husband, my son, my bestie—so much more satisfying, knowing they know and love all of me. Real family is the people who love even when it's not pretty.

Why didn't you go to the authorities?

When I was a child, I told the people who I was taught in school to tell— my mom, my church leader, my best friend's mom—and you know how that went. After The Big Awful, I was convinced the police would not help me because he killed someone and no one cared.

When I was a teen, I was scared to death to go into the foster care system so I stayed silent. I wanted to be with the one person who loved me, my daddy. I thought if I could just graduate and escape, I could leave it all behind.

But they wouldn't let me go. When I got older, every time police were at my house, I thought they would stop it for sure… but they never did. They always believed The Grandfather and The Mother because they are affluent, white, churchgoing folks. There was no one to save me but myself. So I just worked and worked on gaining enough independence that I could expose them safely. I have told these stories on the internet, with my real name and face. Still no law enforcement agency has contacted me. They are not interested in stopping bad behavior within intact families. Hence generational trauma continues.

What happens next?

In June of 2024, I posted a video on TikTok of an audio recording I made while confronting The Grandfather on his deathbed. It is not eloquent. I am a mess standing in his nursing home room with my aunts kneeling at his side like he's a god. My voice is shaking, and I am crying, and I

run out of there like a scared little girl. But it's real, and it captured the attention of millions.

I knew to outwit my family, I had to have this book in the hands of a publisher before I confronted him, so even if he killed me, he would be exposed. It was the first time in my life I had ever stood up to him. The rage in his face when I stood there blurting out my defiance—I knew in that moment he would rip me apart if he had the strength to move. Because he was too weak, he smiled instead and dismissed me. "Who would ever believe you?" he mumbled, confident in his lies and mortality.

No matter how you came to be reading this book today, I thank you for proving him wrong.

I don't know if I will write another book in this way. This is a history of my forgotten pieces, and I think they have been well represented. For the next story, I want to focus on the things I did to build a life beyond horror. I found a wonderful husband, I coached incredible dance teams, and I worked at crazy companies, so many wonderful things to share that I achieved in spite of the nightmare of The Family.

In the meantime, I have signed with a documentary team to tell the next chapter of this story. There are bodies to be uncovered, trophies to be found, and now I have collaborators to help me expose them. Follow my social media accounts to continue the journey with me.

www.sabrinacapper.com

Printed in Great Britain
by Amazon

56751964R00249